DATE DUE

GAYLORD   PRINTED IN U.S.A

"Dear Carrie. . . .": The Civil War Letters of Thomas N. Stevens

George M. Blackburn
Editor

Illustrations by Andrea Lozano

The Clarke Historical Library
Central Michigan University
Mount Pleasant, Michigan
1984

© Copyright 1984, The Clarke Historical Library
ISBN 0-916699-10-2
Publication of this book has been assisted by a gift from Margaret W. Blumenthal.

Table of Contents

Preface

Thomas N. Stevens enlisted in the Army to fight for the Union cause. As is often the case he spent most of his service away from the action dealing with the less glamorous and romantic aspects of military life — the tedium of camp life, sickness of his troops, and constant rumors. His letters to his wife Carrie, carefully preserved and passed down in the family, are an excellent record of his trials and tribulations, but also of his deep commitment to the Union cause. They will be rewarding reading for those interested in the Civil War not because they offer new insight into the key battles but because they show us the level of dedication and commitment of a captain of volunteers and his continuing devotion to the Union in the face of privation and disappointment. Thomas Stevens did not find glory, but he found satisfaction in having done his duty.

The Clarke Historical Library is very pleased to be the repository of Stevens' letters, through the gift of Margaret W. Blumenthal, Stevens' granddaughter, and her late husband Joseph. My predecessor John Cumming recognized the value of these letters and set this book in motion. George Blackburn selected from the voluminous collection the letters published here and has provided introductory essays and notes to provide a context for seeing them in relation to the wider war. Andrea Lozano, Stevens' great-great-granddaughter, has contributed a number of original illustrations that help visualize the setting in which Stevens wrote.

William H. Mulligan, Jr.
Clarke Historical Library

GENERAL INTRODUCTION

Not every Civil War soldier fought in such battles as Gettysburg, Chattanooga, or Bull Run. For many veterans the war largely consisted of dreary months in camp and sustained marches interspersed with a few battles. Such was the experience of Captain Thomas Nichols Stevens, Co. C, of the Wisconsin 28th Volunteer Infantry Regiment. He pithily summarized the principal role of his regiment in a letter to his wife of September 10, 1864, when he wrote that "we are merely holding our position & waiting for events to develop themselves at the east & southeast of us." Indeed, Captain Stevens' regiment spent most of its service on garrison duty in the trans-Mississippi West, a theater of low priority to both the Union and Confederate governments.

That the 28th Wisconsin went to the trans-Mississippi West, and largely performed garrison duty during the Civil War can be attributed in part to circumstance and in part to the ingenuity of a certain general named Clinton Fisk, who is best known as the founder of Fisk University. The circumstance was that the existing Union garrison at Helena, Arkansas, apparently needed reinforcements badly in the fall of 1862. At least General John Pope, commander of the Department of the Northwest at St. Paul, Minnesota, on October 27, 1862, reported that he was "hurrying off the troops for Helena as fast as possible. . . . From Wisconsin the Twenty-Eight goes to-day. . ."[1]

Pope's statement of the departure time for the Wisconsin unit was unduly optimistic, and draft duty at Ozaukee County intervened, but eventually the 28th left Wisconsin and reached Columbus, Kentucky, in December, 1862. Before they could get to Helena, however, the Wisconsin boys faced another hazard — Ulysses S. Grant. Apparently, the latter wished to retain at Memphis the 28th Wisconsin and six other regiments destined for Helena. Writing to his commanding officer at St. Louis, General Fisk said that to forestall Grant he would go to Memphis "in person to-night to drive by and away from that point the troops from your department. . . . If I succeed in running this force by Memphis, I shall consider ourselves very fortunate. I am unable to judge why General Grant is so earnest in his desire to keep us at Memphis. . . ."[2] Grant's forces, claimed Fisk, were adequate.

If Grant had succeeded in capturing these troops, the history of the 28th Wisconsin would have been more exciting. Nevertheless, Stevens' letters have considerable literary value. At the lowest level, he displayed a good command of grammar and spelling. Further, he wished to communicate, and in his numerous letters Stevens demonstrated an ability to express himself with admirable clarity. In addition, as a company commander and the head of a household writing to his wife, he wrote candid letters from a perspective which provides insight on the impact of the Civil War upon individuals. The topics Stevens discussed in his include five major categories.

The first category is the military experience of himself and of his unit. He vividly described the two major engagements in which the 28th Wisconsin was involved, the Battle of Helena, Arkansas, on July 4, 1863, and the capture of Mobile in 1865. He devotes more space to descriptions of marches of the Badger unit. He also devotes considerable space to describing his food, clothing, and shelter, so that his wife and young daughter could understand how "Papa" lived. In most letters, he specifically lists the illnesses in his company and sadly records the deaths. Stevens was so good at portraying nuances of mood that the reader can sense that a particular soldier was going to die from Stevens' graphic description; note, especially, the death of the much respected Sgt. Plympton on August 24, 1863, and also the death of a soldier who was given up July 17, 1864. Finally, he frequently tells of the administrative routine of a company commander, such as filling out requisitions and completing the monthly reports.

A second major category of topics treated by Stevens includes his comments on certain general aspects of the Civil War. He reacted very emotionally, for example, to Abraham Lincoln's assassination. His comments on top Union generals were surprisingly limited; usually he confined himself to hoping that Ulysses S. Grant might bring victory at Vicksburg or in the Wilderness campaign or noting with joy George Thomas' victory at Nashville. He showed considerable interest in blacks; he hired black servants, he described their dress, he rejoiced to see them free. He was less charitable toward Southerners, especially Southern civilians. He was bitter about treatment of Northern prisoners; he believed that Southern leaders should be punished. He showed scant sympathy toward Southerners whose property was destroyed as a result of the war.

In a third category, Stevens' letters might be considered travel narratives. As the itinerary of the 28th Wisconsin shows, that unit traveled through a considerable portion of the Union. In addition, Stevens took a special journey down the Mississippi River on official business. As a result, he had extensive opportunities to observe the country and to write descriptions of what he saw.

In a fourth category of topics Stevens tells much about the impact of the war on the families of soldiers. His second daughter was born while Stevens was in camp. In a sense he had to manage financial affairs of his household from long distance; do not, he said, pay certain debts at this time since creditors would be understanding. His wife became terribly pinched when Stevens' pay was several months in arrears; that happened not once but several times. He offered suggestions about whether she should live by herself, in a boarding house, or with her parents. Be sure, he urged, to hire someone to do the washing and cleaning, otherwise Mrs. Stevens would become tired and ill, and the doctor bills would cost more than the hired help.

Finally, a fifth category of topics relates to Stevens himself; in the candid letters to his wife he reveals much about himself and values. He volunteered, he wrote, out of patriotism and with no desire for personal gain. He showed remarkable concern for his men; this is shown in the detailed lists of ill men and the countless times he visited the sick in military hospitals. He was also certainly concerned about his family. In addition, he was a very moral and religious man. He pointedly noted some officers who drank too much, gambled, and squired Southern ladies. He did not. He attended religious services, though charity did not stop him from criticizing dull, insipid sermons. Finally, he discussed his own personal goals. He was not desirous of promotion in the military; he sought no rank beyond captain. As he suggests, he might well have been promoted if he had played his political cards correctly. He was much more interested in where he might settle with his family after the war; more than once he suggested that he would like to locate in the South.

Perhaps the most revealing information about Stevens himself can be found in the attitude of his men toward him. He certainly had their respect. He raised his company, as he records in a letter to his wife of June 14, 1863, and would have been content to serve in the ranks, but his men elected him captain. During the war Stevens provides hints that both his men and fellow officers respected him highly. Finally, after the war he was elected president of the veterans association of the

28th Wisconsin. Indeed, at the encampment in 1907 Stevens was elected president for life.[3]

* * * * * * *

Thomas Nichols Stevens was born May 6, 1835, at Varysburg, New York, the son of David Stevens (1795–1878) and Nancy Nichols Stevens (1799–1848). In 1852, at the age of 17 years, he left home and migrated to Wisconsin; his father later followed him to Wisconsin. There young Stevens lived at Oconomowoc, Columbus, Stevens Point, and New Lisbon. He married Caroline E. Silsbee, of Columbus, Wisconsin, on January 31, 1857. She was the daughter of Thomas Silsbee (1807–1864) and Jane Howard Silsbee (1810–1885). From Oconomowoc Stevens went into the service as Captain of Co. C, 28th Wisconsin. Certain references in the letters suggest that he was postmaster at Oconomowoc immediately prior to enlistment.

Upon his discharge from service in 1865, Stevens went back home to Wisconsin. As his letters indicate, however, he was restless and thinking of settling elsewhere. Early in 1866, Stevens moved with his family to Greenville, Montcalm County, Michigan, where he engaged in the abstract business. Stevens soon played an important role in the life in his new home; in 1870 he was elected a Trustee of the village of Greenville and in 1874 he was elected Mayor of Greenville.

In 1879 Stevens and his family moved to the nearby village of Stanton, the county seat of Montcalm County. Stevens had been Register of Deeds in 1870 and held that office from 1880 to 1888; no doubt found the location near the court house in Stanton more convenient than a residence in Greenville. He continued managing his abstract business while Register of Deeds; indeed, he was active in his abstract company until 1906, when he sold the business to his son-in-law.

Stevens was an active member of several associations. As his letters amply demonstrate, he was a Republican during the

Civil War and continued that affiliation after the war. In 1880 he was a delegate to the Republican national convention in Chicago. He was not only a member of the Congregational church, but also the treasurer at the time of his death. In addition, he was a member of the Grand Army of the Republic, the Army of Tennessee, the Military Order of the Loyal Legion and the president of his regimental association, the 28th Wisconsin.

He died January 1, 1908, at his home in Stanton and was buried at the family lot in Greenville. He had five children, two of whom predeceased him.[4] Lu, the child he frequently mentioned in his letters, was three years of age in 1862; Mary was born a few months after Stevens went into service. His last daughter was Mrs. Bertha Walker; it was her daughter, Mrs. Margaret W. Blumenthal who gave Stevens' letters to the Clarke Historical Library.

*   *   *   *   *   *   *

The origin of the 28th Wisconsin Infantry Volunteer Regiment can be traced to Abraham Lincoln' call for 300,000 men in early July, 1862. Five thousand men, or five regiments, constituted the quota for Wisconsin. During previous calls, men from Waukesha County, just west of Milwaukee, had joined various regiments, but now residents wanted a regiment of their own. A number of leading citizens visited the governor and secured permission to organize a Waukesha regiment. In villages in the county as well as at school houses and crossroad hamlets, orators urged residents to fulfill their patriotic responsibility. Within two weeks from near the end of August, between 600 and 700 men enrolled for active duty in six companies. Each of those companies was sponsored or "raised" by a prominent local citizen, with occupations ranging from superintendent of schools to district attorney to postmaster (in Stevens' case); each of these prominent citizens was then elected captain of the company.

Since there were no more volunteers forthcoming, the other four companies of the regiment were raised in nearby Walworth County. Lest it be thought that residents of Waukesha County were remiss in not filling all ten companies for the regiment, it should be noted that the 26,000 inhabitants of the County in 1860 furnished some 2,000 men for the army during the Civil War.[5]

The officers of the regiment from captain through colonel are listed below; those who initially held office are listed first with their successors in parentheses.

Regimental Officers

Col. James M. Lewis, Oconomowoc (Charles Whittaker, Edward B. Gray, and Calvert C. White)

Lt. Col. Charles Whittaker, Waterville

Major Edward B. Gray, Whitewater.

Company Commanders

Co. A: John A. Williams, Waukesha, clerk of the circuit court

Co. B: Mandeville G. Townsend, Waukesha, cashier of a bank
(Charles B. Slawson, Waukesha)

Co. C: Thomas N. Stevens, Oconomowoc

Co. D: Edward S. Redington, Whitewater

Co. E: James S. Kenyon, Troy

Co. F: Calvert C. White, Waukesha, district attorney
(Archie D. Montieth, Genessee)

Co. G: Elihu Enos, Jr., Waukesha, superintendent of schools
(Willis V. Tichenor, Waukesha)

Co. H: Herman A. Meyer, Waukesha, merchant
          (James Murray, New Berlin)
          Horace B. Crandall
          (Andrew J. Shiverich, Oconomowoc)
Co. I: Lindsay J. Smith, Troy
Co. K: Ira H. Morton, Janesville
          (Levi J. Billings, Madison; George C. Cowing, Walworth).

The original strength of the regiment was 961; subsequently, 144 additional men volunteered, and thirty two additional recruits were added as substitutes. Of the members of the 28th Wisconsin, five were killed in action, one died of wounds, 231 died from disease. The regiment by the end of the war had lost thirty one men by desertion, eighty one by transfer, and 221 by discharge. At the mustering out the regiment numbered 573 men.[5]

*   *   *   *   *   *   *

The military service of the 28th Wisconsin can be classified under the five major time periods.

   I.   Organization and initial activities
      A.   Organization at Camp Washburn, Milwaukee; mustering in 10/14/62
      B.   Draft duty, Ozaukee County, Wisconsin: 11/12 — 11/30/62
      C.   Camp Washburn: 11/30 — 12/21/62
      D.   Columbus, Kentucky: 12/21/62 — 1/5/63
         1.   Expedition to Hickman, Kentucky: 12/24 — 27/62
      E.   Helena, Arkansas: 1/7/63 — 2/24/63
         1.   Expedition to St. Charles, Arkansas on the White River 1/11 — 22/63
  II.   Yazoo Expedition: 2/24/63 — 4/8/63

III. Arkansas duty
    A. Helena: 4/8/63 — 8/10/63 (repulsed Confederate attack, 7/4/63)
    B. Capture of Little Rock: 8/10/63 — 9/10/63
    C. Little Rock: 9/10/63 — 10/26/63
    D. Pursuit of Confederates to Rickport: 10/26 — 11/1/63
    E. Pine Bluff: 11/10/63 — 11/30/64
        1. Expedition to Longview: 3/27 — 31/64
        2. Expedition to Mt. Elba: 4/28 — 30/64
    F. Little Rock: 11/30/64 — 2/11/65
        1. Expedition to Mt. Elba: 1/22 — 2/4/65
IV. Mobile campaign
    A. Mobile Point: 2/11/65 — 3/16/65
    B. Seige of Mobile forts: 3/17/65 — 4/12/65
    C. Manna Hubba Bluff: 4/13/65 — 4/26/65
    D. McIntosh Bluff: 4/27/65 — 5/9/65
    E. Mobile Bay: 5/9/65 — 5/30/65
V. Texas expedition
    A. Clarksville: 5/31/65 — 6/16/65
    B. Brownsville: 8/3/65 —
    C. Mustering out: 8/23/65
    D. Arrival at Madison: 9/19/65

Thomas Stevens was with his unit except for a period from approximately January until June, 1864. He apparently went home on sick leave, stayed two and a half months recuperating and also engaged in recruiting. Instead of directly joining his unit, the army sent him down the Mississippi River to New Orleans, charged with the responsibility of delivering recruits to various Wisconsin units.

*   *   *   *   *   *   *

There are approximately 367 letters in the Stevens manuscripts; while some letters were written to his father and other relatives and friends, most were directed to his wife. Since the letters to his family largely duplicate information given in letters to his wife, few of them are included in this publication.

Stevens' letters to his wife frequently followed a definite pattern. First, he acknowledged receipt of his wife's letters (or complained about not receiving any for some time) and perhaps made a comment or two about them. Next he described his own and/or his unit's activities. Then he listed those in his company who were ill and those who had died. Finally, Stevens closed with words of endearment to his wife and children.

Clearly it is not possible to print the complete 800-page typescript of Stevens' letters; certain standards were utilized in excising material. First, letters containing duplicate material were eliminated. Second, opening paragraphs acknowledging receipt of letters were eliminated. Usually the third section listing the ill and deceased was eliminated. Finally, the closing words of endearment were eliminated. All deletions within a letter are shown by elipses, though no attempt is made to indicate the deletion of entire letters.

The letters are printed as written, with limited exceptions. At times a word or letter is inserted; such additions are indicated by brackets. Some minor changes in punctuation were made in a few instances without changing the meaning for the purpose of clarity. The salutations, complimentary closes, and signatures have been eliminated, except to indicate when Stevens wrote to someone other than his wife.

For those interested in additional research on members or activities of the 28th Wisconsin Infantry, the following may be consulted:

Isaac S. Bradley, *Bibliography of Wisconsin the War* (Madison, 1911).

William G. Paul, comp., *Wisconsin's Civil War Archives,* (Madison, 1965), describes archival material by office of origin.

Proceedings of the annual reunions of the Twenty-Eight Regiment (Bradley list annual reunions from 1882—1910).

Papers of the following members of the 28th Wisconsin may be found in the State Historical Society of Wisconsin Collections, Madison, Wisconsin:

1. James B. Lockney (Loughney), Co. G, diary 1863—65, correspondence, 1862—65
2. Edward S. Redington, captain, Co. D, copies of letters written in 1862 and 1863
3. Solomon Conright, Co. A, typewritten copy of diary, 1863–65
4. Edward Walden, Co. G, typewritten copy of diary, 1862—63

Service Records

The *Official Records* have a few items relating to the 28th Wisconsin, beyond those listing organizational structure. *Battles and Leaders* is principally helpful in portraying general background.

The National Archives at Washington has service records of individual soldiers, organized by unit.

NOTES

1. *Official Records*, Series I, Vol. XIII, 766
2. *Ibid.*, XXII, Part II, 19–20.
3. Waukesha *Freeman*, July 4, 1907, printed in *Memoirs of Waukesha County,* (Madison, 1907), 137.
4. Biographical sketches of Stevens may be found in John W. Dasef, *History of Montcalm County, Michigan* (2 vols., Indianapolis, 1916), I, 503, and in a memoriam statement by the Military Order of the Loyal Legion of the United States, Stevens MSS, Clarke Historical Library.
5. Accounts of the raising of the 28th Wisconsin may be found in county histories: Theson W. Haight, *Memoirs of*

Waukesha County, Wisconsin. . . . (Chicago, 1880), 514–15; *History of Walworth County, Wisconsin.* . . . (Chicago, 1882), 387–392.

    The list of officers is derived from county histories listed above. The statistics for the regiment may be found in *History of Walworth County, Wisconsin.* . . . 90 (the latter based on a report by the Wisconsin Adjutant General). *Memoirs of Waukesha County*, 139, 140, 141–4 lists those who died in action, died of wounds, and died of disease.

Part I: ORGANIZATION AND INITIAL ACTIVITIES

In the early months of the war, northern states raised the quota of troops assigned by the federal government through volunteers. In 1862, however, Congress anticipated difficulty in securing enough volunteers and authorized the President to call out the militia for as much as nine months; Congress in effect also authorized the President to use a draft if necessary for raising troops. In August, 1862, the War Department called for 300,000 men, 11,904 from Wisconsin. States were to raise the troops through volunteers by August, otherwise a draft was to go into effect.

Wisconsin Governor Edward Salomon assigned quotas to each county and persuaded the War Department to postpone the draft in the state in the hope that volunteers would fill the quota. By October, as a matter of fact, most counties had filled their quotas with volunteers; unfortunately, several counties near Lake Michigan with a large immigrant population had not.

Some immigrants, particularly Germans such as Carl Schurz and Governor Salomon himself, were ardent supporters of the war and the Lincoln administration. On the other hand, many Roman Catholic immigrants were Democrats and unsympathetic to the Republican administration in Washington. Many opposed emancipation and were disturbed by Abraham Lincoln's preliminary Emancipation Proclamation. Finally, many immigrants who had fled Europe to avoid conscription were strongly opposed to a draft.

In several counties, but especially in Ozaukee County, immediately north of Milwaukee, attempts to administer the draft led to violence. Conflict in Ozaukee County pitted rural Luxembourg Roman Catholics against German Protestants and native American businessmen at the county seat of Port Washington. The draft commissioner for Ozaukee County, William Pors, was a German and a Democrat, but he was also a Protestant and a Mason. When Pors started drawing names of those to be drafted, a mob drove him away, burned the boxes containing names of men of military age, and then rioted throughout the town, burning houses of business leaders and the Masonic Hall. Eight companies of the 28th Wisconsin, including Stevens' company, surrounded and occupied the town.[1]

A curious outcome of the riot was the arrest of scores of draft resisters and subsequent litigation regarding their fate. Governor Salomon, who initially had legal custody of the prisoners, turned them over to Major General John Pope, commander of the Department of the Northwest. Some of the prisoners sought release through the writ of habeas corpus, a petition denied by federal authorities because of a Presidential proclamation denying the use of the writ to draft resisters. The prisoners then challenged the President's authority to deny the writ, saying only Congress could suspend it. When Wisconsin courts upheld the prisoners' position, a classic confrontation between federal and state authority seemed possible. Washington officials planned an appeal to the Supreme Court but meanwhile paroled the prisoners. Soon thereafter Congress granted the President authority to suspend the writ of habeas corpus, thus making the draft resisters' case moot. But they remained free anyway.[2]

*   *   *   *   *   *   *

After pacifying Ozaukee County and some further training

at Camp Washburne, Milwaukee, the 28th left Wisconsin for Columbus, Kentucky, in December, 1862. That city, on the Mississipi River just below Cairo, Illinois, where the Ohio River joins the Mississippi River, had been occupied by Confederate forces (the first occupation of Kentucky by either side in the war) in the summer of 1861 as part of the Confederate effort to gain control of the Mississippi River. Ulysses S. Grant then occupied Paducah, Kentucky, to counter the Confederate move; his subsequent capture of Forts Henry and Donelson in early 1862 forced the Confederates to withdraw from Columbus.

While the 28th Wisconsin was at Columbus on the Mississippi River for only a short time, nevertheless duty at that place symbolized the principal role that the Wisconsin unit was to play during the Civil War. Except for the Mobile campaign and duty in west Texas, all of the 28th's operations occurred along the Mississippi River or its tributaries.

Since most of its activities were in Arkansas, to understand the role of the 28th, it is necessary to have an understanding of military events in Missouri and Arkansas. Certain generalizations can help in understanding the somewhat confused operations in those two states. First, they were not major theaters of operation; indeed, the Confederates largely stripped the trans-Mississippi West of the best fighting units and utilized them in duty east of the Mississippi. Second, from the Union point of view Missouri and Arkansas were important largely because control of those states aided Union efforts to control the Mississippi River. Finally, because of the region's relative unimportance neither side gained absolute control; thus Confederate forces continued operations there (notably guerrilla warfare in Missouri) until the very end of the war.

Military operations in Missouri and Arkansas until January, 1863, when the 28th Wisconsin reached Helena, Arkansas, can be summarized quickly. General Nathaniel Lyon took vigorous steps to control St. Louis for the Union cause very early in the war. Ultimately, however, he overreached in trying to control all of Missouri, suffering defeat and death at Wilson's Creek in southern Missouri in August, 1861.

Subsequent Union efforts were more successful. General John Pope secured portions of northern Missouri. After John C. Fremont postured to no avail, he was replaced by Henry Halleck. Under his command, General Samuel Curtis drove Confederate forces from southern Missouri and defeated them at Pea Ridge in northern Arkansas in March, 1862. Although the Confederates subsequently made efforts to reconquer Missouri, thereafter the state was more or less under Union control. At about the same time General Pope was advancing down the Mississippi River, capturing New Madrid and Island No. 10 in March, 1862. Soon after, Union forces captured Memphis, June 6, and General Curtis occupied Helena, Arkansas in July, 1862, some 60 miles below Memphis on the Mississippi River.[3]

The 28th Wisconsin was to spend some five months of garrison duty at Helena.

Camp Washburne, Milwaukee Sept. 18, 1862.

Dear Carrie:

I have been trying since Sunday to write you, but could not get a chance, & am *stealing* time now. It is busy times getting used to *new business*, & arranging everything.

We all got wet as sop night before last, but it don't hurt us. I do not feel it in the least — did not get a bit of cold.

We got our blankets last night. The boys are feeling merry.

If I can I shall try & come home soon. Will write you when, probably. They say I am getting fat. Kiss Lulu for papa & take a lot for yourself. Write often. I hope you are all well. Tell Homer that the position he wanted is filled. Regards to all. I have not been off the camp ground since I first came on. I may try & go to Milwaukee an hour or so this P.M.

Camp Washburne, Milwaukee, Sept. 30, 1862.

Once more I will attempt to write you, though I may be interrupted before I get half a dozen lines written.

I still keep well and am getting along as well as I could expect with my new duties.

Camp life is, indeed a change from the life I have been leading for years — but I take hold of it first rate I think, for a green one. Quite a number of the boys are complaining, but not many of them are much sick. . . . I keep very busy and find it necessary to be so if I attend to things as I should want them attended to if I were a private & had a green captain over me.

Sunday was a lonesome day to me. I attended Church at Milwaukee in the forenoon, walking there and back. Was in camp the balance of the day. . . .

I wish I could see you & Lulu. I miss you both — my dear ones — and I know I am sadly missed at home by my hearts idols. How gladly shall I be welcomed home when I can return and be with you.

. . . .

I don't know when I can come home. I am considerably behind a part of my class & must catch up someway.

. . . .

Our second Lieutenant is a pretty good fellow after all, & takes well with the men, though he has not quite *snap* enough to him — *some like me*.

There, I must close. I hope to have more time by & by.

Camp Washburne, Milwaukee, Oct. 5th., 1862.

As I have a chance to steal a little time today, I will write you in relation to one or two incidents transpiring here recently. I have been very well since I came in, and very busy.

Yesterday noon my company presented me with a beautiful sword, belt, sash & sword knot, the whole costing $57.[4] It is a splendid gift, and coming, as it does, from the men I have known for years — most of them — I esteem it highly as a mark of their confidence & regard. I trust I may never dishonor the gift — nor its donors. I will try & let you see it before I leave.

Yesterday I attended the funeral of Capt. Bloodgood at Milwaukee. I was but little acquainted with him. He had lived in Summit. Myself and three other Captains from this regiment acted as pall bearers. It was the first military funeral I ever attended. The ceremonies were very impressive.

A company of the 26th acted as an escort.

What do you think about coming in to see us? I should be glad to have you come if you think you can endure it. Do you think you could sleep on my hard bunk? Could you bring Lulu? I want you to see us in camp.

How do you all do? All well I hope. I wish I could see you and "papa's baby" today. Give the darling a kiss from papa — yes, a hundred of them — & take as many for yourself.

. . . .

I have just had my company out on parade & read the 101 Articles of War to them, & am tired.

Camp Washburne, Milwaukee, Oct. 9th 1862, 10 P.M.

I have been writing so very busily this week at my *Muster in Rolls* that I have had no time to do anything else. I work late every night. Have just quit for tonight.

The talk now is that we will be mustered in as a regiment on Saturday. I hope so, for I want my pay to commence. It is no fun to command & be responsible for companies at ones own expense.

I am very well. Most of the boys are well, though a few are sick. James Hall & Isaac Bogart are in the Hospital. Lloyd Breck is not very well. Lieut Curtiss has been quite unwell for a few days, but is getting better. He keeps around nearly all the time.

Have you got moved yet? I wish I could help you about it. I hope I shall be able to come home some time next week. Had we better go out to Columbus when I come out or not?
. . . .

Camp Washburne, Milwaukee, Oct. 12th, 1862.

What shall I write to you tonight? I don't know hardly unless I tell you how I have spent the day. Well, I wrote nearly all the forenoon; attended church — or rather Divine Service — in Camp at 11 o'clock; ran about a little after dinner, & we had battalion drill at about 4 P.M. There were a great many visitors in camp today. . . .

Once more we are having such pleasant weather. I hope it will last awhile. We were to be mustered in today, but it has been postponed till tomorrow.

We are mostly well here, & the sick are on the gain.

I am sorry, dear wife, that you suffer so much. How I wish I could do something to relieve you. And how I wish I could press you to my bosom tonight, my own loved one. The time seems very long to be away from you, my own, but I felt it *my duty* to go, dear Carrie. It will not be for *very* long I hope, for I miss your presence, your kisses, & your words of love. And so too, do I miss my little Lulu — *papa's baby* — the dear little birdie. Give her a hundred kisses for me, & take a thousand from her lips & call them from me.

Was Mr. Kreeger willing to let you rent the house? I never thought to say anything to him about it. Are you at Kinne's yet? How does everything go?

I will come home the last of the week if I can get away.

Shall we go to Columbus?
. . . .

Camp Washburne, Milwaukee, Wis., Nov. 1, 1862.

Yours with the bundle came safe to hand yesterday. I am sorry you had to work so late at night to fix up the things, you have so much to do. I am glad that my letter did you so much good, and sorry that you have had no more such, —

But, darling, you must not think that a want of disposition to do so has prevented my writing good long letters to you. My time has been so much occupied that it has been only at odd minutes that I have been able to write. I hope to have more time now as the machinery of the company & regiment gets to running more smoothly, though I am just as busy as ever thus far.

But, darling wife, I think often, *very* often, of the dear ones whom I have left behind — and indeed I do miss them. The warm caress, the sweet kiss, so often bestowed, — I feel the loss of them now, and long for the time when I may once more receive them after having performed my whole duty in another sphere of action. Will you not welcome me with pride, my darling, when I come back to you, if I only merit it?

The papers last night said we would leave this week. It may not be reliable.

A lot of men from several different regiments, (including the 10th and 18th) paroled prisoners, were here today, on their way to Superior, where they are going to spend the winter.

Today we had quite a snow storm. I hope it will clear off tonight, for I am to be officer of the day tomorrow, & want a fine day.

. . . .

I am well as usual, and feel first rate. Can eat my regular rations & am growing fat — so all the boys say.

Soldiering agrees with me. I only hope I may keep as well as now. John Colby was here last week. We have lots of visitors here.

I have got a Record of my Company in which are pictures of the Colonel, Lt. Col., Major, and myself & both lieutenants — also names of the whole company. I intend sending it home the first opportunity.

. . . .

Camp Washburne, Milwaukee, November 8th, 1862.

Though I have not been long away nor long in camp this time to hear news, I will write to you, for I know you are anxious to hear from me as often as possible, and you deserve more than one letter, darling, brave little wifey, for your terrible effort at self control this morning. How much I thank you for it, though I know your heart was full to bursting and your "eyes a fountain of tears." If you had yielded I should have been completely unmanned — as it was I could hardly contain myself, though I tried to keep up a cheerful countenance. When I saw the tears spring to your eyes, dearest, as I parted from you, and heard, as the door closed upon me, that wail from your lips — from the bottom of your heart, as it were — I could have wept — in fact I could hardly refrain from it. Do not think, dearest one, that though I go from you with a smile upon my lips, that I do not regret the parting — that it has no pain for me. Though I smile, my heart is wrung at parting with you, my own, and our sweet little one. God knows I regret the necessity; but the call I could not withstand.

I learn that we have orders to leave next Thursday. I do not yet know our destination. Perhaps we shall not leave as soon as that. If we do I shall not be able to come home again before leaving. If I do not it will not be because I do not desire to, dearest Carrie.

. . . .

8 P.M., Sunday, Nov 9th

This has been a bright, beautiful day. How I have wished I could be with you today, or have you with me. We have had a great deal of Company in camp today, though not in our company. Soldiers wives & friends have been here in any quantity.

There is a report that our regiment, or a part of it, will go to Milwaukee tomorrow to prevent trouble in relation to the draft. Some resistance is expected.

Nothing new about our leaving. I bought a revolver yesterday, costing $22. beside holster & cartridges — a haversack 14/ — & several other necessary articles. It takes *money* to run a Captain's Commission.

I forgot to leave that money with you. I will send it out.

. . . .

Camp Washburne, Milwaukee, November 11th, 1862.

I don't know as I shall have time to write you this morning, but I have got time to commence a letter, — so I'll improve it. It is a rainy, disagreeable morning, though not very cold.

Hope it will not rain much.

. . . .

Nothing new about our leaving. The draft in Milwaukee is said to be postponed for the present.

I shall not go into raptures at present at the appointment of Burnside. We have had many changes, and nearly all have proved of little, or no account. Let him be tried in his new position, & praised or blamed as he deserves.

We are called for drill.

Camp Washburne, Milwaukee, November 11th., 1862
9 o'clock P.M.

We are ordered to be ready to move at midnight. We take the boat at Milwaukee at half past one for Ozaukee we suppose. There seems to be some disturbance there in relation to the draft, and the Governor has ordered eight companies of us there, in order that the presence of 600 bayonets may cool them down. I think that the bayonets will do it without any fighting. Companies A, B, C, D, E, F, G, & H, are the ones which go, leaving I & K here to run the camp, with Major Gray in command here. I suppose the Colonel & Lt. Col. will go with us. The boys all feel good at the prospect of leaving, though it is a stormy time. Several who have been complaining & not able to do duty for a few days, are on hand for a start, though we leave a few behind.

This is to be our first campaign, and I think will be a peaceful one.

I shall miss your loving letters, dearest, which I have been receiving so often lately. Please write me at Ozaukee for a few days, or till you hear from me. I expect we shall be there for a short time.

I shall try & write you often, and hope to hear from you and little Lulu as often.

I sent $15. to you in the letter sent by Colby. I hope you rec'd it all right. I shall probably get no time to write to anyone else. Homer goes with me on this expedition. I presume we shall not be gone long — perhaps 3 or 4 days — perhaps 10 days.

We shall take about 78 men and officers of our company. Some companies will go stronger.

I hope it will not storm any more, though I hardly think it willstop *now*. I expect we will have a *great* time — a *tedious* time.

If it only turns out well — then all right — and I believe it will.

Kiss baby Lulu for me, and tell her to kiss you for papa.

I must rest a little. Good night! dear, darling wifey, Good night!

Head Quarters 28th Wis. Vol., Ozaukee, Wis., Nov. 13, 1862

We have been here about 30 hours, but this is the first opportunity I have had to write you. I am writing this on a window sill at the hotel. We fell into line at the "long roll" Tuesday night at 11 o'clock. At one o'clock we were on the steamer at the foot of Main St. Milwaukee, and immediately left — not for Dixie, but the north. Four companies were aboard the Steamer "Comet", and four on the "Sunbeam." We were on the former. We landed at Port Mao, five miles from here between 4 & 5 o'clock yesterday morning. Just before daylight we disembarked & marched for this place, reaching here at 8 or 9 o'clock. We immediately took possession of the Court House & some other buildings, & Company D. was detailed under proper authority to arrest the leading rioters.

They have had a terrible time here — a perfect "reign of terror." Houses have been sacked, their contents destroyed, citizens almost murdered. I saw fragments of splendid $400 pianos which were completely demolished by the rioters — bureaus, sofas, chairs, bedsteads, tables, stoves & all kinds of furniture, some of it of a very costly character chrushed [*sic*] and torn entirely to pieces. Such destruction of property was the result of mere wantonness — it certainly had no object — It is worse than the work of savages. The people are very, *very* much relieved at the sight of our gleaming bayonets. 600 good men like ours are good for any mob they can raise. How grateful the people are! Passing along the streets yesterday, ladies would run out asking us if we had dined, invite us in to take coffee, load us with food & apples, offer us the use of their houses — & all this without pay. They feel as is released from the power of a thousand devils.

The ladies greeted our battalion, as we marched into town with the waving of handkerchiefs & other manifestations of welcome; while the flowing of tears from eyes of those whose homes & property had been destroyed showed how deeply they were affected.

About 80 of 90 prisoners have been taken. They have been sent under charge of Co. F., Capt White, to Camp Washburne, Milwaukee. They are a hang dog set of devils. Fire arms were used in one engagement yesterday when 40 or 50 were taken prisoners, a short distance out in the County. No one was injured on our side. Only one *secesh* wounded. A few of our company were in that skirmish.

Cos. C. G. H. were called out at half past 9 last night & marched 5 miles west to a place where a mob had threatened to smash a mans house. Reached there at 11 last night & stayed till 2 this morning. Saw no enemy & had no fun.

"The king of France with full 10,000 men, marched up the hill & then — marched down again." We got home at 4 ½ this morning. I had had no sleep of any account for three nights, & was *terribly* sleepy. Went to bed at 5 & got up as the clock struck 12 at noon. Had a fine sleep & feel better. We had no chance to sleep on the boat. The boys are mostly all right & feel good. They all wanted to come — even the sick. Some of the sick got well suddenly when they heard we were coming.

I think we shall have no trouble now of any account.

The drums are beating. I must away & see what is up.

7 ½ P.M.

Back again & got my supper. Nothing but a little business has been attended to this P.M.

I am all well — that is, as well as a man with only one hand to use can be. I yesterday split my thumb open, accidentally, from the end to about half way to the joint. It was very painful yesterday & last night, but feels much better today. It was very bad when I was out last night, but I am bound to go when the boys of Co. C. go, as long as I can walk.

I think it will do well now as long as I don't take cold in it.

There is a report that we are to march to Cedarburg tonight. I don't think it is reliable, but we may go. We are ready for business of that kind every time. We want to do our share of taking the northern as well as the southern secesh.

Homer was unwell yesterday after arriving here, but is well as usual today.

I stand the marching better than most of the boys. They nearly all complain some — nary a complain do I — no sore feet or lame legs.

If we go to Cedarburg tonight it will try some of them, for it is 18 miles, & rough walking at that.

I send some pieces of the keys of the pianos destroyed, which I picked up in the yard.

Well, darling, I have written a long lot of yarns about myself. Now how are *you* & *Lulu* at home. I wish I could look in upon you tonight — it would do me good. And I'd like a kiss if you could spare me one. Guess you'll have to send it in a letter.

I shall look for a line from you tomorrow. Hope I shall get it. There is none today.

Ed. Kinne is a nice Methodist. He was drunk when we came from Milwaukee, though he managed to come along. He was full of his profanity that night. It is bad enough in any one, but in a man who pretends to better things it looks much worse. He spends enough for oysters &c. to help his family *a little at least*. I think that & whisky is the secret of his poor success in California & other places.

What men *some* men are.

. . . .

Ozaukee, Wis., Nov. 17, 1862.

I will commence a letter to you from here, though we are to leave for Milwaukee again this afternoon.

Have seen some service since I wrote you. I rec'd orders Saturday evening at 6 o'clock to pick such men as I wanted from Company C, & go north to the southern part of Sheboygan county to arrest one of the principal leaders of the mob. We left at 8 P.M. Had a dark night for it. Found our plan of destination at 2 A.M. Surrounded the house, arrested our man, & started for Ozaukee again. Visited one or two nests of secesh & Catholics, but took no more prisoners. The one we have is considered here as one of the hardest customers in the country. We got back at 9 A.M. Sunday, having marched 29 miles. Were complimented by the Colonel upon our success, as well as the rapid march we made. He hardly expected we would catch the man, & the citizens many of them thought we would lose him & have a fight with the secesh.

The boys were well tired out when we got back. Homer went along and carried a musket. He is all right except sore feet. I suffered less from the march than almost any one else. Am not sore or lame in the least.

We are to leave at 2 P.M. by the steamer. Will leave 2 Companies here for the present.

I write this sitting & lying on my blanket with an India rubber blanket for a desk. That will account for the chirography.

This is a regular Dutch hole — a hard place. I never saw the quarters as quiet as they were yesterday after our return. The boys were all very Sleepy, & we all slept ourselves nearly to death. My eyes almost "slept out" of my head.

I cannot say I shall be glad to get back to camp, except I can get a chance to run home & see you. I hope I can do so.

Will try & finish this at Milwaukee.

1 P.M. 17th

Just rec'd another order — Co. C. is to stay for a week or so longer —

. . . .

Ozaukee, Wis., Nov. 19, 1862.

My loved one:

I rec'd another of your dear letters yesterday, and I assure you it did me a vast amount of good to read it, and hear from you and darling Lulu. It seems something like having you near me to hear from you often, and the sweet good letters remind me of those I used to watch for so impatiently when we were both younger in years than now — when we were waiting for the day which was to make us one.

I am so sorry Lulu is not well. I hope it will be nothing serious. Tell her papa says she must not be sick.

In my last I did not write as fully as I intended of some of our movements, but you can read my letter to Sara which, I think contains fuller particulars. Since I wrote nothing has transpired worthy of note. We are lying here doing nothing but keep up a guard, drill 4 or 5 hours per day & keep up the forms of a military post — in a measure. I was on duty yesterday as officer of the day. Shall be on now once in three days, as only three companies remain here. The rest of them left yesterday morning. Companies C. E. & H. remain here.

The drafted men from this county have until next Monday to present themselves at this post. After that they will be sent for — i.e. those who don't come in. We shall then have something to do, probably. Homer is well. Lieut. Gilmore is acting Adjutant here, Lt. Col. Whitaker being in command.

Monday evening some 10 or 12 of us (officers) were invited to an oyster supper at the residence of a Mr. Blake, one of the wealthiest of the citizens here. He has a very pleasant family. Had a nice supper & got back to quarters at 9 ½ o'clock.

Some 30 of us attended a supper last week at a Mr. Tomlinson's, whose mill was sacked by the mob. We also had a nice supper pleasant time there.

I split my thumb, accidentally, the day I came here, with a large knife. It is not very sore, but I am not able to use it yet — and my hand but very little. It is my left hand, fortunably for me. I am very well.

I hardly see a paper here. Get no news of importance.
· · · ·

Ozaukee, Wis., Nov. 20, 1862.
7 P.M.

Though I have rec'd nothing from you since your letter of Sunday, I'll try & write something, though my brains feel dull tonight, and I have nothing to write that seems of the least importance. We had company drill this fore noon for two hours, preceded by inspection of ammunition. At a quarter before two I inspected the arms of the company, and at two P.M. went out again for battalion drill. I commanded the battalion until the arrival of Lt. Col. Whitaker. Famous commanding officer you may think. Of course I am. I think our company does the best of any company *here,* to say the least.

I get no news here scarcely. Once in a while I manage to get hold of a daily paper for a few moments. Saw a weekly Tribune for an hour last night. There is a dance here tonight, to which I was invited, as well as the other officers of the Regt. I prefer to stay away. I think but few if any of the officers attend.

I took dinner at a Mr. Goldsmith's today — a very pleasant German family they are — speak very good English. He is a merchant here. One of the daughters — there are two young ladies present, — favored us with some good music on the piano after dinner. We are *lions* here, you see.

. . . .

Ozaukee, Nov. 23/62

. . . .

A company — from the 27th I believe, went down today bound for Kewaunee County to enforce the draft there. Some companies of the 30th are at West Bend for the same purpose. Tomorrow the drafted men from this county are to be here.

The boys are cutting up so that I can hardly write. I get no letters from any one but you. I wrote Cousin Mort some days since. Homer is well.

. . . .

Ozaukee, Wis., Nov. 25, 1862.

Yesterday I looked for a letter from you, but no mail arrived yesterday afternoon, so I am without the letter, but feel sure I shall get one today.

Yesterday the drafted men from this county commenced reporting themselves at this place. I have been unable to ascertain how many reported, but there was a crowd of them besieging the office of the drafting commission during the day. Everything went off quietly. The presence of 200 men here with arms was sufficient to keep good order. I was "officer of the day" again yesterday & was up a good portion of the night. Feel a little sleepy today, but shall probably drill with the company today.

How long we shall stay here is yet unknown to us, though I do not see any necessity of out prolonging our stay longer than Thursday or Friday.

I keep well. You did not believe that I could wear out the *tough farmers*.

I am a better man for work than almost any one in the company. Can out work, out drill, out walk almost any of them — and I find that going without sleep does not affect me more than them. I am a *tough one*, aren't I. *I may make a man yet*, if I keep on.

Some 6 or 7 arrests were made yesterday of men engaged in the late riots.

. . . .

Tuesday, 1 P.M.

I have just rec'd permission to go to Camp Washburne. Col. Whitaker sends me down on special business. I am to return tomorrow, so I cannot come home, even for 1 night. I must get back by tomorrows boat. Homer goes down with me & is going home, so I'll send this by him, probably.

I wish he would give me another day so I could go home, for I so want to see my darlings. Am aboard the steamer Sunbeam waiting for her to start.

I saw a pretty sight here a day or two ago. I counted 36 vessels in sight from the pier, beside 1 schooner lying at the pier. What an immense trade is carried on upon these Lakes. It is coming a time of year when some of these vessels will meet with disaster — Storms & cold weather must soon come — then God pity the poor sailor — & soldier. Will try & write again from Milwaukee. Till then good by —

Head Quarters Co. C., 28th Regt. Wis. Vol.
Ozaukee, Wis., Nov. 27, 1862,
11 P.M.

I saw Major General Pope yesterday in Milwaukee, and had the pleasure of hearing him make a short speech at the Chamber of Commerce. I have faith in him still as a *fighting man*. I don't think he is much of a speaker.

. . . .

Lt. Col. Whitaker, the three captains & Lt. Curtiss were invited to Thanksgiving dinner at Mr. Blake's today. Of course we went. Had oysters, turkey, goose, mashed potatoes, apple & cranberry sauce, mince pie, coffee, biscuit & butter, & lots of nice things. I wish you could have had a good meal of from [*sic*] it. Ate our bellies full & left.

. . . .

I did not see Homer after I came into Milwaukee. Some 300 or 400 drafted men went to Milwaukee from here yesterday. All is very quiet here now. I think we will get away from here soon.

I shot a match with Lt. Col. Whitaker, Capt. Kenyon, Capt. Meyer, & Mr. Goldsmith, today, with revolvers.

Shot by count, and made the best 6 shots, & the best 10 in 12 at 30 paces. I also did pretty well with a rifle at 40 rods, beating nearly all the company (Co. C.) at it.

If you go to Columbus you must let me know immediately so that I can go there if I get leave of absence after going back to camp. I hope I may do so, for I want to see them all.

. . . .

Ozaukee, Wis. Nov. 28, 1862. 6 P.M.

Still we are waiting for marching orders; waiting & hoping they will soon come, for we are tired of staying here. When I say *we* I mean the men — I am fully as well satisfied here as at Camp Washburne, though it is a little out of the way. I don't fancy the idea of guarding prisoners there or drafted men either. We all have our fancies you know — and mine are quite different in this one respect from those of the men — most of them. We drill forenoon & afternoon each day — have dress parade at 4 ½ P.M., roll calls four times a day, & all the regular routine of military posts . . . .

Camp Washburne, Milwaukee, Nov. 30, 1862.

Here I am again in Milwaukee, after the tedious campaign in Ozaukee. Just before noon on Saturday we rec'd orders to prepare to leave for this place. At about 8 ½ or 9 o'clock we went aboard the "Sunbeam," two companies of us, C. & H., and left for Milwaukee. Arrived in camp at about 2 this morning.

Co. E. remained at Ozaukee, the boat being heavily laden, so that they could not get aboard. They will probably come tonight. We had a very pleasant trip back to camp. Rather cold when we got here, but a fire soon warmed us up. Had quite a snowstorm today, so it really seems like winter once more. I really did not expect to see snow fall in Wisconsin this month, but the Regiment has been delayed time and again till winter is really here.

. . . .

Tomorrow I have got to select a lot of men & give them furloughs. All want to go home, and all who do not get a furlough will be mad, but I can't help that. Shall be obliged to stand it. I am wondering tonight if you have gone home yet. I almost hope you have, for I want you to have a good visit there. I wish I could be with you. Perhaps I may before you come back —

. . . .

Camp Washburne, Milwaukee, Wis., Dec. 7, 1862.

Another week is gone, and still we linger here, though we have orders to be ready to move at one days notice. When that notice will come is uncertain, but it seems to be the opinion of the officers here that it will come as soon as Thursday of this week. The boys will be glad to have it come, for they long to be in "Dixie" this cold weather, instead of tarrying in the ice-bound north. They will never be easy till they go, though they don't appreciate the fact that they are much better off here, and they will doubtless be just as anxious to come back in less than three weeks after here. It is very cold here in camp, but the hardships are nothing to what we must endure before we are long in the service.

. . . .

Lieut Curtiss has resigned. I am glad of it, for, although a good man, and meaning well in everything he does, he has been a perfect incubus upon the company. As an officer the men all dislike him — have no respect for him. The Sergeant Major, S. S. Alvord will probably be appointed 2d Lieut., & Lieut Gilmore 1st Lieut. They will make me a good team, both having seen service, and will make me better off in that respect than any other Captain in the regiment. The company is mostly well, except some men who are home.

. . . .

God bless you and our own baby, my darling. It is hard for me to do, but harder for you to let me go. Only a sense of duty to my country could have called me from your side, my own — that duty performed, and the piping times of peace returned, and we will be so happy together, with our own little ones. Keep a brave heart till then, sweet Carrie, and I hope you may have reason to be proud of you soldier husband. I go not to win honor, but hope I may deserve it. . . .

Camp Washburne, Milwaukee, Dec. 10th, 1862, 1 ½ A.M.

I am up late you see. I have just been out to a party again. Col. Page of Milwaukee invited several of us officers to his house last night. Have just got back after a pleasant time.

The news is that we will leave here now very soon. Some of the officers think we will go tomorrow (Thursday.) I hardly think we will go before Friday, & perhaps not till Sunday, but we will doubtless get away by the first of next week, and probably this week. We expect to go to Memphis first. Shall probably stop at Cairo on the way down there. We go without receiving a cent of our pay. What we shall some of us do for money I'm sure I don't know, but presume we shall get along some way.

. . . .

Camp Washburne, Milwaukee, Sunday, December 14th, 1862.

Another Sabbath has come, and we are still in camp here, awaiting orders to leave for "Dixie." The 24 hours notice of our departure is still delayed, and the boys are getting *anxious*. It is amusing to hear their speculations. Some assert that they positively heard one of the field officers say that we would leave tomorrow, & consequently they know that will be the time; some think we will not leave before the last of next week; some are offering to bet that we will not leave next week; & still others that we will be here till after New Years; while some pretend to think that we will not leave the State at all.

"Who shall decide when doctors disagree." I can hardly

"Who shall decide when doctors disagree." I can hardly form an opinion in relation to the time of our departure, and shall venture none at present, but can only say that we intend to be ready at all times to leave at a day's notice.

. . . .

Camp Washburne, Milwaukee, Wis., December 18, 1862.
11 P.M.

We have at last rec'd marching orders. This afternoon, as I did not feel very well, I got leave of absence to run out & see you & return in the morning. Went to Milwaukee, & was just stepping aboard the train, which was then under motion, when a messenger reached with a dispatch to the effect that we would leave at 10 tomorrow morning, & requiring me to return to camp immediately. So back I had to go. On account of want of cars we will be obliged to wait till Saturday morning, but it was not known in time so that I could come out, — so dearest, I shall be compelled to go without seeing you again. I had hoped that since we had been detained here so long, we would now be here till about the first of February at least, so that I might be with you — but it seems that it is differently ordered.

I sent to you today by express $55 — I wish I could leave more for you, but I could not raise it at present. I hope we shall be paid off before it is gone, so that you may have sufficient for your wants. Dear one, it is hard to go & leave you & the little darling, but we will hope the separation will not be for a long time. I wish I could see you once more before leaving, but it is hardly possible I think.

You will give my love to Pa, Mother, Em. & the boys, & to all other friends. Tell En' to send me a *Journal* occasionally, and all of them to write me often, for I shall be anxious to hear from all. Tell En' to keep the "Major's" colt, for there is no knowing when it may be wanted. (Ahem!)

We go to Cairo from here.

Tomorrow we shall be busy packing up & getting ready to leave what has been our home (what a home!) for over three months.

. . . .

Camp Washburne, Milwaukee, December 19, 1862

The want of cars to carry us has kept us here another day. We leave at 7:45 tomorrow morning for Cairo. I learn that the Quarter Masters Stores are marked for Memphis. I presume we shall go there. Pa is here tonight — came in this morning. Write to me directing to Cairo, Ill. *"to be forwarded"*. I think I will receive the letters. I will let you know where to direct as soon as I get a chance & can find out. Supose you number your letters at the top of the sheet, commencing with "1" so I may know when any are lost, I hope none will be.

Please send me the "Daily Wisconsin" while it comes. I have written to Frank to send one copy of the Tribune — Reading matter will be worth having down there I presume. The boys nearly all rejoice at the prospect of leaving.

It may be well enough to tell you what debts I have contracted lately. I owe $125. at Waukesha Co. Bank endorsed by H. Hurd, for money borrowed — nearly due. $55.40 at Wells Simonds & Co. Milwaukee for clothing, Due next Monday — endorsed by E. Hurlbut. $25. to Henry Hitchcock for money borrowed, due on demand.

They will probably all wait till pay day — they will have to.

I don't think you will be troubled about them. Don't pay any attention to them even if you are.

We are packing up. Will write again soon. . . .

Cairo, Il. Dec 22 1862, 2 A.M.

We left Milwaukee yesterday noon by rail road for this place — left Chicago at 8 P.M. & arrived here at about 11 ½ last night. We are on board the steamer for Columbus, Ky, and I supose will leave for that place sometime this morning. We had a pleasant, though rather tedious time on the way here. The men are in fine spirits. The weather is much warmer here than at Milwaukee, being quite comfortable without an over

. coat. I have no time to tell of the great prairies of Illinois over
. which we passed, nor of my opinion of the country.
  . . . .

Columbus, Ky., Dec. 23, 1862.

I went to bed on the steamer at Cairo after writing to you,
went to sleep in no time, & waked at 7 o'clock in the morning
to find our boat "tied up" at this place, a point already noted in
the history of this rebellion. I have taken a look at some of the
points of interest here. The principal fortifications are upon a
bluff next the river some 200 feet high I should think, and
nearly perpendicular. This is just above the town which is on
low ground just by the river, the mighty Mississippi, which
sweeps alongside. The large number of cannon of all sizes; the
large quantities of shot & shell & other military "traps," are
far beyond what I expected to see. There are lots of "contra-
bands" here, also, of all *sizes*, & shades of color. There are
some 3500 troops here.

At 2 P.M. yesterday our regiment left here by the Memphis
R.R., with detachments of the 21st Missouri & the 111 &
119th Ill., notice having been rec'd here of a raid upon the
road some distance below here. We went as far as Union City
without being disturbed, contrary to our expectations. There
we stopped for the night — the other troops occupied log huts
&c — One reg't occupied an earthwork which had been erected there. We had our blankets only (besides the sky) for
covering. Slept very quietly & not very cold. There was no
frost at all, I believe — quite a change from Wis. weather. We
were not disturbed at all during the night. Early in the morning
we fell into line at the tap of the drum, a dispatch having been
rec'd requiring our presence at this place again — so aboard
the cars we went, left about sunrise & arrived here at 9 this
morning. The distance is about 26 miles. Union City is the
place where Lieut Tanberg's company had an engagement at
one time. It is only a small place. On our return here we went

immediately aboard the boat again, & are now here waiting for further orders. It was expected we would go down the river this P.M., but have rec'd no such orders yet. When or where we go next is a mystery. The boys are mostly well — 2 or 3 of my Co. complaining.

. . . .

The talk is that we will go to Memphis — all guess work. Darling I think of you. Will write whenever I can. It hardly seems that we are 520 miles apart, — but so it is. . . .

4 A.M.
Columbus, Ky. Dec. 24/62

We are ordered out on another expedition — to leave at 6 o'clk — for some point in Tennessee south of where we went (Union City) day before yesterday. How long to be gone we don't know, only that we are to fill our haversacks with all the provisions they will hold & carry our blankets. Knapsacks & other things to be left here aboard the steamer till our return.

Frank has finally concluded to return by the boat this morning, & I take the opportunity to write again. You will get a pretty full supply of mail when he arrives — He takes a large bundle of letters.

We hope to be as fortunate this time as on our last expedition. Three more regiments arrived here last night. The 25th Wisconsin is said to be among the number. A lot of secesh prisoners went down last night to be exchanged. The weather continues fine. Hope it will remain so.

. . . .

Columbus, Ky., Dec. 26/62

We fell into line Wednesday morning after I wrote you for a trip somewhere — were to start into the country. Just at daylight a report was rec'd that a large party of rebels were near, & that we would be attacked here on that day. Hence we

were sent onto the bluff in the rear of the fortification &
assigned our place. We laid there till about 3 P.M. when our
reg't was ordered in hot haste onto the flat next the river &
ordered to dig rifle pits along our front. The men went to work
with a will, & I never saw work done so fast or quickly as was
the work on those fortifications. Before dark we were all ready
for an attack from that quarter. As there were some
$10,000,000 worth of Govt stores here, it was expected the
enemy would attempt to capture them, even if they did not
storm the fort.

We found the ground dry for the position — men put up
their rubber blankets for tents — but last night came on a rain
storm & such a wet muddy place! Lt. Gilmore, Homer & I had
a good plan & kept dry. At 11 this A.M. we rec'd orders to get
ready with 1 days rations & our blankets for another tramp.
Fell in at noon & started for the steamer. Will try & finish this
when I get back.

On board Steamer Black Hawk
Mississippi River, Dec 26/62

After going aboard today we stood down the river convoyed
by a gun boat & went to Hickman to destroy some guns, gun
carriages &c. Arrived there at 3 P.M., rolled some large guns
into the river, burnt some gun carriages; captured a 6 pound
rifled gun, 6 mules & a horse — had no fight & saw no enemy.
Returned to the boat at dark & left again for Columbus — &
here we are at the dock.

The principal productions of this country, as far as I can
discover, are secesh & niggers. The water we drink & use is
from the Mississippi river — you cannot see the bottom of a
tumbler filled with it, much less a pail — it is full of the
washings from the banks of the rivers & its tributaries. I
thought I could not drink it, at first, but now it goes very well,
for I can get no other. I rec'd your & Lulu's letter this morning

— it was mailed Wednesday — only about 48 hours coming. I also rec'd one from E. H. Jones. He & Mrs. J. ask to be remembered to you.

Homer is not able to stand the fatigue & exposure incident to camp life. I shall send him home soon — tomorrow if I can — & get me a good contraband. There are lots of them here, & I can get one cheap.

. . . .

Columbus, Ky, Dec 27.

Darling: Here we are in camp again. We slept on the boat last night. Have just got my wall tent & put it up & have been cutting a lot of brush for a "feather bed" to lay on the ground. Had to carry them nearly a mile. I am feeling finely this morning. It is a very pleasant day & the mud is drying up.

In Camp, Columbus, Ky., Dec. 28, 1862
(Sunday, 2 P.M.)

I write you again from this place. Homer starts for home by the boat this afternoon, with Mrs. Lewis & Mrs. Savage. I am sorry he is not able to go along with me, but do not think it advisable to take him any further, as he would not be able to stand it, & I might not be able to send him home by and by. Last night was a very cold night — had a very hard frost — the first I have seen for a week. Today is very pleasant & warm — a bright beautiful day — such as we used to enjoy so happily together. I hope sincerely that we may enjoy a return of the same — I *know* we shall, darling — I feel it sure. Dear, darling one, how I wish I could be with you New Years, & for three weeks following. I would make almost any sacrifice to be able to do so. I pray that you may be brought safely & easily through the agony that awaits you. I do pity you, dearest, *all alone*, as it were, — away from me — or rather I away from you. Keep a stout heart dear one. Our happiness by & by will compensate for all. How is darling Lulu, as well as yourself? Tell her she must not be naughty while Mamma is sick — that she must make her no trouble — for papa loves his dear baby girl.

I am writing in my tent, without a coat, & with no fire, and am warm enough. Homer says "it is so warm in here," & has gone out to cool off. I gave him $20. to go home with — to pay his fare if he cannot get passed free, which is very uncertain. I may need some of that money — if I do I will send for it. I hope we will stay here a week or ten days, for if we do I shall expect some pay, & that "will do me good." Don't you hope I may get it?

I wish I could find something here to send home to you, — but is is "Nichts" so far, — will try & look again before the boat leaves. I must at least send some candy to my baby. I expected a letter & paper today but got neither. Perhaps they will come tomorrow.

The boat is going, Good bye

In camp, Columbus, Kentucky
Jan'y 2d 1863. 11 ½ A.M.

I just this moment rec'd a letter from Cousin Jennie, and also one from Lavantia, both announcing the appearance of a little daughter at our house. Dear one, I am glad to know that you have passed safely through the trial. I have been thinking of you all the time, and wishing I could only be with you. But it could not be, and I was obliged to wait here anxiously wishing to hear from you often. I have only rec'd one letter from you, and I begun to think it might be you were ill.

Darling, to us is given another jewel — a priceless gem — something to guard & guide & cherish. — May we discharge that duty aright. Dear, darling wife, I fancy I can see that dear little head pressed close to your heart, the little hands nestling in your bosom. Would I could *really* see it, if but for a moment, and give you each a kiss, not excluding from such favors another little one — our little Lulu.

Do not fear that I, being absent, will not love her — and you too, dearest — for is she not "papa's baby girl" as well as our older one? "Bone of our bone, flesh of our flesh," we will cherish & love her always, dear loved one.

You know, love, we had wished it might be a boy — but what difference makes it so she is *our darling baby*? None in our love toward her or toward each other.

You must be very careful now, love. Better let some expense be made now for care & help, than by & by twice as much for doctor's bills &c. Though a letter written by the dear hand I have so often pressed in mine would give me unfeigned pleasure, I had rather receive them from another's hand than have you make the exertion too soon, for you *must* be *very* careful.

I shall now think of you more than ever, & shall hope to hear from you *very* often. Cannot you have Mrs. Whitney, Mrs. Brown, Lavantia, or some one send me a line, *every day*, be it ever so short, for I want to keep posted, and know just how you are. I *must* hear.

. . . .

Jennie says I must *send home a name* for the little one. What shall it be? I am puzzled. How will *your name* do? or Mary? or both? There are *many* sweet names, but *few* seem fit for *our* child. Proud parents we? I like *Sara* very well, but *not Sarah*. I had rather *you* would name her. Suggest some name, will you not?

Kiss our little ones for me, my own wife, & may our Father watch over you all, & unite us again ere long.

Love & kisses to you & *the babies*, dearest. Kind regards to all friends. Tell the Doctor he must take good care of you. Ditto to Mrs. Whitney & the rest. Be careful, darling one.

Once more good bye.

Columbus, Ky., Jany 4, 1863

. . . .

I am feeling much better than I have been. Am somewhat

weak from my diarrhea, but will be all right in a day or two again. I have been living on a little milk thickened with flour & *black pepper* (a *delicacy* for me you know) for a few days — & have eaten but little of that. Milk is 10 cents per quart — strong butter 30 cents per pound — & other things in propor- tion. We get no news here — don't know what is going on. — There is some talk of our going to Memphis tomorrow — it may be so & may not — I do not think we shall go at present. Troops are arriving here & passing down the river almost daily. The rain last night makes our camp quite muddy today, so I can't run around as much as I would like to, — but there is not much to be seen here.

. . . .

Columbus, Kentucky, Jany 4, 1863. 7 P.M.

We have just rec'd orders to take the steamer tomorrow morning, but where we go I do not know — probably to Memphis, Helena, Vicksburg, or some other point. The report here this evening is that Vicksburg is captured — that it is burning &c.

. . . .

Helena, Arkansas, Jan'y 7, 1863.

Passing down the river we arrived at Memphis after dark last evening, & remained there till daylight this morning. It being night I did not attempt going ashore, as I could see but little in the dark. Memphis is quite a fine appearing city from the river, and is the first place I have seen since leaving Chicago which I could call a city without compunctions of conscience. There are some very fine blocks of buildings there, I am told. The city contains, as near as I could ascertain, about 30,000 inhabi- tants. Coming down the river the towns are all small, with very few exceptions, & those few are nearly all much smaller than one would suppose judging from their situation upon the river.

We arrived here at about two o'clock this afternoon. Helena is quite a town, and from appearances from the boat there must be quite a body of troops here. A part of the second Wisconsin Cavalry are here. I hoped to see some of the first cavalry here, but am told that they are all at Cape Girardeau, Mo.

. . . .

Helena, Arkansas, Jany 9, 1863

I wrote you from here day before yesterday. Since then nothing has transpired of any importance. We have come ashore and pitched our tents — and *here we are.*

. . . .

We are encamped about a mile below the town here. There must be some 10,000 men here I should think. There were 26 steamers "tied up" at the levee here when we came in. Quite a fleet. I have as yet found no one here that I know. I may possibly run across some one.

. . . .

Helena, Arkansas, Jany 9, 1863

Dear Father:

. . . .

Passing through Illinois, over the great prairies, it struck me that I should never fancy them for a home. "Out of sight of land" for hours at a time, not a tree or shrub in sight, it seemed very desolate to me.

Cairo I saw nothing of, as we arrived there just before midnight, & went immediately aboard the boat for Columbus.

Columbus, and, indeed, all the river towns I have seen, except Memphis, are one-horse institutions — greatly disappointing me in their appearance, having judged previously from the amount of business reported to be done in them. Memphis I only saw from the river, but should think it a fine city.

Helena, where we arrived on the afternoon of the 7th is

quite a town, but nothing of a city. There must be about 10,000 troops here I should judge. We get but little news here, & that little you get sooner than I could send it. We hope to get a mail from home today.

. . . .

Camp near Helena, Arkansas, Jany 10, 1863. 8 P.M.

My dear Wife:

Once again we are to take up our traps & move — down river I presume. We rec'd the order about sundown today to be ready to go aboard the steamer at daylight tomorrow morning. Conjectures are numerous as to our destination, but we generally think that Vicksburg, or at least its vicinity will be our next stopping place.

Several regiments are to move at the same time — some 8 or 10 I should think from what I hear. The 29th is now here, and is also going, as I am told.

. . . .

Col. Lewis commands our brigade. I don't really know what other regiments are brigaded with us. Shall probably find out tomorrow. Everything is to be packed tonight except blankets and tents, so we must be at work, and then rest a little, so I can write but little more now.

. . . .

On board steamer Imperial, opposite mouth of the White River, Jany 12, 1863.

Although we were delayed until about dark before embarking yesterday at Helena, we did finally get aboard the boat, and at about 9 P.M. moved down the river.

This boat is the largest I have yet seen on the Mississippi, and is finished in splendid style.

I woke at 6 this morning to find the boat "tied up" here, in

company with some 25 or 26 others which form part of the expedition — quite a fleet I assure you. Our boat has a heavy load of Commissary stores on board, a battery of artillery with horses & all, & some cavalry — besides which she carries *the ten* companies of the 28th Regt. *on her upper deck.*

I have been unable as yet to ascertain what regiments are along, except the 29th Wisconsin.

The object of the expedition is still a secret — from me at least — but we shall probably know soon.

Yesterday was a beautiful warm day, so warm that while waiting after striking our tents, I laid down in the open air upon a little bundle of hay & went to sleep with only my over coat around me, & woke up as warm as need be. — Quite different this from a northern winter.

Soon after daylight this morning squads of men were sent ashore to make coffee for the companies, which they are still at.

. . . .

On board Steamer Imperial, White River, (Arkansas,) Jan'y 12, 1863.

It was one of the grandest sights I ever witnessed when the twenty seven steamers composing this expedition got under way, and, leaving the Mississippi, passed into and up the White River.

The morning sun never shone brighter, and it was so warm that over coats were a superfluous article as we stood about the decks. It is now 3 P.M. We started this morning at half past 10. Have moved slowly and have probably not made more than 20 miles yet, as we "tied up" an hour at noon. The weather still continues very warm & fine — too warm for this time of year. If this is January, what will August be?

Various are the conjectures as to our destination & the object of the expedition. Some assert that we are to land soon &

march across to Arkansas Post on the Arkansas River & attack that point; some think we are to go as far up as Clarendon, & march thence to attack Little Rock, the Capital of Arkansas. I apprehend that the latter is the more likely of the two, though it may be we have nothing to do with either.

These dirty streams! How human beings can be satisfied to use the water for drinking & cooking purposes seems a mystery — at first. How I have longed for a draught from the little well of ours at home. How it would refresh me — how it would cool the parched lips & throat - & wouldn't it be grateful to the stomach after being doused with *mud & water?*

. . . .

The channel of the White River is very crooked. The banks are covered with a growth of cottonwood & other trees from 20 to 50 ft. high — slim and straight, & standing very close together. In some places the undergrowth of Cane brake make it almost or quite impossible for a man to penetrate it. The 20th regiment is supposed to be beyond Little Rock — it may be that I may meet Lieut Rockwell & some other Oconomowoc boys there. It would be pleasant.

. . . .

On board Steamer Imperial, St. Charles, Arkansas,
Jany 14, 1863.

Passing slowly up the river with the fleet, without any particular adventure, we reached a point some 5 miles below here last night, where we tied up till morning. Two gunboats came on ahead this morning to this place, where we expected to meet with some resistance. We found it evacuated however — the fox had left. Nothing scarcely is left here. St. Charles is a small town on the west bank of the river, & some 50 miles from its mouth as near as I can learn.

The houses & shops are entirely empty — a sawmill was burnt & one or two other buildings. The guns if they had any

upon their earth work they must have taken with them or
dumped into the river.

. . . .

On board Steamer Imperial, St. Charles, Arkansas, Jan'y 15th, 1863.

. . . .

We learned on Tuesday morning by some of the natives, that
Arkansas Post, a point on the Arkansas River, which we were
to threaten from the rear, had been surrendered.

We now learn that the rebel forces who evacuated this place
made for that point, being unaware of the surrender, and were
quietly "gobbled up" by our army there.

The rebels had fortifications here to a considerable extent.
Some of our men —*not* of the 28th — went to work yesterday
& last night & burnt several of the best houses here. The had
better far have waited till we get ready to leave here, and so use
what there is here as long as we want it.

The 28th Wis., with the 1st Missouri battery of Artillery, &
some 200 Cavalry are to remain here for the present, occupying St. Charles. Col. Lewis is appointed post commandant.

The balance of the forces here are to go up the river to
Clarendon, as near as I can learn — thence probably to Little
Rock.

Monday & Tuesday were very warm days — so much so that
we sought for the shady side of the pilot house while riding
upon the hurricane deck. Tuesday night it commenced raining
in the night & continued nearly all day yesterday & into the
night last night. The men had a hard time of it in the rain,
having no adequate shelter — none in fact.

On rising & looking out this morning what was my surprise
to find the ground covered with snow to *the depth of some four
or five inches.* We begun to imagine that we had been trans-
ported to Wisconsin again during the night, but we have finally

concluded that we are still in the "sunny (?) South." Terrible changes in the weather these are, and they come hard on the boys. It is quite cold today.

St. Charles is some 50 miles above the mouth of the White River, as near as I can learn.

It is a village of no considerable size, but probably has done some business for a small town in prosperous times. It was evacuated upon the approach of our fleet, without the firing of a gun on either side.

I heard this morning that this boat, which is much the largest of any in the fleet, is to remain here, all the rest leaving with the other troops. The Imperial is 280 feet long & has a carrying capacity of some 1,600 tons. She is altogether to large a boat for this river, and, it seems to me, ought never to have been sent here. There are many sharp bends in the river where she had difficulty in turning on account of her great length. She is also deeply laden, drawing some nine feet of water.

I hope we shall be able to provide comfortable quarters for the men here — but am afraid we shall not if the other regiments are permitted to burn all the buildings.

The men are ashore except the sick and the few necessary for a guard over the boat. I hope we shall have better weather soon.

. . . .

St. Charles Arkansas, January 19, 1863

. . . .

I came ashore from the boat on Thursday. Several of the companies, mine among the number, are occupying quarters built by the secesh before they left here. They are built of logs & poles, but were not chinked up very well. Our boys went to work & chinked them up with mud, put in some boards for floors, when we could get them, fixed up the stick chimneys, work & chinked them up with mud, put in some boards for floors, when we could get them, fixed up the stick chimneys, and are not quite comfortable situated, with our bunks nailed up at the sides, rough tables made from pieces of boards picked up around town, & other things in the same style.

Some of the companies have been sent out foraging. Quite a number of beef cattle have been brought in, so that we are having fresh beef occasionally. Chickens & turkeys, sweet potatoes &c have been found, but only in limited quantities. Tobacco is a scarce article, & the boys are feeling terribly that they can't get enough to chew & smoke.

. . . .

Negroes are coming in every day, bringing horses, mules, wagons & other property. They are kept within the lines, and will be fed, & kept busy if we have work for them to do. I have tried to get hold of some little curiosity to send home, but have been unable to secure anything yet.

. . . .

Had some pancakes yesterday & this morning, made from *flour* & *water* with a little soda mixed in, making them as tender as leather & as light as lead. They were a luxury, eaten with some 30 cent butter I brought from Helena. Had beef soup yesterday. Am going to have a big boiled *rooster,* (some call him a chicken — for fun,) for dinner today or tomorrow — *when* will depend upon how soon he can be cooked. I suspect it will take a couple of days or so.

I drink nothing scarcely but tea, here. Coffee is not as good for one with diarrhea, & I don't want another turn at that. I hear that there is a chance to send our mail out sometime today, so I hope to get this off. I hope my letters get through safely to you, for I know you will all be anxious to hear from me.

When the payment comes due on the house, tell Mr. Kreeger he must wait till I get some pay, for I have not got a cent yet. I guess he will be fair about it . . . .

Jan. 19, 1863

. . . . The Surgeon told me today there were three belonging to our reg't in hospital that he thought would die. So they go, poor fellows! sacrificed for liberty. May it not be in vain! How I wish the soldiers could get hold of the copperheads at the north. I wish you could hear their opinion of them — it would be expressed in language more forcible than elegant, I assure you. What can such men mean? They are no less *Traitors* than Jeff Davis & Co. themselves. Will the *people* at the north permit them to carry out their nefarious schemes? *If so, wo to that people!*

. . . .

On board Steamer Imperial, White River, January 21, 1863.

The fleet having returned from up the river, we rec'd orders yesterday to cook three days rations of meat & be ready to go on board the steamer again at five o'clock this morning.

Last night about 9 o'clock a row of buildings on the levee, being the principal business buildings of the town, were set on fire, accidentally or otherwise — I think purposely — by some of the soldiers. It is supposed that some of the 28th Iowa reg't were the ones. The buildings were completely destroyed, and the fire came very near communicating to our boat, with its immense load of commissary stores, ammunition &c. If it had taken fire it would have burned like timber, & doubtless many lives would have been lost, & a very great amount of property, for several other boats were in close proximity to her, and she was in a position where it took more than half an hour to get her out into the center of the stream.

I was on board, & I tell you I felt a little streaked for a while.

This morning the regiment was marched on board soon after daylight & the fleet started down the river soon after 8 o'clock.

What this expedition has accomplished to compensate for the immense outlay it has occasioned, I am at a loss to imagine. We have done nothing of any account, that is certain. I do not *know* that much was expected of us, but I supposed we were to do *something*. Since our landing at St. Charles it has been disagreeable weather continually. Today the clouds seem breaking away somewhat, & I hope for fair weather, though I suppose I must not expect much of it at this time of year.

Not a word of news yet from home or any other quarter. How long it seems to wait. How sweet are thoughts of home when so far from you all. I do hope I may hear from you soon.

Our destination I do not know, but presume we will first report at Helena or Napoleon, preparatory for some other service. If we go to Helena I shall feel sure of hearing from you, but may be disappointed.

. . . .

Helena, Ark., Jany 22, 1863.
11 ½ P.M.

We arrived here today soon after noon, and I assure you I was very happy to receive the letter from you, written on the 11th. Though I expected later news, yet was I pleased to receive even that, assuring me as it did of your returning health.

. . . .

Jany 23, 8 P.M.

We landed & pitched our tents (on the ground we occupied when we were here before) early this morning . . . .

In Camp near Helena, Ark., Saturday, January 24, 1863

My darling little Lulu:

Did you think because you have received no answer from

papa, that he had forgotten to answer your sweet little letter, or that papa did not think of his dear baby? I have not forgotten you, dear one, but papa has had so much to do, and written *so many letters to mamma*, that he could not get time to write any more. Now he is going to write *you* a good long letter and tell *you* what he has been doing since he wrote to dear mamma. Day before yesterday we came up here on the great big boat, which is about as long as from mamma's room over to Mr. Kinne's store. There were a great many men on the boat, and horses, & guns, and a whole lot of things. We staid on the boat all night, and yesterday morning we came on shore & put up our tents, and are living in them. Don't you wish you could see papa in his tent? It is about as big as a bedroom, and I have a stove in it, and a little table, made by driving four sticks into the ground, and putting a box on the top — bottom side up. Then I have a box to sit on when I eat, and write letters. I spread my blankets on the ground inside the tent and sleep on them. Two men — my lieutenants — sleep with me in the tent. We stand our swords up in the corner, or hang them up, and put our valises in the tent, and it is very nice, but crowded.

. . . .

Helena, Ark., Jan'y 25, 1863 8 P.M.

My dear Carrie:

. . . .

Do not fear for me, my loving little wife. I may meet danger, but my thoughts of the dear ones at home will prevent my incurring any unnecessary risk. You speak of my not wearing my "crimson sash" if I go into an engagement. I probably shall *not* wear it at such a time, as it is too plain a mark for sharpshooters. Officers usually leave them behind, I think, on such occasions. I intend to do so.

. . . .

We heard tonight that England, France & Russia had demanded of the rebels that they give up the struggle in which they are gaining no ground. I shall not believe it untill I hear more about it, but if it is so I hope the war will soon be ended, for I am indeed very anxious to be once more with my dear little family — and I am sure my wife & little ones will welcome me with open arms.

. . . .

Helena, Ark., Jany 27th 1863

The expedition down the river towards Vicksburg which I expected we would be off with before now, has not yet started, and from what I learn I think it will not start at present — at least that is the prevailing impression in camp. It now seems probable that we will move back from the river, perhaps 3 or 4 miles, and go into camp for present. However, we cannot tell what an hour may bring forth, and tomorrow may put an entirely new face upon matters here.

. . . .

Mr. Feller intends to start for home tomorrow on business, so I am writing this tonight to send by him. He says he will take charge of a box if *the folks* wish to send us one, so I'll tell you what I want. Well the, *first*, I don't want those *old stockings*.

If you can send me a little dried fruit it would be very acceptable. Lavantia wrote that she would send me some dried currants &c. if she had a chance. A can of almost anything would go good — something for a *relish* you know. If I had only been *posted* I could have brought along something of the kind — I have learned *now* how I could have worked it through. It will be a good chance to send along some newspapers in the box.

I wish Doct. White would put up for me a few bottles of remedies for diarrhea, dysentery, typhoid fever & colds, *with directions for using*. I know it will be some trouble, but tell him its for the *poor soldiers* & I guess he'll do it, though I've got no money for him *now*. I am in need of no clothing except a pair of boots, & am not very hard up for them just yet. Ed Kinne, Lt. Alvord & others will probably want some things sent. I don't know how much the freight will be. If they could be sent I'd like a bag of *fried cakes* — that's so! — and a few ginger snaps, & a good apple pie if it could be sent without *messing* too much.

I want Frank or Homer to make me *six tin cups*, made so that they will pack into each other & not take up too much room, 6 tin plates, 6 iron spoons, a tin pepper box, & one or two tinned dishes for cooking rice & such things in. Our Iron mess pans are too greasy.

I want a pound of black pepper — ground & a little ginger.

A little *black* tea would not come amiss — but I will not ask for so much, for I know your money & *my credit* will not hold out — and I only mention these things so that if there are some few of them that can be sent as well as not — why all right. I could not find room to carry around much more than what I could eat up — but we are *good at eating*.

O! I want some *little bags*. One to hold a pound of tea, one for 5 pounds of coffee, one for 5 pounds of rice, & 3 or 4 little ones holding a quart or two, would be handy for different uses. A loaf of home-made bread would taste good. A small can of fresh butter *ditto*. Am I not asking for a "heap of things?" But I haven't got through yet.

. . . .

Have Homer make a little tin case for the medicines so that the bottles will not become broken.

Helena, Ark., Jany 28th 1863 8 o'clock P.M.

Mr. Feller has delayed his departure for home till tomorrow, so I have time to add a few lines to my letter of last night. . . .

I'll tell you one thing the "Ladies Soldiers Aid Society" can send to our company that will be worth its weight in gold to us. That is, *a bottle or a part of a bottle of quinine*. We need it badly, & the Surgeons are out of it a great deal of the time. Col. Lewis rec'd a little — 16 grains — from the Medical director this morning as an *especial favor*.

Can you send me some sort of smoking cap arrangement for a Camp cap? — or, politely speaking, a *night cap*? Anything that will go on my head & be soft & easy to sleep in will do. It is not a very pressing want, but I have seen a few nights when it would have been very convenient & comfortable. I don't think of anything else. I must *stop* thinking or I'll want more than the steamer can bring down the river.

. . . .

In Camp near Helena, Arkansas, February 6th, 1863.

Dear Father:

. . . . Our Brigade (2nd Brigaade 5th Division) consists of the 28th Wis., 29th Iowa & the 33rd Mo. Regts. under Brig Gen Fisk.[5] At present Col. Lewis is acting Brig. Gen. We have been moving our camp back from the river this week, which has kept us quite busy. During the day it is very muddy. When the mud dries off I think it will be pleasant enough here, though it looks desolate now. We get no news here hardly. I presume now we will be paid off while here, up to the last of Dec. Probably we shall not see the paymaster again in 4 or 6 months, if we get that much now — which we may not. A little money would be very acceptable to us, and no doubt our folks at home would be glad to get some. I shall not try to pay my debts at home out of this first payment, for my family needs *something* to last till next pay day — so the banks must wait.

. . . . This morning I took a notion that I wanted a little milk, so I went over to a "nigger settlement" about a mile off & bought a little. *I only had to pay 25¢ for a quart*! Fact! I sent to Helena for a dozen eggs. Had to pay 30¢ per dozen for them, & only 6 out of the dozen were good! Only 5¢ each! Corn meal costs 2 ½¢. *Corn is worth $1.20 Wheat 75¢* & poor at that. But little wheat is used by the natives here. Butter sells for 30¢. I presume we will be here a month yet, but we may move in 48 hours. There is considerable sickness from diarrhea & fever. The Reg't. has lost 3 men from sickness, also 1 Lieut., since leaving Wis., but has not seen an armed rebel . . . .

Head Quarters Co. C., 28th Wis. Vol., 2nd Brigade. Fisks Division. In Camp near Helena, Arkansas, Tuesday morning, Feby 10th, 1863

My loving wife:

. . . . I am sorry indeed that you are being driven about "from pillar to post" at such a rate during my absence, by reason of change in boarding places. It is indeed too bad, and I do feel very bad about it for your sake. I hardly think you had better go to keeping house, it will give you so much to do in addition to your care of the dear children — I really don't believe you had better attempt it. You are not able to do the necessary work.

As to going to Mr. Topliff's to board, it would suit me if you could feel at home there.

If I could get what is due me on the first of March I should be able to make the payment on the house then, but I don't expect to get more than the pay up to Dec. 31. In that case I could not make more than *part* payment if any. If Kreeger will wait, & you can rent the house, I think it will be the best way.

You speak of visiting Columbus this summer if you could hear as often from me there. As for that letters will reach Columbus the same night that they would reach Oconomowoc, and I could *write there just as often*. Do as you think best.

If I could only get my pay I could tell better what to do; but I

havent a cent yet, and I have no idea when I shall get any —
perhaps not in three months — though I *hope* for some sooner.
If I *don't* get some I really don't know what I shall do, but I
don't care about it on my own account half as much as yours,
for I know you must be about out of money — and I *can* get
along without it here, while you *must* have it there *to live*. . . .

Ed Kinne cooks for me & the Lieutenants. We get along
very well. Usually have pancakes for breakfast, pancakes for
dinner & pancakes for supper. A little pork & bean soup gets
mixed in now & then. Yesterday he baked some bread. Had
pretty good luck with one or two small loaves, & the rest was
tough. We would think the same of all of it at home — & the
pancakes too . . . .

Head Quarters 28th Wis. Vol.
In Camp near Helena, Ark., Friday night, Feb'y 13, 1863,
11 o'clock

. . . .
Poor young Lt. Mead . . . passed away this morning. I had
watched him every since I have known him in camp, and had
been led to respect him for his virtues. Quiet & unassuming,
strictly moral in all his habits, his was a character which all
might well be glad to imitate. His body will be sent home. He
was the only child of his aged & wealthy parents. He has died
for his country — let his name be honored. Two men — one
from Co. E, & one from Co. H — died last night in the
hospital.

Theron M. Smalley of my Company whom I mentioned as
being in the hospital, is almost gone. I think there is no hope
of his recovery, if, indeed, he lives till morning. He has been
deranged for some days. He recognized me this afternoon,
however, but is nearly all the time insensible.

We are lying here still, improving our camp, and drilling a
little. I learn that we have been transferred to another brigade,

to be under the command of Brig. Gen. Salomon, a brother of
our Gov.[6] What other regiments will be with us I do not know
. . . .

**Head Quarters 28th Reg't. Wis. Vol.,
In Camp near Helena Ark., Feby 18, 1863.**

. . . .

War presents its dismal aspects here to some extent. Could
you see the amount of suffering presented by our *one* little
regiment, and then compare it with the large number of regiments in the field — consider how little of hardship we have
had to endure as compared with hundreds of other regiments,
it would make your warm heart bleed. The hospital, we sometimes think, is not as well conducted as it might be, though it is
easy to find fault where a *few* have *so much* to do. Our sick do
not, however, number near so many as in most regiments near
us. It is affecting to one of tender and humane feelings to look
in and see the poor fellows stretched upon their cots, and feel
that we cannot assist them — that their friends are looking to
us, their commanding officers, and in a measure holding *us*
responsible for their lives, and we powerless so far as any
ability exists to raise them up — & the surgeons much of the
time without proper remedies for the treatment of their cases.
Poor fellows! some prostrated with fevers — some dying of
consumption, their bright eyes sparkling with such an un-
earthly light — some talking incoherently from hour to hour,
of everything; one could fill a volume with the thoughts called
up. We (that is the regiment) have lost eleven men and two
lieutenants since leaving Wisconsin.

My company has been called upon to mourn the loss of one
its members. Poor Theron M. Smalley breathed his last on
Sabbath afternoon at four o'clock. He was a good man — one
of the best in my company — a true soldier, always ready to do
his duty. I am proud to say of him what I can say of but very

few, that *he never gave me occasion to reprimand him.* His brother faithfully cared for him, watching by his side by day & by night during the last days of his illness. It will, I am sure, be a hard blow to his parents, who reside at Aztalan, Jeff. Co. It seems hard that he should die here. If his mother, a sister, or a dearer one could have watched by the bedside of the sufferer, smoothed his dying pillow, and like an angel of love & mercy soothed him with words of tenderness and affection, it would not seem so hard. He was, however, insensible during most of the last four days of his life, though he recognized me several times when I called in to see him, as I did several times a day, and spoke my name. We buried him upon the hill-side in the shadow of the giants of the forest, and placed a board at the head of his grave to mark his resting-place, Lieut Gilmore & myself having engraved upon it his name, age &c. "Peace to his ashes."

. . . .

Our regiment has been transferred to another brigade, which is composed of the following regiments, viz: 47th 46th & 43rd Indiana, 28th Wisconsin & 1st U.S. Regulars, commanded by Brig. Gen. F. Salomon of Wis., a brother of Gov. S. Our officers think it will be a "bully" brigade. We are the "First Brigade, Thirteenth Division, Army of the Tennesee." I don't know where the balance of the brigade now is. We shall probably go to them, or they come to us.

. . . .

In Camp near Helena, Ark., Feb'y 18, 1863.

I have already made out a long letter — a sad one perhaps in some of its details, — but I'll try and add something to it yet. Perhaps you would like to know how we live here in the *Captain's tent.* I'll tell you. I usually get up at reveille, which should beat at 6 A.M. Sometimes Lieut. Alvord is up first, but not usually. Now and then "Ed." comes & builds a fire before any of us start. Lt. Gilmore generally lies in bed — or *bunk* rather — till breakfast is ready. He is getting lazy. Ed Kinne cooks for us. Fries pork, makes a kind of flour gravy for the cakes (*loss gullion* we call it) & bakes pancakes for breakfast. Our pancakes are light & good now. They are made of *salt risings*. We have coffee, & sometimes milk in it. I go nearly every morning to the nigger shanties on the "branch," about a mile, for milk. Sometimes I get it & sometimes *not*. It costs *only twenty five cents a quart*, & we are glad to get it at that price. Ed. bakes bread (salt rising) about every day, so with bread & pancakes, pork & coffee, we fare sumptuously every day. *Gravy* (& molasses when we can get it) fills the place of *butter* to *perfection* — don't it? We occasionally have bean soup for dinner, and twice we have had dessicated potatoes, (we get no fresh ones here.) They taste good I tell you, and are easily cooked, looking some what like hash when cooked — *but the meat is not there*. For supper bread & coffee is usually the great staple, but pancakes has been our "stand-by" for the past three weeks, morning, noon and night.

The Col. is having a regimental baking built, but I think it will not be used much by us, for I fear it will not be done in time. Ed. does our washing "once in a while," assisted by some one of the boys. *The ironing does itself.*

We have enlarged our tent by building up an addition behind it of rough slabs, or "puncheons," split out with an axe, and covering it with out tent "fly." It gives us almost double the room. We have built us a table, stools, benches &c., & have the floor of the tent "carpeted" with "shakes" split out from logs with an axe. So we are really quite comfortable here.

Company drills in the forenoon when pleasant. We have had no battalion drills here yet, on account of the weather. Dress parade every afternoon at half past four.

My Lieutenants have *bunks* built one above the other at one side of the tent, where they sleep, while I have my "cot"

(which I bought at Milwaukee for $4. and have been able to transport thus far) to sleep on, which is very comfortable.
. . . .

Helena, Ark., Feb'y 19, 1863. 8 A.M.

. . . .
We are looking forward anxiously to see a blow struck — a vigorous blow — that will be of some effect toward suppressing the rebellion & ending the war. Oh! that it might be struck quickly, that the loss of so many lives from disease & exposure might be prevented. O, Lord, how long! how long must this terrible strife rage among men who ought to stand shoulder to shoulder as brothers? Let us hope, dearest, that it may soon end.
. . . .
We have orders to be in *readiness to move*, as I understand. Where to I don't know, but I presume we shall leave here very soon for some point. Some think we will go up to Fort Pillow, near Memphis, while some think we will go to Vicksburg
. . . .

Helena, Ark., Feb'y 23, 1863

Yesterday I was officer of the day again & did not get time to write you as I intended. The regiment was also paid off, which made me some additional labor & consumed some time, as the commissioned officers have to see to the payment of their companies.

We still remain here in the same camp, but expect to move down in the vicinity of the fort either this afternoon or tomorrow, preparatory to sending off the effective men of the regiment to the "Yazoo Pass." At least that is what I expect. The sick and disabled men will probably be left at Helena, while only the effective men will go. "Yazoo Pass" opens from the Mississippi River some 8 miles below Helena. It has been closed up by a levee built at a cost of about a quarter of a million, several years ago. It has now been cut out, and the water from the river passing out into the "Coldwater" river & thence into the Yazoo, it is expected will allow gunboats and small transports to pass down to the rear of the fortifications behind Vicksburg. I think we will leave for there to clear out the channel, in two or three days.

Our payment yesterday was only up to October 31, so that I have now nearly four months more pay due me. I however rec'd pay from date of Commission, (Sept. 2d) so that I got a little money. I shall pay up what I owe in camp, & then send you all I can — Probably $150. or so. I wish I could have enough to pay up Kreeger — & all my debts — as I might if I had what is due me to date.

Feby 23, 11 P.M., 1863

I got cut short in my letter writing this morning, and have only now found time to re-commence. We have orders to move. Tomorrow morning at five we are to strike tents, and we are to be aboard the boats with all our baggage by 8 A.M., at which hour the boat is to leave. We take 15 days rations, along with us. As near as I can learn we are only going to "Yazoo Pass" & vicinity at present. Any further information which I can obtain I will forward as soon as possible to you.

Capt White remains here in charge of the disabled men &c. He has money to send home, & has kindly taken charge of some for several of us officers, and will send it if he has a chance. If not he will keep it till our return. I left $170 with him, and hope you will receive it soon, for I know you will need it, or at least a portion of it, by this time. I have paid the $25. I borrowed from Henry Hitchcock, and about all the other little bills I owed in camp. Shall probably settle *them* tomorrow. I am compelled to keep for my own use more than I like to, but I don't know when I shall get paid again. It may be several months. I rec'd $245.30 yesterday. If Kreeger will take $50. now & extend the time on the balance due M'ch 13th you had better let him have that amount, if he won't wait without. I think I can pay all I own on the house by next January. Use the rest of the money as you need it. I shall hope to send more soon. I don't wish to carry much money south with me, as it might be lost if Secesh should "gobble me up" & find the Green Backs about me.

. . . . You will, of course let me know when you get the money. *Keep it as quiet as possible.*

Ballard & Haight are no better. I think both will die. Clark is better. We leave 23 men here unfit for duty, including the three mentioned — cases of diarrhea &c. 52 men will go with us, of my company. Well! it is almost midnight & I have but 3 hours to sleep.

. . . . .

NOTES

1. Richard N. Current, *The History of Wisconsin, Vol. II, The Civil War Era, 1848-1873* (Madison, 1967), 312–19; Current cites several titles of monographic studies dealing with the riots in Ozaukee County. These draft riots were extensively reported; the Detroit *Free Press*, for example, printed accounts of the disturbances for several days.

2. Current, *The Civil War Era*, 318-19.

3. For accounts of the fighting in Missouri and Arkansas, see relevant portions of Robert U. Johnson and C. C. Buel (eds.), *Battles and Leaders of the Civil War* (4 vols., New York, 1884–87). More recent studies include two excellent studies of Sterling Price: Albert Castel, *General Sterling Price and the Civil War in the West* (Baton Rouge, 1968) and Robert E. Shalhope, *Sterling Price: Portrait of a Southerner* (Columbia, 1971). See, also, Jay Monaghan, *Civil War on the Western Border, 1854-1865* (Boston, 1955).

4. Mrs. Margaret W. Blumenthal presently has the sword in her personal possession.

5. Clinton B. Fisk, 1828–1890, had been a banker in Michigan but was in St. Louis when the war began. Named colonel of the 33d Missouri, September 5, 1862, and brigadier general, November 24, 1862. His principal military service was in Missouri. After the war he helped found Fisk University at Nashville.

6. Frederick Sigel Salomon had fled Germany with his brother, Edward, the future governor of Wisconsin, and another brother Charles Eberhard. Both brothers became generals. Frederick Salomon is frequently mentioned by Stevens in his diary.

Part II: YAZOO PASS
EXPEDITION

One of the major Union objectives of the Civil War was to gain control of the Mississippi River. Many of the early Union activities in the West were directed to that goal, such as Grant's capture of Forts Henry and Donelson, his movement to Shiloh, Union operations in Missouri, capture of Island No. 10, Memphis, and Helena, Arkansas, and, of course, Admiral David Farragut's capture of New Orleans in April, 1862. The net result of these efforts was that by the summer of 1862, the principal obstacle to Union control of the Mississippi River was the Confederate stronghold at Vicksburg, which fell to Ulysses S. Grant on July 4, 1863. The 28th Wisconsin Infantry was involved in one phase of Union efforts to capture Vicksburg.

Grant was appointed commander of the Department of the Tennessee in October, 1862. He planned a two-pronged thrust against Vicksburg. Troops under his personal command marched south from Grand Junction, Tennessee, along the line of the Mississippi Central Railroad. His advance was blocked when separate Confederate cavalry forces under the commands of Earl Van Dorn and Nathan B. Forrest raided behind his lines, seizing supplies and disrupting his communications so that Grant was forced to retreat. A second force under the command of William T. Sherman landed at Chickasaw Bluffs north of Vicksburg, attacked the Confederates in December, 1862, but failed.

Logically, Grant should have reformed his forces and tried to advance along with the Mississippi Central Railroad, to allow him to attack Vicksburg from high ground west of the city. But a complicating factor was the arrival of General John B. McClernand at Vicksburg; Grant had little confidence in McClernand's fighting ability, yet he outranked Sherman. Consequently, Grant himself came to Vicksburg and took command.

His problem was how to get at Vicksburg. The Confederates could utilize bluffs, swamps, and rivers to foil an attack from the Mississippi River. Grant ingeniously tried several devices to overcome the difficulty. At separate locations he tried digging two canals, each of which would divert the Mississippi into a new channel, thus leaving Vicksburg high and dry. Both failed. His engineers tried to cut a course through bayous and obscure rivers, so that a Union fleet would have an alternate route around Vicksburg. This, too, failed. Then he tried sending a fleet up the Yazoo River, which enters the Mississippi a few miles above Vicksburg from that direction. But that maneuver also failed when Confederate land forces almost captured the fleet in a very narrow, tree-clogged waterway.

The 28th Wisconsin was involved in still another effort to capture Vicksburg. The plan was for a joint army-navy expedition to go through the Yazoo Pass, some 300 miles north of Vicksburg, proceed via the Coldwater, Tallahatchie, and Yazoo Rivers, and reach high ground east of Vicksburg. The fleet was composed of two iron-clads, six tin-clads, and two rams; accompanying the fleet were 4,000 men in a division commanded by General L. F. Ross, including the 28th Wisconsin. Grant later ordered 30,000 additional troops to join the expedition, but because of delays only a small part of this force joined the expedition.

Indeed, other delays severely hampered the expedition. Levees separating the Yazoo Pass from the Mississippi River were blown up on February 3, 1863. Since the difference in levels was eight or nine feet, a torrent of water poured through, and it was several days before it was practicable for vessels to navigate. Meanwhile, the Confederates felled trees along the Pass, which further delayed the Union advance. When the fleet reached the Coldwater River on February 28, difficulties continued. The stream was narrow, and the current was swift; overhanging branches caused extensive damage to the ships, further slowing the advance. The fleet entered the Tallahatchie on March 6, and four days later reached the junction of the Yazoo and Tallahatchie Rivers, where the Confederates had constructed Fort Pemberton.

Union attacks on the fort were unsuccessful. The Confederates had sunk the *Star of the West,* of Fort Sumter fame, as an obstruction in the channel. The guns of the Union fleet were unable to subdue the fort, and Ross's men could not find enough firm ground to land on. As a result, the Union fleet withdrew on April 5, its mission unfulfilled.

Stevens graphically described the Yazoo Pass expedition. His letters bear abundant witness to the narrow streams and the hazards of overhanging branches. He attributed the failure of the expedition to the delay between the time of arrival and the attack on Ft. Pemberton, a delay which allowed the Confederates time to develop ample fortifications.

Members of the 28th Wisconsin were not the only persons disappointed with the results of the expedition. The health of the naval commander, Watson Smith, failed so badly during the attack on Fort Pemberton that he was sent back and died soon thereafter.

All of Grant's ingenious plans had failed, yet he did not give up. He marched his forces south of Vicksburg, ordered the fleet to run past that city, and then ferried his troops across the Mississippi to the high ground he had so assiduously sought. There then ensued one of the most brilliant military campaigns of the Civil War, a campaign which culminated in the capture

of Vicksburg on July 4, 1863. As we will see, the 28th
Wisconsin during these stirring events was on garrison duty at
Helena, Arkansas, and on the same day that Vicksburg fell
defeated a superior Confederate force.[1]

On board Steamboat Diana, "Ross Landing" Yazoo Pass, Miss. Thursday, Feby 26, 1863. 8 o'clock, P.M.

Are you at all surprised to hear from me way down in the State
of Mississippi? After writing you last Monday we rec'd orders
to be ready to leave camp at 6 o'clock Tuesday morning, and to
be on board the steamer at 8 A.M. I had to do so much that I was
unable to write again. I was at work nearly all night, as were
many others of the officers, but the usual delay occurred so that
we only embarked at 3 o'clock P.M., and left soon after, going
down the Mississippi some 8 or 9 miles I think, then entered the
"Yazoo Pass", and steamed *out into the country* — at least it
seemed so as we left the River and slowly crept down the narrow
channel towards the close of the day — and a beautiful day it
was. Just before night we emerged into a sheet of water called
"Moon Lake" — a beautiful sheet indeed by moonlight. I sat
for a long time on the guards feasting my eyes on the fair
scenery, the moonlight being reflected by the ever moving
waters of the lake — the dark shades of the giant trees which
border upon the water — the fleet of some 25 steamboats and
gunboats moving hither & thither — it was well worthy of a
passing thought, at least — and so I sat and dreamed, with open
eyes; thought of the many other lovely spots I had seen —
Thought of the dear ones at home who had gazed with me upon
scenes of beauty; and wished that *one* fond, loving one, might,
under other circumstances, also look upon "Moon Lake" & its
surroundings. There I dreamed till the roll of the drum & the
shrill voice of the fife called me away from dream-land at
"tattoo." I was officer of the day (and night!) *that day & the*

next, having the general supervision of the boat & troops on board to attend to, so my hands were pretty nearly full. The night was quite warm, and at midnight I wrapped a blanket about me & laid down upon the deck, where I rested quite comfortably, & free from cold, till half past three. The morning brought a very heavy rain, and many of the men got a good soaking. It continued a good share of the time till this afternoon, when it cleared off again. We make slow progress, — are probably not more than 20 miles, by the course of the stream, from the Mississippi river. The channel through which we are passing will probably average 60 feet in width, and is very crooked, and some of the larger boats find it difficult moving with any speed. Our boat is a very small one for six companies to occupy, and an old one too. However we expect no difficulty, as far as the boat is concerned. Six of the companies under Lt. Col. Whitaker are on this boat, while Col. Lewis & 4 companies are on the St. Louis — a boat three times as large. All right!

This Division (consisting I think of two brigades) is commanded by Gen Ross.[2] Our brigade by Gen. Salomon. We probably are about 6000 strong, (Infantry) beside having some artillery & several gun boats along. As near as I can learn we are bound for Vicksburg & vicinity. Report says that the rebels are already aware of our movement, and that we *may* meet them before reaching "Yazoo City" — but we expect nothing of the kind. The stream down which we are passing runs through heavy timber, so that we cannot "see out" any where scarcely — seldom see a house — & then only log ones. No inhabitants in sight. I bro't but 51 of my men with me, having orders to bring only well men. The rest remain at Helena. Some are quite sick. Ballard & Haight were very low when I left. Clark was better. Clausen was badly off with diarrhea. The rest were unwell, but not much sick. Christy & Hitchcock are among them. I think some are more *cowardly* than *sick*. Those I have with me I believe are *true blue*. We can get poor board on the boat for 50 cents per meal. *Only* $10.00 per week! I took 3 meals, & then fell back onto *hard bread & coffee*. I am getting fat — cannot wear my pants buttoned around my waist, with any comfort, and if I keep on, shall need a new dress coat very soon. I weigh more than I ever did before.

I have had no trouble with my men — why do you ask?

I left $170. with Capt. C. C. White at Helena, to be forwarded to you. Our allotment dont work yet. He will send it if an opportunity presents itself, or if he can buy exchange there. I hope you will get it soon. Don't go to paying any of the notes against me, if asked, for you may need it yourself. Capt. White will inform you by mail when he sends it. I have been very busy making out Company Clothing Returns, returns of Arms, Ammunition &c. for several days, at least all of the time that I could get. It is busy & hard work. I have also just completed my 4 copies of Muster Roll. I have to make them out every two months.

Provisions of some kinds *cost* here. Cheese 25 cents per lb by the whole cheese, Butter 40¢, dried beef 20. I have bought of the Commissary 65 Ham at 9¢ 2 Bu. Potatoes at $1.25 per bu. I have seen onions which cost 5 cents apiece. Some eatables would bring almost any price. I am sorry that the Sutler did not get along with those things. I don't expect now to ever get them. They may come, however. Did you ever write me what you had sent? I never found out yet what there is for me. Just as we left Helena I rec'd 2 Tribunes from home & a Wisconsin from Dora. The Tribunes come quite regularly — I have missed but 2 up to Feby 13. The Lt. Col. has just called for me, so I must stop for a while. Will write more tomorrow if possible. . . . .

On board Steamboat Diana, "Yazoo Pass",
Mississippi, Friday eve'g Feby 27, 1863.
10 P.M.

. . . .

I am not risking my life here merely for freedom for the Negro, though that may be one of the fruits of the war, but for the preservation of our constitutional liberties. Last night and today have been very pleasant. Today has been quite warm. This morning in company with two other Captains of our regiment I went in our boats yawl to several of the boats of the fleet. We passed some 15 of the transports & gun boats. I went to the commissary boat & bought some provisions. I have Lieut Gilmore to feed which takes some money, as he on account of some informality in his accounts &c. drew no pay at our last pay-day, and is out of money. He also owes me a little. We have made but little progress today — the channel of the stream being more tortuous than ever — winding about among the giant cottonwood trees. Sometimes as we are passing along we can see through the woods just ahead another boat headed in an almost opposite direction. To-day day [*sic*] about 4 or 5 o'clock we passed a plantation on the right bank of the stream, on which was a splendid house with weeping willows & evergreens all about it, with walks laid out beneath them, *and several ladies standing* beneath their shade. There was also the usual sprinkling of niggers, big & little, *black & white,* and, as a methodist preacher would say, of *all sexes.* The 29th Wis. Infantry we also found encamped there, they having left their camp near Helena last Saturday, and been sent down here. Capt Bryant, E. H. Jones' friend, was sick and unable to come along. I saw his 2d Lieut today, (Lieut Townsend, Cousin of Capt. Townsend of our regiment.) He had also been sick, but was just going down to join his regiment.

We have no surgeon with us on board the boat, and no medicines. I hope the people of Waukesha & Walworth counties will make up and send us all the hospital & sanitary stores they can — and send agents along with them, so that we may get them. I do so wish I had what Feller has for me & the company. James Hall & Charle Waller are quite ill in my Co. James is threatened with a fever, but is feeling better tonight. Some others are complaining.

Darling, it would pain you to see the anxiety manifested by seven eighths of the soldiers to get beer, liquor &c., every time they have a chance. I shut up the bar the day we came aboard, but the Lt. Col. has allowed it to be opened to the men to drink occasionally — as often as the officers request it for them. *That I won't do.* I have three or four times drank a glass of beer by advice of the doctor, in place of this terrible water, but I have about made up my mind to touch no more of it, even as a medicine, on account of the pernicious influence of such example. It is indeed medicine for me, for I do not like the taste of it.

How do you get along, darling, I pity you when I think of your being alone, almost, at home. But I hope you may get along well. Don't try to do that washing. 'Tis cheaper to pay some one to do it, by far, so get it done. Be very careful of yourself, & I know you will care for the babies. Tell pa, Lavantia & all that I am all well, even if I don't write every day. I can't get time to do that, for I have work to do. Tell them I am fatter & heavier than I ever was before — it is the truth. Why need they be eternally worrying themselves & making themselves & *every one else* miserable. *Show them this.* It is all nonsense to *fret* so.

. . . .

On board Steamboat Diana, Coldwater river, Mississippi, March 2, 1863, 9 P.M.

Another day's duty is about done, and before I lay down to take my rest as usual on the deck, I will write a few lines again to you. We are now, as you see by the date, in the Coldwater river. The map which I have puts down this stream as running into the Mississippi. This is an error. It empties into the Tallahatchie. We reached the river from the "pass" about 10 o'clock this morning, and have been lying here ever since, building barricades upon the sides of our boats, with Timber rails &c. One more gunboat, two rams, & a mortar boat have passed us during the day, so that we have, I believe, 5 gunboats, 3 rams & 2 mortar boats in advance of us. I do not know

General evidently anticipates it somewhere, and wishes to be ready for it. I suppose we have some 20,000 to 25,000 troops along with the fleet. The gunboats look sullen with the brass pieces looking out from their portholes. The mortar boat carries one 13 inch mortar, which weights over 17,000 pounds, & carries a 220 pound ball some 4 miles. I have been "officer of the day" again today. My turn comes often here. Today we rec'd some mail again from the north, but it was old — mailed in Jan'y. I got none. Most of the boys are well. This stream is small, and I presume we shall move slowly yet, though probably faster then we have been doing. Some days we have moved no more than about two to two and a half miles. It has been a tedious voyage thus far, but I have had some time to finish up some of my writing. That has made it endurable. I have heard nothing from the men left at Helena since we left there. Those with us here are mostly well. Some have a little diarrhea. Our only surgeon who accompanies us is Dr. Smith. He is on the other boat, and has no medicines of any account. We are poorly used, I think. The boys are hoping he will get killed or something will happen so that we can have a surgeon good for something. I really begin to think he is not as good as some.
. . . .

On board Steamboat "Diana,"
Coldwater River, Mississippi,
Friday, March 6th, 1863, 9 A.M.

Once more I am enabled to write you, and still from on board the steamer which we have occupied since a week ago last Tuesday — a small, rotten, uncomfortable, unmanageable concern, — fit only for a tow boat, which is her business. I had no idea, when we came on board, that we should be so long cooped up here as we are. The men — sick & well — as well as the officers want room; room to sleep & room to stand; room to walk & room to eat.

Passing down these small streams is slow & tedious work.
We are still some 12 miles above the mouth of the Coldwater,
but the stream is so much larger here that we are able to steam
along faster than we have been doing, so that we shall probably
arrive at the mouth of the river about noon, if we have good
luck. We have met no opposition yet. Yesterday one of the
boats confiscated a lot of cotton at a plantation a few miles
back. What a lot of negroes there were about! Little & big —
dark and light colored — "boys" & "girls" — it was an
interesting crowd to look at. Today we have some fresh beef,
which was "*found*" ashore last night.

The boats of the fleet have been badly used — most of them.
Smoke stacks knocked off, railings torn off, parts of the decks,
wheelhouses, &c. carried away by trees & overhanging
branches on either side. It is a wonder that no one has been
injured on any of the boats. My health continues *very* good.
My brother officers congratulate me every day upon my improved appearance, physically. Perhaps *dirt may* make some
difference in looks. Really, I have not been as well for a long
time. I think I have seen the worst part of it here, so far as
health is concerned.

. . . .

Possibly we may encounter the enemy before I am able to
write again. If we do, I shall go into battle confident that I shall
yet return to you & all the loved ones at home. I have no fears.
"Let not your heart be troubled," my own darling. "There is
no sorrow for the earnest soul, That looketh up to God in
perfect faith." Let that faith be thine, dear Carrie, and all will
be well. Surrounded by the din of battle, the rattle of musketry,
the roar of cannon & the screeching of shells, I shall think of
you, & hope I may bear home honors of which *you* may be
proud — if only that of having served faithfully my country.

Some of our officers think that if this expedition results
favorable it will be the decisive blow of the war — for we are
advancing against Vicksburg — that fallen, and we hope that

Jeff Davis & his fellow traitors are conquered. I hope we may succeed. If we do, the honor of having been a part of this army will be enough for me.

. . . .

On board steamboat Snella, Tallahatchie, (50 miles above its mouth) Sunday, March 8th, 1863 9 A.M.

Yesterday morning my company & Company I were ordered aboard this boat at 10 minutes notice, to go on a foraging expedition — and off we went. We passed down the river in advance of the fleet, landed at a plantation and "took" 85 bales of cotton. Went to another place & found 4 bales stowed away in a shanty, killed a dozen pigs & 7 beeves. During the day the boat took on board 160 bales of cotton, worth at least $400 per bale, amounting to $64,000. There is any amount of cotton in this part of the country — a great deal to say the least. One day — Wednesday I think — they took 200 bales at one plan[tation]. We use it for barricades upon the sides of the transports & gunboats. We put a lot of it aboard 2 boats this morning, and are now off for another *haul*. There is no force of the enemy here, though they had scouts here a week ago. I don't see why this cotton has not been burnt. We found some that had been set fire to & the ends scorched. The bales are very solid, & will probably weight from 450 to 600 pounds. We incur no danger from the rebels here on this duty, though we may do so further down the river. We shall probably be relieved in a day or two, and some other companies take our place.

At the mouth of this river we are told that there is a battery of 17 guns. Our gunboats & mortar are enough for that, I'll warrant you.

There are some fine plantations here. I have visited several, but have found nothing that I would take exchange for a good

"eighty" in Wisconsin. Peach trees are in blossom. I wish I could have some of the fruit when it is ripe. Winter wheat is 3 or 4 inches high, but we see but little of it. Salt, coffee & quinine are scarce articles among the *natives* here. One man offered $10 for a 25 pound sack of salt.

. . . .

I am anxious to see you all love, but can't promise when I will come home. If you want to see where we are, take a map, & make the Coldwater run Southeasterly into the Tallahatchie. Then you can find about our locality. A slave that I saw the other day inquired what cotton was worth. The capt. of the "Diana" told him "a dollar a pound." Said he "Golly, if dat's so, they'll make dese niggers *get up and shine*." He said he could pick 250 pounds of cotton per day. We see but very few whites here, but lots of niggers. They are quite intelligent, as a class, as I expected to find them. You know I am not especially a "niggerito."

. . . .

This cotton that we take is first rate for barricades on the boats, & then is worth a *pile* in cash at the north, besides being much needed there. I hope we may continue to get it — and in quantities worth taking, too. The Quartermaster receipts for it to the owner, when requested. If he proves his loyalty he will be paid for it. Doubtless lots of *traitors* will have no difficulty in proving anything necessary to save the price of their cotton.

I like being on this duty very well — better than lying idle on a transport. It gives one a little exercise, — and we all need it. As often as possible I will post you as to our whereabouts & condition. I am feeling well and doing well.

. . . .

Near mouth of Tallahatchie river, Miss.,
(In the field, on picket.) Mch 12, 1863 9 A.M.

We landed yesterday two miles above here, and marched down here about 3 P.M. The Gunboats were one or two of them in advance. While we were marching down, one of the gunboats opened upon the rebel battery, which almost immediately replied, and here we had our first sight & heard the first sounds of real war, except the burning of cotton which I will mention & try to describe to you hereafter. The first shot fell just at my left & opposite the head of my company, as we were marching down the rivers bank, striking in the water, about 4 rods from me. The next passed just over our heads. The third struck a tree in front, bringing down some dead limbs about Col. Lewis horse's heels. Those were the closest shots to us. The 43rd Indiana was in advance as skirmishers & had 3 men wounded by rifle shots. One of our gunboats met with quite an accident, & hauled off. They were loading, when a shell struck the shell they were putting in when they both exploded, killing one man and wounding 18. 3 have since died. This was all there was of the engagement. Our regiment was out on picket all night, and are yet. We are to be relieved at 11 o'clock today. It was a cold night — a heavy cold dew fell, & we had a cold time of it lying out with only our blankets. I was worse off than most of them, as I had nothing but my coat & rubber blanket. Had to get up every little while & jump, run & stamp around to get warm & couldn't do it at that. I have heard of but one man among us who slept warm.

Coming down the river on Tuesday we passed a great deal of cotton, burning along the banks, having been fired by the rebels or the owners. Just at night we passed a steamer loaded with cotton and burned to the waters edge. She must have had at least $1,000,000 worth of cotton on board when fired. As her guards burned away the cotton had fallen off & the banks of the river were lined for miles with the burning bales of cotton. It was a sight worth a thousand miles travel to see. All night, after wead [*sic*] *tied up* for the night, the flaming masses continued to float past us, carried by the current. Once a burning bale caught under our guards, but a little exertion on the part of a few men relieved us from danger. The steamer was owned by rebels, and found herself followed so closely by us that they burned her to avoid capture. Millions of dollars worth of cotton have I seen destroyed by fire. I begin to *see* what I have never been able to fully realize of the effects of war in a country where carried on. May we at the north never feel such dreadful effects from such a cause. Well, Carrie, I have heard the barking of the "grim dogs of war." Ears ever accustomed to the "sweet voices of the children of peace" have listened to the booming of cannon, the screeching of shell; the plunging of shot; Have heard the sharp report of the rifle bringing down the solitary picket in the forests of Mississippi. The rattle of musketry in battle I have not yet heard — though I *may* ere this days bright sun shall set. The sounds I have heard are very much as I expected from the descriptions I have read of them. The sensations, thus far, are not, to me, so *very* dreadful, though it seems a careless way to throw balls into a crowd of men. Col. Lewis was out with the reg't yesterday, & again this morning, though he slept on the boat. *He* & also Col. Whitaker, are better.

Noon, Mch 12th

We are now lying in the woods supporting a battery, consisting of 1-32 & 1-12 pounder, which were placed in position by our forces last night & today — a part of the men working all night, rolling cotton bales &c to build breast works. Our big mortar & this battery will probably open on the rebels this afternoon again, assisted by our gun boats. I think we will experience no great difficulty in taking it. While writing this (which I do seated on the ground, with my haversack & knee for a writing desk,) two guns have been fired from the rebel battery, probably to "feel" of us & find where our position for battery has been chosen. We have not yet replied, & probably will not till we get fully ready. The sun is shining brightly & quite warmly down upon us; the birds singing in the branches overhead & on every side, and one not *posted,* if dropped down here, would hardly realize that we are just ready to engage in battle. But we shall, probably, and may God defend the right.

. . . .

All but four of my men here shouldered their muskets & marched out yesterday. *One* of them is a *sneak,* one has the mumps, one the diarrhea and one fever. The river water is bad here. I do not drink any of it till boiled, but may be compelled to. My drink is tea & coffee. My supper on picket last night was hard bread & cold tea. For breakfast this morning I had cold tea, raw bacon & hard bread — quite a variety. I get along well on it, & am vain enough to think I can appreciate a *good meal* when I get back home. Get one ready in time, Carrie.

I am now with my *reserve.* They lie around me, some sleeping — some talking. All, nearly, are anxious to have the ball open. Some apprehend that the *secesh* will evacuate & burn their works, which are, I learn, built of cotton to a great extent. Well, if we can capture the place without a fight, so much the better, though *I'd like to save the cotton.*

1 ½ P.M. I hardly think there will be a fight today. No appearances of it now, though it *may* begin in 5 minutes. I don't know when I can send this, but hope to do soon. You can tear off this half sheet & let our folks read the first 6 pages & I will not have to write it all to all of them — and, more than that, I can't get time to do it. Ed Kinne has brought us a canteen of tea, a loaf of bread (full of Salacratis) & some slices of raw ham. They make a good dinner. Darling wife, don't worry about me. I came out expecting to endure hardship & exposure to some extent, but have got along well so far. I shall probably realize my expectations to some extent, but feel confident I shall come safe through all, and return to my loved ones again. You know I have always felt so about it, and I hope *you* will also. . . .

Thursday, 3 P.M. The fight has begun I suppose. Our gunboats have just fired 2 shots, to which we have yet no reply. Our reg't has been moved down to a new position, & each man ordered to take shelter behind a log or tree for protection from shot & shell from the enemy's batteries, as some of them will probably pass in our direction — probably directly over our heads. We will probably be out all night. I have just sent for my blankets, so as to be prepared for the cold this time. Sergeant Brown of my company came near being shot last night by a rebel picket, while out reconnoitering, the ball passing within a few feet of his head. Capt. Meyer of Co. H. also had a narrow escape this morning.

9 P.M. — Well, dearest, we had no more fighting today, after all, but we now expect that the gunboats will open in the morning. Our reg't was relieved at dark, and we are now on board the "Diana" again. How soon we shall be called out again I don't know. I inclose a leaf of holly. The trees (holly) are green as can be with them. I wish I had a flower or something of the kind to send you.

. . . .

In the field, near mouth of the Tallahatchie River, Miss., Mch 13, 1863. 12 o'clock M.

We were relieved last night, as I wrote you, went on board our boat up at the landing & went to bed without cooking anything but coffee, expecting a chance to cook this morning, but at daylight this morning we were ordered out again, merely taking time to take a little bread & raw meat along. We marched down to our present position, which is a little above the ground we occupied yesterday, & were ordered to stack arms & send back a detail of men to cook for the companies, so that they had something to eat & drink about 9 ½ or 10 o'clock. I write now within hearing of the guns of the enemy. The fight between our gunboats & batteries & those of the rebels is now going on. We are out of range of their shell, though they are continually passing a little to our right and bursting in the woods near our picket lines. Our boats & mortar opened on them about half past ten. I don't know whether any particular damage has yet been done on either side. It is a warm, beautiful day. I am sitting on the ground with my overcoat for a cushion, writing, & perspiring quite freely. Col. Lewis & Col. Whitaker are both out, though neither are well. Col. Whitaker being sick, I have been in command of our boat most of the time for several days. I slept but little, though situated very comfortably last night. I see no prospect of any fighting on our part at present, though we may be called on at any time. I suppose we will support our battery if it should be in any danger of capture by the enemys infantry. The boys are in fine spirits. D. R. Thompson will return by the first boat, I hear. There is no knowing when it will go up the river. I picked up one or two articles the other day which I want to send home by him if I can get them ready and put them up in time. Ed. just bro't me out some tea & fried sweet potatoes, so I shall not go without my dinner.

Saturday, Mch 12, [14] 1863, 8 A.M.

We laid in the woods till towards night yesterday, listening to the roaring thunder of the guns, both ours & the enemys. Our two best gunboats, the Baron deKalb & Chilicothe were engaged. The latter was struck some thirty times, I am told, by the enemys shot & shell. She is but slightly damaged. She had two men wounded. One was wounded on the Baron deKalb, I hear. The fight lasted from 10 ½ till 5 yesterday, with but little interruption. No one was hurt at our land batteries or among our forces on shore. Just before sundown we fell into line, marched up to the boat & were given 15 minutes to fill our haversacks with provisions & fall in again ready for a night in the woods. It was dark before we got back & took position in rear of our battery to support it in case of an attack by rebel infantry during the night. Stationing our guards we laid down in our blankets on the ground. I had rather an uncomfortable bed & did not rest very well, but feel well this morning. There was no alarm during the night, so we were not called out.

We could hear the rebels at work all night. It is said they have erected another battery during the night. We could also hear their steamers running back & forth. They kept them busy. *Our side* was also busy upon the gunboats, preparing for a renewal of the attack.

. . . .

In Camp, **Near the mouth of the Tallahatchie, Sunflower County, Mississippi, Sunday, March 15, 1863.**

. . . .

I wrote you last from "the field" yesterday morning. But little was done yesterday in the line of fighting. Our battery opened upon the enemy at about half past three P.M., & there was considerable firing on both sides for about half an hour, with an occasional gun on either side after that till about night. We were directly in the rear of the battery, & the way the shot & shell flew over our heads for a while was a caution. The tree tops fell about us, cut off by 64 pound shot — . . . one limb fell between the knees of Sergeant Brown of my Company. I had no hair breadth escapes to mention, though a fragment of a shell passed within 20 feet of me I should think. We were pretty secure behind our trees, & no one was hurt. At night we were relieved & marched up to the boat, where we remained last night. Today we have pitched our tents on shore & gone into camp. What will come next no one of us can tell. I think the rebels have a strong position, & that we can never take it without reinforcements. Their battery is said to be so situated as to command both the Tallahatchie & the Yazoo. So far as I can see it is almost impossible to approach it with infantry. Still we will hope for success.

. . . .

Near the mouth of the Tallahatchie river, Mississippi, M'ch 19, 1863. 9 A.M.

For three or four days I have been unable to write, on account of being very busy. Sunday we landed & pitched our tents, did lots of police work. Monday we went out & made a reconnoisance on the left bank of the river, the weather being very warm, & came back tired. Yesterday I had charge of a detail of 50 men to fix up the camp, & worked hard at it till 3 P.M. when I was ordered to take command of the right wing of the regiment & come out & relieve the left wing which had supported our land battery Tuesday night & yesterday. I got ready, came out & relieved our other companies, but did not get to sleep till about Midnight. Yesterday was very warm — about like the last of June in Wis. I should think, & the fore part of the night was also warm. I laid under a tree, gazing at the stars, & dreaming of the dear ones at home. After having a couple of hours sleep I was wakened & ordered to call up my command without noise & fall back up the river some half a mile & take up a new position between the Gunboats and the river. I immediately marched down there, & *here I am.* Our land battery was removed during the night, and has been placed upon the gunboats.

What our next movement will be — whether up the river — of if we are to move at all, I do not know. I think, however that we are to leave here. What unseen object our Generals may have in sending out this expedition, I cannot see — doubtless they had an object. I find that we bro't only some 7000 men, & there are now, probably, less than 6000 effective men in the expedition. I think the rebel fort could have been reduced &

taken by us during the first 3 days we were here, if all had gone
to work; but time was wasted & the rebels improved it in
bringing up men & cannon, planting batteries &c. till they
have a strong position, & doubtless more men than we have, as
they can easily bring them up the Yazoo river from Yazoo City
& Vicksburg. I regret that we have achieved nothing yet, &
hope that we may yet do something. Of course I do not know
the plans of our commanding Generals, & all these movements
we have made & are making may lead to something of which
we little dream. I shall be glad if they do lead to something of
which we may be proud, but I must say I do not expect it now.
We shall see.

I still keep well, and continue to grow fat. I presume I shall
not be so large that you'll not know me when I get home. I
succeeded in getting a couple of hams the other day. Also a
little flour, 5 lbs sugar, 3 lbs dried apples (at 25¢ per pound) &
some cheese (at 20¢). Also some pretty fair black tea. Coffee
& sugar are scarce. *"Iron Clad"* (hard crackers) & *"Sow
belly"* (Bacon) constitute the principal diet of our men. I can't
go the Pork & Bacon, though I can eat the hard bread when I
can get no other. It is hard food for sick men, but they get
generally a little tea or coffee, sugar, rice or hominy, beans or
peas & vinegar. They get no molasses lately. It would do you
good to see the peach trees in blossom here. I inclose some
blossoms I found in the woods. The trees on which they are
found are quite large — say 15 to 20 feet high. I don't know
what it is.

3 P.M. I have just been on board the U.S. Gun Boat Baron
DeKalb. A Milwaukee man who is serving on board showed
me over the boat. He gave me a piece of a rebel shell which
burst on board of her last Friday, during the bombardment,
after striking one of her guns & killed a master's mate & two
men, & wounded 3 or 4 men. I shall try & preserve it & bring
it home. We shall probably be relieved & return to camp about
5 o'clock. If I have a chance I will write more. To you, dear,

dear, darling Carrie, to Lulu and our *little* baby I send much
love. In your letter you forgot to say how much money you had
left. Have you rec'd the $170. from Helena?

On board Steamboat "Diana,"
Tallahatchie River, Mississippi,
Sunday, March 22nd 1863.

I wrote you last from "the field," I believe, last Thursday.
We went out about 3 P.M. on Wednesday & were not relieved
until about 7 P.M. Thursday, — so we had to go back to camp
after dark. The guns from our land battery had been removed
on board the gunboats during the day. We had been in camp
not more than ¾ of an hour, I think, when the order came to
pack up, strike tents, & put our baggage & men on board the
boat immediately. I had all day anticipated this movement, so I
was not surprised by the order.

At daylight day before yesterday we started up the river,
leaving the scenes of our *glorious* (?) [*sic*] exploits in the rear.
I can't see what we have accomplished. We made a run of
some 75 miles yesterday. About 4 P.M. we met the Mail boat
coming down, with quite a mail for us. I rec'd yours mailed
March 11th & 12th, one from Frank 9th, one from Cousin
Jennie Stevens 6th and one from (will you believe it?) Cousin
Allie Pratt mailed the 11th. Yours, as always, were *read first*,
and I assure you they do do me good, be they ever so short. I
am afraid, though, my own darling, that you are not as well as
you would have me think. Don't deceive me, dearest. If you
are sick do not fear to let me know it. I wish to know just how
you are. I am glad to learn that the money has come through
safely, before you were quite out. If I can send some more by
& by, I'll pay up my debts about home — on the house &c.
Frank wrote no particular news. The same may be said of
Jennie & Allie. Just before night we met a fleet of steamboats
bound down, *bringing us reinforcements*. We immediately

"about faced," & here we go at 2 p.m. on our way back to our late camp, and, I trust, further down the river. How much force we now have I don't know, but I presume from what I hear, the reinforcements amount to 4000. With these I think we should achieve a victory at the mouth of the Tallahatchie.

As to the house, you can't do better than to let Tom have it. I hope he & Libby may be as happy there as we were — don't you. Have him put up the fence if you can, even if you have to pay $10. or $20. towards it in money, to buy lumber &c. . . .

On board Steamer St. Louis, before Greenwood, Mississippi, March 27, 1863.

. . . .

Still we are here in our old position, getting ready for the seige of the fort of which I have written you. Our forces are getting siege guns mounted, bringing down more guns from above, making reconnoisances &c. &c. More troops are expected down soon, so we shall have quite an army here. I expect it will be some time ere we capture the fort, but I think now it will have to come down, though we shall probably see warm work first. The principal fighting will be with artillery I apprehend. Two large guns were bro't down by the boat that brot the mail today. Our regiment, except company C, with 4 companies from another reg't & an artillery company have gone up the river today. I suppose the intention is go across the country after going up the river the necessary distance, & occupy the town of McNutt, the county seat of this county. What other movements are being made now I don't know. I am unable to get much information in relation to movements here, not being one of the *favored* officers, & consequently not admitted behind the scenes as some of the captains are. Well, there's nothing like *leather!* and I trust I shall be able to *wear* as long as some of the *polished cloth* in the regiment.

Spring is coming on apace here. The green leaves & grass

— the fragrant blossoms, look and smell so refreshing — so sweet. The weather is warm — some days *very* warm. The weather seems much like the fore part of June at the north. And all this while you are having a cold, dreary month at home. How different from this climate down in "Dixie."

. . . .

Corporal Theadore Leavitt met with quite an accident last Tuesday. The regiment was out on picket, and he in handling his gun, carelessly shot himself in the arm. The wound is both above & below the elbow. It is not a very serious wound, though he will not be able to use his arm for weeks. Half an inch more to the right, and his elbow would have been shattered, & doubtless he would have lost an arm. He is able to run around camp, & feels but little pain from it. I am glad it was no worse. He is young — only 18 — but plucky. He took it very cooly — *never whimpered*.[3] I sent one sick man to Hospital at Helena Wednesday — James Bare, ill with fever.

Before Greenwood, Miss.,
March 29th 1863.

. . . .

The work of investing Greenwood is progressing slowly. Ordnance, supplies, & men are arriving every day. Two boats came down yesterday, & one this morning. On Friday our regiment (except my company which was left behind as a guard,) went up the river a short distance, & thence across the country some 10 miles to McNutt, the county seat of this county. McNutt is a small village — has a neat court house & square with a few houses on other streets.

The Reg't. returned yesterday. They report having had some fun chasing *butternuts* — had no fight — captured 12 prisoners, a few arms, horses, mules &c., & destroyed some powder. They also found some letters from which we derive information more or less important. A few relics were bro't. in as well as a lot of chickens &c.

. . . .

Before Greenwood, Mississippi
Saturday, April 4, 1863.

When did I write last? 'Tis not long since, and during the time nothing of much interest has transpired. "All is quiet along the" Tallahatchie, except that we now and then hear of a boat being fired into along the river while coming down. We have been building a fortification upon the land next to the slough or *bayou* south of the "Clark house" as marked on the map, and still south of our battery marked "6". The left rests on the river, and it extends back from the river some two hundred feet or more. It is intended for about 10 guns I hear. A part of another division is following Gen. Quimby's down the river, and will probably arrive in a day or two — if some of them are not already here.[4] I heard this morning that the 6th Wis. Battery had arrived, and that the 8th Wis. Infantry were on the way down. This is the Reg't. in which Tom McPherson's brothers are, I believe. We are kept pretty busy with picket & other duties. I have not been out yet on duty, but intend to try it the next time the company goes out — which may be tonight. The rebels continue to fire upon us as we are at work on the fortifications. Shot & shell reach us there quite profusely at times, though they usually fire only once in half an hour or so, except they discover some party of men moving in that vicinity, when they fire oftener. The firing is mostly to drive out the workmen. I hear that two men of another regiment were killed there this morning. The Quartermaster of the 46th Indiana had his hand broken all to pieces & shot partly off this morning by a fragment of a shell. The missile afterwards passed through his vest & coat, sideways without otherwise

injuring him. Gen. Quimby is fortifying on the left bank of the
river, I learn. He is a little above us on the river, & on the other
side. Fisk's brigade is ordered up the river, I hear, and a part of
it is just embarking. There is a rumor that Salomon's brigade
will also be sent back in a day or two. I do not credit the
report, but many of our officers do. Whether it is thought best
to evacuate here entirely, or whether we are to go upon some
other service & let Quimby & Co. finish the work we have
begun, is more than I know. Some seem to think that we will
go to Columbus, Ky. The sick of the regiment are increasing
somewhat, but only two of my men *here* are in hospital —
Leavitt, with wounded arm, & Chaffee of Summit who is able
to be up around. Some others are sick enough to be excused
from duty — 6 or 7 I believe. Neither of my Lieutenants are
very well. Christy, Thompson, Chaffee (Wallace) & Kinne are
well. So are Plympton & Frank Ludington. Perkins is still at
Helena. I have heard nothing from the boys there since the half
dozen came down last Monday, nor from the boys at
Memphis. We have had no mail since a week ago today. We
expected one last night or this morning, but it has not come. I
hope it will get along soon, for it seems a long time since we
had one, we have had them so often for the past three weeks.
We hear that the rebels are invading Kentucky again. I hope it
will not be necessary to recall all the troops from this way to
drive them out. The rebels are not idle here. They are continually throwing up works and mounting batteries, receiving
reinforcements &c. Every little while as I write, I can hear the
booming of one of their guns and the explosion of a shell
thrown at some part of our works, or the woods where our
pickets are. No one of our reg't has been hurt yet I believe
though one of Co. F. had his musket bent by a cannon shot
yesterday, as it stood against a tree at his side. Will write more
by & by.

On board Steamer "Diana," Apr 6, 1863.

As I had anticipated we were ordered on board the boats Saturday evening, and at daylight yesterday morning our pickets were called in, and we left for Helena — or somewhere else. The failure of the expedition through the Sunflower river, with which we were to cooperate rendered this one of too little importance, so the Generals say, to expend any more time or lives upon it, so an order was rec'd on Friday or Saturday for us to withdraw our forces from before Greenwood, & return up river. I think the rebels could have been captured if a persistent effort had been made to do it, but it may be as well as it is. I must say I disliked to leave there till we whipped them. We have left something like a dozen dead upon the banks of the Tallahatchie — that is our regiment — none of my Co. Other regiments have probably lost as many in proportion.

We stopped this morning & buried one man from Co. K. this morning. A boat ahead of us was fired into by guerillas yesterday, and the captain & two men killed. The boat stopped & landed a force, so of course, they, the rebs, *skidaddled*. The soldiers burned all the buildings on the plantation and left. . . .

NOTES

1. Literature on the Vicksburg campaign is, of course, extensive. See, for example, Bruce Catton, *Never Call Retreat,* Vol. 3 of *The Centennial History of the Civil War* (New York, 1965), 80–92, 193–205, Catton, *U. S. Grant and the American Military Tradition (Boston, 1954), 94–108.* For the Yazoo Pass expedition in particular, see James Russell Soley, in *Battles and Leaders,* III, 561–64.

2. Leonard Fulton Ross, 1823-1901, a lawyer, participated in the Mexican War and then became a judge. He raised the 17th Illinois, fought at Fort Donelson and Corinth and was promoted from colonel to brigadier general. He commanded the 13th Division, 13th Corps, February 8-May 25, 1863. He resigned in July, 1863. His division included some 4,000 men. *Battles and Leaders*, III, 562.

3. Leavitt was the first man in the unit to be wounded during the war; ironically, the wound was self-inflicted.

4. Isaac Ferdinand Quinby, 1821–91, served in the Mexican War, raised a New York regiment early in the Civil War then returned to civilian life. Named brigadier general in March, 1862, he held various commands in the West, including the 7th Division, XVII Corps, January 20-April 14, 1863, during the Yazoo Pass Expedition. The initial plan for the Yazoo Pass Expedition called for only troops from General Ross' division. Grant later enlarged the plan to include General McPherson's corps of 30,000 men; only a small force under General Quinby, however, actually took part in the movement. *Battles and Leaders*, III, 562.

Part III: ARKANSAS DUTY

Military events in Arkansas, where the 28th Wisconsin was stationed during almost all of 1863 and all of 1864, illustrate the standard military judgment that operations west of the Mississippi River were subordinated to operations east of the river. This was especially true, local southern sympathizers bitterly charged, of the Confederate government.

After the defeat of the Confederates at Pea Ridge in March, 1862, Confederate forces in Arkansas under Generals Earl Van Dorn and Sterling Price were ordered to reinforce the army of Albert Sydney Johnston at Corinth, Mississippi near which the Battle of Shiloh was fought in April, 1862. Not only did they arrive after the battle was fought, but their departure left Arkansas virtually undefended from Union assault. To remedy the sitaution, General Thomas Hindman was put in charge of Arkansas. With great energy he created an army and supplied it.

Meanwhile, Union forces were not idle. After his victory at Pea Ridge, General Curtis moved his army to Batesville, Arkansas, where he threatened Little Rock, 100 miles to the southeast. With growing Confederate forces in Arkansas and guerrilla activity threatening his supply lines to Missouri, however, Curtis resolved to move to Helena, Arkansas, on the Mississippi River, where his supply lines would be more secure. He reached that point August 13, 1863.

Temporarily ignoring Curtis at Helena, the Confederates gathered a substantial army to invade Missouri. This invasion failed, however, as Union forces defeated the Confederates at Prairie Grove in December, 1862, north of Little Rock; in January, 1863, Union forces forced the Confederates to retreat from Fort Smith to Little Rock.

While Confederate forces were retreating from Fort Smith, an equally great disaster befell Confederate arms with the capture of Arkansas Post, a strongly fortified position on the Arkansas River 50 miles above the mouth of the river and 117 miles below Little Rock. This place was taken by Union forces under the command of General John McClernand. The net result of these actions was that thousands of Union forces in Missouri and also at Helena were freed to join Grant in his expedition against Vicksburg.

The Vicksburg campaign continued to dominate military events in Arkansas for the first six months of 1863. The Confederate government urged a diversionary attack on Federal forces, which resulted in an assault on Helena on July 4. Fortunately, for the Union, their position was very strong and well fortified; they could also count upon the Union fleet for firepower. The Confederate attack, on the other hand, was poorly planned; in addition, heavy fog and rough terrain hampered Confederate coordination. Though the Confederates outnumbered the Union defenders 7,600 to 4,000, Confederate losses of 1,636 vastly exceeded Union losses of 239. Ironically, the battle at Helena occurred the very same day that Vicksburg fell, July 4, 1863.

With the capture of Vicksburg and Port Hudson, Louisiana four days later, the Mississippi River was now in Union hands, and the federal government was in a position to consolidate its control of Arkansas. Major General Frederick Steele was sent to Helena with additional troops, and moved toward Little Rock on August 5. On the way he was reinforced with troops from Missouri under the command of Brigadier General John

Davidson. The Union forces numbered over 10,000 men, while the Confederates at Little Rock, now under the command of Sterling, had only 7,700. Wisely, Price abandoned Little Rock without offering serious resistance and retreated southward to Camden without pursuit. At the end of 1863 Union forces occupied all of Arkansas except for that portion of the state south of a line drawn through Camden.

In 1864 there were two principal campaigns in the state. The first occurred with General Nathaniel Banks' abortive Red River campaign to capture Shreveport, Louisiana. Union forces from Little Rock attacked Price's Confederate troops to lend assistance to Banks. When the latter abandoned his efforts to take Shreveport, the Union forces retreated to Little Rock.

The second major event in 1864 was Sterling Price's raid into Missouri. Collecting a considerable body of men, he marched from southern Arkansas into Missouri, unsuccessfully sought to attack St. Louis and Jefferson City, then retreated to Arkansas with one-third of the men with whom he started the campaign. The Price raid was the last major military campaign west of the Mississippi River.

Of the six major military actions in 1863 and 1864, the 28th Wisconsin participated in two: the defense of Helena and the capture of Little Rock. Understandably, Stevens was jubilant over the Union victory at Helena and wrote detailed accounts of that battle. He also wrote detailed accounts of the capture of Little Rock. The 28th Wisconsin, however, was not involved in either of the major campaigns in 1864; for almost all of that year, the regiment was on garrison duty at Pine Bluff, Arkansas, on the Arkansas River between Little Rock and Arkansas Post.[1]

Helena Ark., Apr 9, 1863

We are once more here safe & sound, thank God! I did not expect to bring back all of my command to Helena when I left here six weeks ago last Tuesday, but all of them are here. Most of the companies have lost men during the progress of the expedition — one, (Co. K) has lost *four*, but we have been highly favored. Some of the men have returned sick, but none are dangerously so, I think. I mailed to you yesterday a letter written during the passage up. You see there *was* a possibility of *retreat*, & we got safely through. Our boat, the Diana, was the first here. The balance of Ross' division arrived during the day yesterday. We arrived here at about 9 A.M. yesterday. Gen Quimby's Division has not arrived unless it came after dark last night.

Well, we have had rather a hard, rough time, and may well congratulate ourselves upon our fortunate arrival here. . . .

Helena, Ark., Apr 12/'63.

Still we are here, and still the hearts of our brave men turn to their northern homes — the homes we have gone forth to defend. Of news I have none. Since writing last I have rec'd one more letter from you. You state that you are *packing up* at the house. What a job it is! But I wish I could help you do it. We went into camp on Thursday & Friday. Yesterday, (Saturday), we moved our camp *twice* — in the dust & wind in the forenoon, and in the rain & mud in the afternoon. It was a hard day for our tired men, but the last move was much better than remaining for even one night in the place where we went in the morning. We nearly all got wet, and as dirty as we could be. Today we have been mustered, and also fixing up our camp into which we got late last night. I am tired, but my health remains first rate, though some of the boys are sick. Sergeant Tucker was taken with inflammation of the lungs last night & is very sick. I got up at half past 11 last night & was with him two or three hours. He is some better today. Corporal Plympton tried the virtues of Homeopathic remedies on him & with good success last night. The surgeon attends him now.

Day before yesterday we rec'd our boxes of *goodies* from Wisconsin. They were in a pitiable plight. Jars & cans of fruit smashed & run all over everything else, — bread, cakes, pies, turkeys, cheese, &c. &c. mouldy & rotten — whew! But some things were good. My boots & Quinine came safe & sound, & are all right. I've not had a chance yet to try on the boots. The case of medicines never came to hand. I could find it nowhere. I am very sorry for I calculated to cure lots of the ills which the flesh of my company is heir to with that box of *sugar pills*. I want you to get me another case, put it up so that it cannot break, (or so that the bottles will not be broken) & send to me by mail. It will be letter postage & will cost something, but I want them. The 29th Wis. & other regiments forming Gen. Hovey's[2] Division embarked yesterday & the day before for Vicksburg. We will not go in that direction — at least not at present. Aren't you glad?

About the rest of those things.

Nearly all the canned fruit was *busted* — the tops were off the cans & all the contents distributed among the packages in the boxes. The raspberries had lost all their juice, but were not sour. The cans packed in the box with the jar of Butter which Hattie sent, were nearly all open & spoiled. Two were good. I have not opened *them*, nor the three good ones in your box. The dried currants were nearly all good. A few of the cakes sent were barely eatable, but not good. The paper & envelopes all soaked & spoiled. I found only one letter from you — that was a *long one*, dated Jany 31 to Feby 6th. The night caps were all right & looked natural. Handkerchiefs soaked, stained & O.K. Stockings *ditto*. Hattie's jar of butter was not broken for a wonder & was good. The things Lavantia & Co. sent were some of them in pretty good condition, but mostly spoiled. The apples were all rotten but two. The best things to send us are dried fruit & such clothing as we need & can use, medicines such as are wanted and asked for, canned fruit, if soldered up so that it will not break open, & butter when it is cool enough so that you can send it & not have it melt.

We were very glad to get what we did that was good. How grateful were we to the kind friends & loved ones who had so liberally remembered us. We shall not forget them.

The war seems to be wearing a new face in some respects. A *"Negro Regiment"* is being formed here. Some of the officers have been appointed, and a lot of the darkies are drilling & preparing for service. This, I think, is as it should be. Let us use every means we possess to conquer a peace by putting down this infernal rebellion.

Gen'l Ross is new in command here. Wallace Chaffee, Kinne, Plympton, Christy, & Thompson are well, as are all the "Cooney" boys I believe. I have a log cabin for my quarters now, which was *turned over* to me by *Capt.* Johnson of Co. C, 24th Iowa. I saw him & he said he wanted the Capt of Co. C to occupy it. It is very comfortable. I have not yet pitched my *tent.*

. . . .

Helena, Arkansas, April 14, 1863.

. . . .

I would be glad to come home & see you, dear Carrie, but it is not to be thought of. Perhaps one or two of the Captains of the regiment may get furloughs home, but your husband is not among that number. I am not of the favored ones. I hope to see a change in some things in our regiment before I leave it — *time* will set all things right.

There is much dissatisfaction just now with some officers and some practices with us. I hope the thing will be stirred up till it is remedied. I[t] would be contrary to *regulations* for me to charge anything against my superior officers, so I will forbear.

Chaffee, Thompson, Christy, Kinne, Perkins, & Plympton

are well. I think the company is improving in health. Sergeant Tucker is much better. Corporal Cobb is ill, but I hope not seriously, though he gives right up to it & thinks he is almost used up. If a man gives up here, he is but little better than dead, but a stout heart will cure more than medicine. It was what kept me up I assure you. Credit me for *that*.

One more of my men is gone. Halvor Knudson, one of the men I left here when we went down on the Yazoo Expedition, finally died in Post Hospital last Saturday. Diptheria & diarrhea caused his death. So they go, one by one. Not a man of our regiment has been killed in battle, but scores have fallen by disease. So it always is in war. . . .

April 17, 1863, 6 A.M.

. . . .

Rumors prevailed in town yesterday to the effect that Hooker had been surprised & cut up in Virginia; that Rosecrans had been defeated with a loss of 80,000 men; and that our force before Charleston have been repulsed.[3] It was also stated that northern papers had been prohibited below Memphis for the present. I have feared a repulse before Charleston, but the rest I cannot think true. I believe the whole thing is a *canard*.

I am to be on duty today in a new position for me — as *"brigade officer of the day."* I have to report to Gen. Salomon's headquarters at 8 A.M.

. . . .

Head Quarters 28th Wis. Vol.,
Helena, Ark., Ap'l 21, 1863.

By the mail today I rec'd another of your dear, kind, loving letters, and though tired tonight, and sleepy too, I will try and write a little something, be it ever so poor an apology for a letter. First, as an interesting item, let me tell you that on

Saturday last our regiment was paid four months pay, which is up to the last of February, so we are in funds again. I had an opportunity yesterday to send my money with Cap't Meyer's of Co. H, so I have sent it again to the Waukesha County Bank, but hope you will not have so much trouble to get it as you did the other. I send $650 — of which amount $450, you will retain, and pay out the other $200 as follows:

To Michael Carr	$45.	To Mrs. Ed. Olson $30.
To Mrs. Christy	$45.	To A. B. Hall $40.
To Sam'l Breck	$40.	

They will present receipts for the several amounts which you will take up and preserve. Mark them "Paid" with ink across the backs. I wish I could send home more, but my expenses are necessarily considerable here, and an officer cannot get along without some money. I assure you, however, that I spend but little money needlessly. I think of the dear ones at home, and how many comforts my savings can buy for them; I think of the time when we may be in our own home, and how much a little money will do to "help us along." I wish you to use whatever you want of the money, & obtain those things you need so much, my own. Don't go so much without, dearest.

. . . .

I am glad to learn that the Copperheads were defeated in Oconomowoc & Summit, as well as throughout the North generally. Let the men who love our country put them down by the ballot, and if necessary, by force. I am hopeful still for our country. It may be that this Union is to be destroyed, but I cannot yet believe it. That there has been a great amount of mismanagement no one can doubt — but I hope for better things in the future. I hope to see our nation rise from beneath this burden of trouble, war & sacrifice, a mightier stronger nation than ever before. God grant she may — and soon.

. . . .

Ap'l 22, 5 A.M. Another beautiful morning has dawned — a morning as bright as the bright mornings we used to enjoy.

Would we could enjoy it together, my own. How happy we would be. O! about those boots you sent me. They fit me to a *t*, and are just the thing. You are a good dear wife to send me so many things I wanted. The Handkerchief, too, came just in time. I was about to pay 75¢ for a cotton one. The peaches were excellent — as good as I ever ate. Tell pa that the dried beef was as good as could be — nice & tender. The currants sent were most of them good. Thank them all for their kindness. Hattie's jar of butter was *tip top*. We are using it now. I wish I had more such. . . .

HeadQuarters 28th Reg't. Wis. Vols., Helena Ark., May 2, 1863.

But for business which could well be deferred. I should have written you more often of late. Our officers for duty are few, some being sick, others detached or detailed for special duty. We have but three Captains for duty just now, and, I believe, but two 1st Lieutenants, while we have about five or six 2d Lieutenants. We have to furnish three of these officers *every* morning for duty, *four* every other day, & yesterday we had *five* of them out, besides the Major, on guard, picket, fatique & brigade duty.

We have no items of news to record, with the single exception of a little fight near here yesterday. The story runs like unto this —

Yesterday morning a party of the 3rd Iowa Cavalry were sent out scouting some ten miles in rear of the town, where they were ambushed and attacked by a band of guerillas, numbering according to different accounts, from 150 to 800. Our cavalry seem to have been completely surprised, and almost entirely surrounded, but fought their way out and fell back upon Helena.

Two couriers came dashing down the bluffs through our camp, into town, just before noon, and reported the facts to head quarters. In a few minutes all was excitement — from the different camps came dashing out along lines of cavalry heading for the scene of the conflict, while the "assembly" was being beaten in the Infantry camps, and regiment after regiment fell into line, ready and eager to be led against their enemies. The 28th was one of the earliest in line, while the 33rd Iowa was equally prompt, and, having rec'd orders first, passed us on its way to the front while we were waiting for instructions.

Maj. Gen. Prentiss seeing us in line, directed us to occupy a line of rifle pits directly in front of our camp, upon the top of a long ridge running at nearly right angles with the road over which the cavalry had passed out, to defend a battery which was being completed to defend that road. The guns were placed in position after we were placed there. Another position at the left has not rec'd its guns yet.

The 33rd Iowa was ordered out to support the cavalry, & passed over the winding road out of sight, while ambulance after ambulance went rolling out to bring in the wounded.

Soon after the wounded commenced arriving — some on horseback, being able to ride in assisted by their comrade — others in ambulances and private carriages pressed for the occasion — some with a shattered hand, arm, shoulder or leg — some with more serious wounds. One poor fellow I saw was shot through the right breast, the bullet having passed entirely through him. He is doubtless dead ere this, for he seemed almost gone as he was brought in propped up in a carriage, and supported by a fellow sufferer who had rec'd a less serious injury.

Presently came in portions of the party who had gone out in the morning — scores of them with no hats upon their heads, having lost them in the desperate charge by which they effected their escapes many without their arms. &c.

Riderless horses, too, came in with them, some wounded themselves, their saddles & sides red with the blood of the "brave boys" who had gone out with them in the morning, but who were now either dead or disabled. It was sad to see them. They were badly cut up, and badly scared I should judge from what I can learn thus far. The cavalry who went out to support these scouts had rode some 15 miles out, but the enemy had, as usual, *skedaddled,* leaving behind nearly all the prisoners they had taken. Last night this morning [sic.] the forces sent out nearly all returned. Col. Rise with the 33rd Iowa marched eleven miles out, when he met the returning cavalry, upon which he *"about faced"* marched two or three miles & stopped for the night, coming into town again this forenoon. How many men we have lost is yet unknown, but is estimated at forty men killed wounded & missing. I think it will prove to be less than that.

And so stands the affair at present.

Some of our officers think that such a band may be only the advance guard of a larger force of the enemy approaching with designs against this post, and are half inclined to believe we will soon be attacked by them. If so, let them come. I think we can hold the place against any force they can bring against us. *I* do not think they will attack us in this stronghold, though our force here is not large at present.

Things are quiet today, though we have orders to be ready to "fall in" at a moments notice. We have seen "stirring times" often, but they never amount to anything serious with us, and this is like all the rest I dare say. If it prove otherwise it will at least be a *variation* — and "variety is the spice of life" no less in the army than otherwheres.

Our men turned out at short notice yesterday, and were all ready to fight — even the *sick* some of them asking me if they *might go* when they learned that there was a prospect of getting a sight at the *rebs.*

We are having a great deal of rain now. Yesterday & this morning were pleasant, but now (1 P.M.) it is raining again.

Maj. Gen. Prentiss is here. Gen. Gorman was yesterday

relieved from command of the forces here.[4] Gen. Salomon will probably assume command of our Division. Gen. Fisk commands the second brigade.

The fortifications about Helena are being completed & new ones are being built. Gen. Gorman having a short time since been directed to put Helena in a complete state of defense, as no more troops could be spared at present for its protection. What is coming next? we all ask. We shall see what we shall see. The negro brigade is being made useful with the spade & pickaxe (the drill is "*hard*-ee" instead of Scott!) building forts &c., &c. "Long may they wave" *while they help us*.

No mail down today. Hope 'twill come soon. Will write more this evening.

**Helena, Ark., May 5, 1863,
11 ½ P.M.**

Things have till now continued to move along in the same channels. Today we went out target firing, and returned about 5 P.M., when we received orders to prepare to march at 6 o'clock tomorrow morning on a scout of 6 days into the country. With so little time to prepare we have been kept very busy, and I have been with the Lt. Col. all the evening since 9 o'clock arranging with him & the other officers the details for the expedition. As I am the ranking Captain now with the regiment, (Capt Townsend having gone home sick) I am placed upon the right of the line. We carry no tents — no extra clothing — nothing but our blankets and rations. We take 60 rounds of ammunition per man. How far we shall go I don't know, or how far we are expected to go. I presume we may have a skirmish before we get back, though I hardly think it. I assure you I don't fear it. Lt. Gilmore is now Acting Adjutant.
. . . .

It is now past twelve. *Today* I am 28 years old. Another year is gone — A new one before me — would that with its commencement I might begin a better life. I must to bed for we march early. . . .

In the woods 12 miles from Helena, Ark., May 13, 1863.

Since writing you on the fifth, just before starting our on our present expedition, I have had no time or opportunity to communicate with you. As you have doubtless rec'd that letter I improve the first chance to sit down with this sheet of paper, soiled by being carries in may haversack for a week, upon me knee, and write you, knowing your enxiety to hear from me. We left Helena on the morning of the 6th (my birthday) in a rain storm, but it stopped raining before night, although that day and the next were quite cold. We took a north-westerly direction from Helena, our destination being the vicinity of Cotton Plant, a small village some 60 or 70 miles distant, where a band of guerrilas were reported, to be. Our force consisted of about 400 men from the 28th, 450 from the 33d Iowa, two pieces of artillery from Capt. Hayden's (Dubuque) battery, and some 200 cavalry. A detachment of some 600 cavalry also went out at the same time on another road and joined us on the fourth day out. The first day we marched 18 miles — 20 the next & so on. We passed through some beautiful country — the most pleasant I have seen in the south. I wanted to keep a diary of the expedition, but was too tired & had no time after getting into camp at night to write at all, as we started by 6 o'clock or about that in the morning and marched till 5 to 7 at night, and then had everything to do. It was a hard march for our boys, but we all stood it much better than I expected, though we have got lots of sore & blistered toes and feet among us. I am well, though pretty tired. We marched out 4 days. On the fifth our advanced scouts of cavalry returned to us with the information that there was no enemy at Cotton Plant, so we about faced & returned to this point. We have rec'd information that Marmaduke with his force is endeavoring to reach us & cut us off from Helena.[5] We are anxious to have him come on, and had it not been that our 6 days rations of bread were about used up we would have stayed 22 miles back where we camped Monday night & awaited an attack. We have been on short rations & at hard work, and were compelled to forage, so we gobbled chickens, turkeys, geese &c. & killed some beef, but still we had not enough to eat a part of the time. We sent to Helena for provisions last night, and shall stay here till we get orders, unless we hear that we are needed to support the cavalry which is in our area & is liable to be attacked. It was attacked 2 or 3 nights ago & the 5th Kansas lost 1 killed & 4 wounded.

On the third day out Co. C. was in advance of the whole column a part of the time, the advanced guard of Cavalry having been sent back to scout in our rear. We were halted about 9 ½ o'clock A.M. & I had pickets out on each side, when two shots were fired at them by guerillas, the shots passing over the heads of the company. Ed. Kinne was one of the pickets & says the shots were fired at him, but he *forgot to return the fire*. I formed my men as skirmishers & skirmished down along side the road through the woods about a mile & back, but found no bushwhackers — they had fired & skedaddled. Our pickets saw the two who fired & 2 shots were returned, but no damage was done. We heard often that the enemy was but a few miles ahead of us, but we never could reach them — they were always gone. The citizens are about all *secesh* here so far as I can learn. Quite a number of darkies came in to our lines, bringing horses, mules, &c. — The last 4 days have been hot — yesterday was *very hot,* and didn't it start the perspiration? Water is scarce & very poor. We have been compelled to use swamp water a good share of the time — & were glad to get that. I have used water here which I wouldn't let a cow drink at home. I rec'd letters from you the morning we started, dated Apr 26, 27, & 30 — and they were indeed welcome to me just then. I presume there are three more at Helena for me, but when I shall get them I don't know. I hope it will be soon. I am very sorry your health is no better, darling wife. You must not work too much. Keep as quiet as you can. I know you have a great deal to do to take care of the children. It is too much for you to do on your own loved one. You had better have someone to help you. Have you rec'd that $650. yet? I hope so. I rec'd 8 stamps in the letters.

I am out in the woods today ½ mile from the camp, acting as a picket guard with my Co., or rather holding an advanced post.

Hurrah! A squad of cavalry has just arrived from Helena, who bring news that Richmond is ours. I hope it may be true *this* time. Once more Hurrah!

13th 2 P.M. The bugle & drums are sounding the assembly — I wouldn't wonder if we have orders to move to Helena. If so I shall get news from you soon, my own.

Helena, May 14, 1863.

I had but just written the other page full when an orderly rode up with an order for me to fall in my command & join the regiment which was in motion before I could reach camp, *en route* for this place. It had commenced to rain a very little, but we did not get wet, though we found it had rained very hard between there & Helena. We started soon after 2 P.M. & reached here at 7 — and a hard march it was in the mud up to our ankles a good part of the way.

. . . .

The General commanding here expected we would have a hard fight before getting into Helena, and probably all be captured, as he learned that a heavy force was on the way to cut us off. He had everything ready here for a fight, as Helena would doubtless have been attacked if we had been whipped or cut off. Every man who could carry a gun was ordered out.

When we arrived you ought to have heard the cheers & hearty greetings we received. They came from the *hearts* of brave men. We were glad to get back after our long and fatiguing march, and glad to get *full rations* of something good to eat. We slept in the open air while out, with nothing above us but our blankets & the sky with its clouds & stars — ah yes! we 2 or 3 times slept under a tree! I never slept or felt better, except that I was very tired sometimes, especially on one occasion when I marched all day, was out all night as Chief Officer of the Picket & *marched the next day*. The Col. let me take a horse a part of the second day.

. . . .

Helena, Arkansas, May 15, 1863.

My dear Father & Sister:

. . . .

Troops are passing down towards Vicksburg every day. Some 5 or 6 loaded transports went down yesterday forenoon. I hope they will be able to capture that place before the hot weather of July & August. It is pretty warm here now — the sun just *fried* us while on the march. We heard day before yesterday that Richmond is ours. I doubt it. If it is taken it is quite unexpected news to us at this time. I hope it may be so. Reports are circulating here that we will go to Vicksburg soon — that we will go to Minnesota soon &c. &c. I consider one just as reliable as the other.

I received the two jugs of horse radish & the onions you sent me. They were *just the thing*. We need such things here & cannot have too much. A large lot of vegetables for the regiment were received at the same time, & the health of the men has visibly improved since then. The soldiers will remember the true friends who thus remember them. Vegetables and dried fruit of all kinds are the best articles to send us, though some other articles, such as dried beef, fresh butter, eggs &c.,

when they can be sent safely & in good condition, are first rate. If you can I wish you would get a few pounds of maple sugar for Carrie to send me.

Eggs are selling here for from 35 to 40¢. Poor butter 40¢ — none fit to eat to be had — dried beef 20¢ to 25¢. Potatoes have been retailing at $3.00 per bushel. Everything is *up*. Eight of my men have died since leaving Wisconsin. Two, — Harshaw & Rendall, both of Summit — are very sick in hospital. Their disease is Typhoid fever. I fear Rendall will not recover. Harshaw is getting better.

Some of the other boys are unwell, but are mostly getting along. Hitchcock & Carlin are still sick at St. Louis in General Hospital.

My health is first rate. I am heavier than I ever was before. Two weeks ago I weighed 150 pounds with no vest on. I think I have held my own since then, so you see soldiering agrees with me — I presume we shall remain here this summer, though I dread to, as it is a sickly place.

. . . .

Helena, Ark., May 18, 1863.

Dearest:

. . . .

So Kinne's folks *could not* board you, but could take in Guy's folks. That is just their style. What a good opinion we must form of the honesty & consistency of such people — professing a most ardent feeling of friendship for you & me, they turn my wife & babies away, to make room for the family of a man whom, or at least whose *principles* they *pretend* to despise. Well! perhaps we shall know our friends by & by. When you see Kinne's folks you need give them no more of my regards, if they will treat us thus. I am sorry for you, darling. But keep a *stiff upper lip* and a brave heart for a while yet, and I hope all will be right.

. . . .

We are living very well here just now. Lt. Col. Whitaker messes with us, & we have pretty good *feed*. How long it — *or our money* — will last I don't know. We have Potatoes, Ham, Eggs, bread, Tea, Coffee, Sugar, Dried apples, peaches, currants, cherries & blackberries &c. Last night we extravagant men had *four* kinds of sauce & an apple pie for supper. *Isn't* that great? We[sic], darling, I shall not spend *all* my money for eatables. Eggs are getting cheap. I hear that we can buy them now for *twenty five cents per dozen*. Don't you think that reasonable?

. . . .

Helena, Ark., May 19, 1863.

. . . .

Young Harshaw is very low and will probably not last more than two days longer. Sad news again to send to our northern state. It is the hardest work I have to do, — this writing home to loving parents about their poor sick, dying and dead boys. Only think! *Nine of our men have died from disease — not one by the bullet*. Is it not terrible? I feel as if I would prefer to lead them to the cannon's very mouth, than see them lying here wasting away in agony — burning up with these fevers — which are almost certain death to every one attacked.

Capt. White of Co. F. has gone home sick. He is the third of our Waukesha captains who have gone home sick & are now absent, while I, whom every one thought last winter would soon be gone, am tougher, healthier, than for years before. So it is.

In relation to selling the house and lot, I hardly know what to say. If we are going back there to live I would prefer to keep it; but under the existing circumstances & uncertainties perhaps it would be as well to sell it, if I can get back the money & interest invested, *and especially if I could get a little more with it — I'm selfish yet, you see.* If you think so too, you can write to Frank to that effect. Do you know how much he could get for it?

. . . .

**Head Quarters Co. C. 28th Wis. Vols.,
1st Brigade, 13th Division, 13th Army Corps,
Army of the Tenn., Helena, Arkansas,
Friday evening, May 22, 1863.**

. . . .

We have a great many sick in the regiment just now. Eighteen of my company were unfit for duty yesterday. Some 10 or 12 of this number are able to be about and do light duty, but are unfit for drill or other heavy duty. We are kept at work, — those of us who are able to work. Lieut. Collyer of Co. E. also went home today on a furlough. He is unable to do duty, and has been a great part of the time for 3 months. I would like to *go home,* but don't want any of these *southern fevers* on me for the purpose of getting a furlough. Capt. Townsend will be back soon I hear. I don't hear much about Capt. Williams lately. I hope he will be able to join us soon. I don't think Capt. White is very sick — I think he has another object in getting home must now. I may do him injustice, but I think he is looking for *promotion more than health on this* trip. If so I hope he'll not succeed, that's so!

Col. McLean of the 43rd Indiana Infantry now commands the brigade, Gen. Salomon having assumed command of the Division — Gen Ross being in command of the post. Col. McLean is not much of a commandant for a Brigade. Like our Col. Lewis, he is *green at the business.* Time will give him a chance to improve I presume. There is *room* for improvement. I hope we shall not go into action at present with either of them at the head of the brigade. The latest report we have from Gen. Price is that he is massing troops at Little Rock and awaiting an attack from us there. Our Generals are just as badly scared and are hourly expecting an attack here. Neither dare get within 100 miles of the other. So mote it be!

. . . .

Head Quarters 28th Wis. Vols. Infty.
Helena, Arkansas, May 23, 1863.

Last night we received orders that a grand review of all the troops would take place this afternoon — consequently we were compelled to postpone moving camp for today, and prepare for the *big show*. During the forenoon I was engaged down town attending Court Martial. This afternoon was very warm. At 1 o'clock we fell in and marched to the ground and formed in line. We had two brigades of infantry, 4 regiments of cavalry, and some artillery, present. The pageant was quite imposing to *green ones* who never saw the like before, but it was rather hard on the men to be out three hours in a broiling sun with blankets & knapsacks on their backs — *in heavy marching order*. The review was held upon the flat above the town and near the levee. Didn't the hot sand burn our feet though?

Major General Prentiss, & Brig. Generals Ross, Fisk & Salomon were present. Col. Lewis commanded our brigade today.

We have just got through, and we are all tired. Our regiment, and particularly my company, did well. Lt. Col. Whitaker was by as a spectator, and told me that not a company in the whole army present presented a more soldierly appearance than Co. C. — a high compliment.

What do you think of my taking a position in one of the negro regiments? I have some idea of it. My position is not entirely pleasant here. Jealousies exist among the officers to some extent, and as I am a little *backward* about crowding myself *forward*, I sometimes stand a poor chance for anything ahead. We shall see.

One of my Sergeants had made application for a commission in the black brigade. One negro regiment has already been sent down the river from here. The second is filling up fast. I presume we will move camp on Monday.

I hear that the news of the capture of Haine's Bluff is confirmed. We today have news that Vicksburg is ours. General Salomon says that he thinks the report is perfectly reliable — that a dispatch boat went up with the news, and was in too much of a hurry to stop here except long enough to leave the news. I shall continue to doubt it till it is confirmed. But I do hope it will prove to be true. If it is, how many shouts of joy will go up over the achievement. Now for Richmond, Charleston &c. May this dreadful war soon end. It has lasted too long — had desolated too many homes already — and every month is adding thousands to the terribly long list of widows and orphans, made so by this rebellion.

. . . .

Helena, Ark., May 25, 1863.

. . . .

I write in haste just after breakfast and before drill — Can spend but little time this time. Shall send this letter up by Lt. Col. Whitaker. I hardly think he will return to the regiment again unless Col. Lewis should resign. (*This is in confidence*). I am sorry to have him go away.

. . . .

Head Quarters 28th Wis. Vols.
Helena, Ark., May 28, 1863.

It was impossible for me to write you by the last mail, though I tried hard to do so. I was rising over the picket lines & inspecting the camps of the different regiments in our brigade, & reporting to Gen'l Ross' Head Quarters nearly all day & night — and when I did get a couple of hours to spare — (9 to 11 P.M.) the wind blowed so hard that I could not keep a candle burning in my tent, and I had hard work to keep the tent from blowing away entirely — and didn't the dust and sand fly?

Last Monday morning a cavalry scout of ours was attacked again some five or six miles out from here — by a party of guerrillas — and lost between 30 & 40 killed, wounded & missing. The alarm soon reached us, and in a few minutes the troops here were in readiness to fight. The 28th was the only regiment of Infantry that went out to the scene of the conflict, though others were in order of battle, ready to support us. I was down town on business when they went out. When I returned I put on my t-*rusty* sword and started to join the regiment, but when I arrived at the picket lines they refused to let me pass. I had walked 2 or 3 miles under a burning sun, and all to no purpose. Rested awhile & started back. Met Dr. Miller going out with an ambulance — piled myself in and got through the lines *this* time but we soon found the road so obstructed by fallen timber that we could not get through, as the regiment had then two hours the start, I concluded I had better go back. We finally started out on another road, and after going out about 2 miles met the cavalry (a large force had gone out upon hearing the alarm) coming back, with ambulances bringing in the wounded. We passed on to their rear where we found the 28th had returned to town by the same road they went, so back we went. The bushwhackers had, as usual, made a speedy *run* after falling upon our scouts & surprising them. They never stand up and fight. The only way to put a stop to this is to sweep the country *clean* for 25 miles around here. I begin to wish they would do it. The 28th was highly praised for its promptness in marching out on so hot a day. The men did well. The reg't. has a high reputation here for efficiency & discipline.

Col. Lewis started for home again this morning. He goes on account of his wife's health he says. The reg't. is now in command of Major Gray. Capt. Townsend of Co. B returned from home this morning. He is better. I rec'd a line yesterday from Mary announcing her safe arrival at Paducah and saying she had shipped the box from Cairo — so I expect to be up to my elbows in fresh butter in a few days.

By "General Order No. 1" from Brigade head quarters, issued this day, we are now to drill 6 hours each day — from *5.30 to 8.30 A.M.*, & from *4 to 7 P.M.* We are getting fixed up partly comfortable in our new camp. It is much better than our old one.

. . . .

Carrie, dear, I want you to do something for me. I know you have your hands full, but I want some *linen collars*. I can't afford to wear 3 paper ones every day at 6 to 8 cents each — that's so. Let them be like the one I send — ¼ inch longer from button hole to button hole, & only trimmed off from about the place I have marked with a pen. If you can send me 8 or 10 such, I'll kiss you for them when I get home! *Now* you'll do it, won't you? You can send them, one or more at a time, by mail. I can't get any but paper ones here. Don't work too hard to make them. Now I think of it I'd *rather* you *buy* some of some kind, for you have *too much* to do with the two babies to care for. Several boats went up this morning with five or six thousand prisoners taken in the vicinity of Vicksburg.

. . . .

Helena, Ark., June 2, 1863.

. . . .

Did I tell you in my last that we had *moved camp* again? On the 24th we moved from the hill down to the levee, worked hard and got everything nicely fixed up, streets graded, evergreen & other trees set out on both sides in front of the tents — when last Saturday about 6 o'clock we received orders to strike tents and move back to the hill again. We were *mad — all* of us. I had that day gone with a 6 mule team & got 2 loads of brick & Lt. Alvord & I had just finished laying a brick floor in our tent — well, it vexed us you may well think. I was assigned the duty of the disposition of companies & baggage in the camp to which we were moving again — a duty which kept me busy till about 5 o'clock next morning, as I had to be up till the last load was hauled & disposed of, and everything was moved during the night & morning. Sunday morning we commenced to "fix up" again. At noon I was ordered out with my company to relieve a company of the 33rd Mo. which was on outpost duty about 3 ½ miles from town on the Lower Little Rock road, a point outside the chain guard & infantry pickets, & near which a number of straggling, prowling bushwhackers had been seen the day before, — so I got the company ready, drew one days rations, marched out and took out position. I assure you I saw to it that my *videttes* & guard were wide awake that night, for there was not even a scout between us & the enemy — though how near the enemy might be we couldn't tell. We were not disturbed, however. Next day, (Monday) a great many persons from the country were permitted to enter our lines and visit Helena, mostly for the purchase of goods &c. They were nearly all *women* and Negroes. The women many of them are bitter in their hate of the Union soldiery, and made many severe remarks to us, as I was obliged to halt them and question them & examine their passes when they had any. Some of them, however, were *ladies* in their deportment. One reminded me very much of Nancy Comstock & *looked* like her.

In the afternoon we were relieved and marched back to camp. I did not sleep a wink that night while on outpost, so that when Monday night came I was ready to do some strong sleeping. On the way in I met a negro wench with some nice blackberries to sell at 10¢ per quart. I got a quart, and they were nice for supper I can tell you. Immediately upon arriving in Camp last night I rec'd an order detailing me to act as a member of a Court Martial here. I am associated in it with a

Brig Gen (Garrard of Ky.,) 1 Col (Clayton) 2 Majors & 3 other Captains.[6] We met this morning. I presume we may be engaged several weeks in this duty — perhaps months. I am sorry I am detailed, as it takes me away from the company, and as Lt. Gilmore is Acting Adjutant Lt. Alvord is alone in command of the Co. I prefer to be with them, & they had much rather I would. The box you sent from Columbus has not arrived. I am still looking for it every day. Helena is not yet taken by Price — the 28th is not yet gobbled. Price seems to be threatening us, but will not attack us I think.

. . . .

Helena, Arkansas, June 5, 1863.

. . . .

Well, we have had another scare. Last night at 11 o'clock I was called up and an order handed me to take Companies C. A & K of the 28th & take them in the trenches on the flanks of Battery "B" in front of our camp. News had been received that Price was once more before Helena, & the whole command was ordered to be under arms & ready to march to the front at a moments notice. I went out, placed my command in position & was ready for the "rebs." We laid there till 3 o'clock this morning when I was relieved by two companies under Lt. Smith of Co. I. At 5 Co. D. went out, and soon after the rain begun to pour down in torrents & the wind to blow a regular gale. The storm continued about two hours. Some of our tents were torn down by the wind, and nearly everybody got wet. It was a terrible storm, & I pittied poor Co. D. It is very warm again since the rain, & I think we will get more. There was any amount of thunder *mixed in*. Quite a number of the sick of our reg't. are sent north to General Hospital today on board the "Gladiator." Charl Waller of my company is among the number. I don't expect he will ever return, though he may finally recover his health at the north.

Our Court Martial is still running, & will probably last for some time. It is a dreadful bore to me — that's so. (I forgot to say that no *Price* was seen or heard of again this morning.)

We have heard by way of the northern papers that *Helena is not* taken! Glad to hear it — ain't you?

The news from Vicksburg is very favorable I think. I have conversed with two Generals from there who say they have all confidence that it is only a question of time — that Grant has got them this time. A terrible bombardment was going on at last accounts — the news is to Tuesday morning. I do hope that we shall succeed there soon — *and I believe we will.* I rec'd a line from Mary stating that she sent the box to me from Cairo, but it has not come here yet. No Express goods have been rec'd here for several days, as no regular boats are running. I hope it will "happen around" before long.

Darling, *I want some money.* If you can, I want you to send me a draft for $100. — If not, then $50. will do. I had to let the boys have money to go home with, and though they promised to send it right back (Nickles & Knox) I may need it before they get around — & the paymaster is not here yet. Send draft on New York payable to my order & send by mail. When pay-day comes I shall have some to spare again — a couple of hundred or so. . . .

Head Qr's. 28th Wis. Inf'ty. Helena, Ark., June 7, 1863

Sunday has come again, and it is the first one for some time that we have not had to work hard all day. Today I am lying by & trying to rest a little, though it is so warm and the flies are so thick that it is but little use to try — so on the whole I though I had better try and write again to you, darling.

Well, for news I have to say that Governor Salomon reviewed us yesterday and addressed a few kind & flattering words to us, for which we thanked him. When he closed we gave him three cheers that fairly made the valley of Arkansas ring.

The resignation of Lt. Col. Whitaker having just been received, the Governor immediately commissioned Major Gray as Lt. Col. Now there will be a fight for the Major-ship. Capt. Williams has not returned, and as is it [*sic*] thought he will not be able to resume active duty, the line officers have recommended Capt. Townsend of Co. B. as next in rank for the position vacated by Major Gray. Capt. White of Co. F. evidently expects the place, and has been *laying pipe* for it for months; Col. Lewis is supposed to favor his appointment (I *know* he does) and the Governor labors under the impression that Capt. White raised the 28th regiment, so I have no doubt he will receive the commission. If he does, there will be *fun* here. Col. Lewis established our ranks as captains in Camp Washburne. Promotions, generally, should be made according to rank — and for Col. Lewis to try to repudiate his own decision as to our rank, after we all have submitted to it for months, is, to say the least, a little inconsistent. I think I see trouble ahead in this regiment. Capt. White is no more entitled to the position for other reasons than rank, than any of the five officers who rank him, and his appointment, if it is made, will produce general dissatisfaction. A committee of the line officers, after a meeting yesterday, at which Capt. Townsend was recommended for promotion, waited upon the Governor & stated our wishes; he frankly expressed his preference for Capt White, but said he would make no appointment till he arrived home — but I'm sure White is the lucky man.[7]

I have had reason to *know* it would be so since last January, so I am not at all disappointed, the more especially since I ask and expect no favors. If I am graciously permitted to do my duty & remain Capt. of Co. C., it is all I need expect, *and I know it* ——

I am still engaged upon the Court-Martial. We have disposed of several cases already, and have a long session each day except Sunday. Of news we have none except the little I have already written you.

Governor Salomon has been to Vicksburg. He says that the

Wisconsin Regiments have lost heavily there. He leaves for Memphis tomorrow to make arrangements for removing the sick and wounded to Wisconsin. I am expecting that we shall be ordered to move camp again within a week or so. Pity we could not move *every day!* Wouldn't it be fun? Charl Waller of my company has been sent north to hospital. I think he will, & ought to be discharged.

I keep well — first rate. I weighed myself last Thursday and turned the scale at 151 ½ — a big weight for me. As fat as I am and with my hair cut short you would hardly know me. By the way I must get a spy glass and see if I can find any hair long enough to cut off & send home to you. I will try & write more before this goes. I think of you always, darling, and do feel sorry for you, my own, if I do not always express it. . . . .

Head Quarters 28th Wis. Vols.
Helena, Ark., June 11, 1863.

Though but little has transpired since I wrote last that will be interesting to you, I have no doubt you will be glad to *hear* from me, even in my letter should contain but little knews.

One interesting circumstance I will mention. On Tuesday the paymaster appeared in camp paid us off for two months — March & April. We were nearly all of us *short,* and he was gladly welcomed. We will make up a package of money to send home in a day or two, probably. I think we will send it by express. I will send $200. to you I think, and then if I need money, send for it. Can you get along on that?
. . . .

Helena, Ark., June 13, 1863.

. . . .
We were ordered up, and under arms at 4 this morning to repel an attack again. The enemy continues to threaten us here,

but unless he brings a very much larger force than we have, he will not attack Helena. We are strongly fortified here.

Troops continue to go down the river. Some 6 or 8 regiments went down yesterday. They were N.Y., Penn, N.H., & Mass. regiments. The boys here talked a little mean to them — telling them that it was no use for them to go down the river — that they hadn't any *wooden guns* there, but had got some *real iron ones,* with which they sometimes *hurt* folks when they fired them. I mention this as a specimen of the *fun* they enjoy here.

I am still on the court martial, and think it will last several weeks yet. I heard yesterday that Lt. Col. Whitaker is married. Whew!

Lt. Gilmore got paid this last pay day. It is the first pay he has had since he has been in the regiment. Lt. Alvord also got his pay. He has had none before except his Sergeant Majors pay up to Oct 31, 1862. *Now* I've got *my* pay of *them.* Ed. Kinne cooks for met yet. He keeps perfectly straight now. He sends $35. to his wife this time. Christy is not very well — nothing serious I think. The boys are usually pretty well. I am tough as usual.

. . . .

I have just been to breakfast. We had fresh fish, Potatoes, bread & coffee — with milk. It is about the first milk we have had in a long time. We live pretty well now, & it costs us less than $2 ½ pr week each.

As I write (6 ½ A.M.) detachments from two cavalry regiments are going out through our camp into the country on a scout. They have three howitzers with them. Other detachments have gone out on other roads, so that if there is an enemy near in force, there may be some fighting before night. If there should be I will endeavor to write so that you can hear from me by next mail. I don't anticipate any conflict here, however, but no one can tell. If there should be a fight, it is not probable that I shall be engaged in it, being on duty down town — but my duty to the men under me would call me to go with them if I can. I think we would be placed behind the breastworks to support Battery "B", if we are attacked here. Don't be at all uneasy about me.

. . . .

Helena, Sunday Eve, June 14, 1863.

It would do you good to be here on Sunday, and especially if you could take a drive through town in the afternoon and see the darkey women out in their *finery. They do dress though, to kill.* Whether they get the garments which their mistresses have worn, or whether they manage to steal or buy new I can't tell, but you can see them wearing their fine silk dresses, Lace shawls & mantillas, fancy hats "with buttons all over" them. Oh, it is gay! Black as the ace of spades, with lips on which you could hang a hat, they get on their fine attire on Sunday, and aint they grand? They are that! White women are nowhere. I wouldn't believe one could see so much finery among them if any one had told me so, or if I had read of it. It is a sight to see, as one can, from 50 to 100 of them going to or from their meetings, dressed up *"within an inch of their lives."*

I have got a big boil under my arm-right in the arm-pit — which is very sore and painful. I can hardly put on or take off my coat. Hope it will get well soon. I think I will have it opened tomorrow. Ed. Kinne makes a poultice every night for it. I can't wear them daytimes very well.

The 3rd Iowa Cavalry left here today for down river, and other troops are passing down daily. With the force that is being concentrated in and about Vicksburg, I think that Grant ought to have a sure thing of it. May he soon take that rebel stronghold is our hourly wish, for we are all anxious to see home and friends once more. We are willing, *anxious* to fight to hasten the glad moment, and long to be led against the foe.

Perhaps we will never get into a fight — but if the war lasts long we probably may. If we do I trust we shall all do our duty.

. . . .

**Head Q'rs. 28th Wis. Infantry.
Helena, Ark., June 14, 1863.**

Dear Father:

. . . .

The force here is not large now, but Helena is strongly fortified, and we could hold it against a much larger force than ours. We have been expecting an attack for some time by Price and Marmaduke; their forces have been reported near here several times, but the attack has not been made. I do not believe it will be very soon, but we are ready to meet them at any time. Troops are passing down the river every day — thousands of them. Vicksburg ought, I think, to fall, and I believe it will fall soon. I think Grant has got them. The 20th Regiment went down the river last Tuesday. I saw Lieut. Rockwell, Sergeant Carpenter & the rest of the Oconomowoc boys. They all looked and felt well.

We have "heaps" of niggers here, of all colors, sizes & *shapes*. The principal productions of this country seem to be darkies & mules.

. . . .

**Head Quarters 28th Wis. Vols.
Helena, Ark., June 14, 1863.**

My own Darling:

. . . .

I have left you, love, because I felt & *knew* it my duty to do so. I have always been one who would rather choose a lowly, quiet position, instead of placing myself, or being placed in a prominent place, & I really dreaded being put at the head of my Company — but, darling, if I had not, I tremble to think what the company I had raised might have become. With Curtiss as Cap't. & the officers as the are — pshaw! I needen't talk. I'll tell you more about it when I come home. I will only say that many of the boys say that if I should leave the company they will get into some other company or regiment as soon as possible. For *one like me*, this is a prominent place, though I am only one among some 10,000 captains in the army.

I think the poet must have meant me when he wrote —
"The gentle heart that thinks with pain,
"It scarce can lowliest tasks fulfil;
"And if it dared its life to scan,
"Would ask but pathway low and still;
"Often such lowly heart is brought
"To act with power beyond its thoughts."

Until I tried it I never would have believed I *could* have filled the place I now occupy, though I think I could, while my health permitted, make an obedient *soldier* in the *ranks*. And, dearest, thus far in the performance of my duty, I have not been obliged to deprive my loved ones of the *necessaries* of life, at least. I am now enabled to provide for them, and at the same time be paying for our home, while serving my country. Such being the case, we are both particularly fortunate in that *one* respect, but I know that my absence makes it very unpleasant for you in many other particulars — that there are some things which it is hard to endure. In this I sympathize with you — pity you — my own; but darling I feel that for my sake you will bear all, endure all — and when I come home happiness shall take the place of such discomfort. Remember, dearest Carrie, I feel for you in all your sufferings — ever bearing you in mind.

. . . .

I don't think I shall go into a colored regiment, though if the war would close soon, *and I knew it*, I would get into one as soon as possible, for it would be a pleasant & paying situation after the war, & I could have you with me — as my home would be with the regiment.

The *scare* of yesterday has not amounted to a fight. The cavalry which went out yesterday brought in two or three prisoners whom they had picked up. All was quiet last night, & it is so today.

. . . .

Helena, Ark., June 18/63

Again, with nothing new or exciting to write about, I seat myself to fill out a short letter to you.

Things still remain as they did when I wrote last. I am, as usual, well, though I am having a tough time with a nice little cluster of *boils* under my arm. They are very painful, and *almost* make me sick. *Only three* have come to a head & broken yet, while one or two are getting ready. They are in the armpit — just under the right arm, — and I can hardly use it at all. It keeps me howling half the time, day & night. I keep them well poulticed, & hope to get rid of the "pets" before long.

Christy is quite sick. I hardly know what ails him. I'm afraid he is going to be clear down — we are doing all we can for him. I really hope it will be nothing serious.

The weather is hot & sultry, though we have an occasional rain.

I see by the papers that the democrats of Ohio have nominated Vallandigham for Governor. Now if the *people* don't clean him out at the polls they deserve — well almost anything bad.

. . . .

Helena, June 20/63

No, dear, the 28th is not disbanded, and will not at present. I don't see from what the *yarn* could have started, unless Col. Whitaker thought that his leaving would break it up.

You may send me 2 pairs of stockings — that will be enough for the present.

. . . .

Helena, Ark., June 20, 1863.

Again this morning I was cheered by the arrival of your dear letter of the 10th and 11th. I am always so glad to hear from you, love, and to know that you are usually well. I am so sorry to hear that our darling Lulu is sick, and hope to hear by your next that it is nothing very serious.

And Mary's little teeth are beginning to peep through, are they? It *would* do me good to see her now; but it cannot be at present. However much we may wish to see each other, I cannot get away from here now. At present no one can get leave of absence without a certificate of ill health from the surgeon, approved by the medical director &c., and then they (officers) get only half pay, while absent. So it would, with loss of pay, cost me at least $150. to go home and be gone a month. That I can't afford unless *I* am sick, or *some of you* are.

As to your coming here, I positively forbid it, for the following reasons:

First: It is almost sure death to at least 1 out of 3 of all unacclimated persons who come here, except late in the fall or in winter.

Second: I could not provide for you a comfortable place except by going down town — and I could get leave to be there but a small portion of the time — and then it would cost be from $2 ½ to $4 per day — an expense *we* cannot afford.

Don't think that I do not wish to see you, darling, because I am able to present these reasons for your not coming here. If it could be consistently, I should be happy to have you with me — but wouldn't it be a little unpleasant for us to lodge in the same tent with *two lieutenants?* — we & our babies!? You will

not attempt to come here unless I should be ill & send for you.
Then you may hasten to me, but till then may be some time —
I hope to be home first.

Christy is quite ill, though better today I think. I will send a
line to Mrs. Christy, which you will please forward to her.
. . . .
Please send the note to Mrs. Christy.

List of L. H. Christy's Effects.

Cash $9.00	3 Knives
Stamps	1 pr Mittens
1 Pocket Book	3 pr Socks
1 Silver Watch	3 Shirts
1 Gold Ring	1 pr Pants
1 Portfolio	1 Over Coat
1 Needle book	1 Dress "
1 Ink stand	1 Blouse "
1 pr Boots	1 Hat

He was buried in his blanket & gave his gold pen to George
Cole.

Helena, June 22, 1863.

Mrs. Christy:

I can send all the above articles to you by express (except
the hat which will not pack well in the box,) or such of them as
you wish to have sent you, & dispose of the rest here at some
rate.

Whatever you say I will do with them. Please let me know
what disposition to make of them.

June 1863

There sounds the solemn funeral march again — the shrill
fife & muffled drum. Another poor fellow is just being carried
to his last long home along side his comrades who sleep so

quietly upon the bluff just back of our camp. His marchings & picketings — all his duties & sufferings for this life are over. Another of the brave men who rallied around the honored banner of the free, is numbered with the patriots who have died to uphold that flag. May he rest in peace. He was a member of Company H. Last week he went aboard the boat to go up river on a furlough, but was too sick to go, & now he is dead. Surgeon Smith returned from Wisconsin this morning. He is just in time, for Doct. Miller has been sick abed ever since Monday morning & we had no other one here.

Why have you to change your boarding place? Can't you & Squire Harrison get along? I am very sorry you are tumbled around so much, & hope you will find some good place where you can stay awhile. Dearest, I do pity you, if I don't *always* say it.

I send "one of my curls." My hair is *long* now, so I'll send this before I have it cut. Wouldn't you like to see me with my hair cut short? I think there is enough of it for you & Lu. I received Lulu's in your letter.

My company has gone out on outpost in charge of Lieut. Alvord. It rained hard when they went out & bids fair to be a wet rainy night. They will be gone till tomorrow at 5 P.M.

You say you do your own washing and ironing. I had rather you would hire it done. It would be cheaper I think when you have so much to do, for I'm afraid if you do so much you will make yourself sick. I sent a picture in my last for Lu. I presume she will think it is *terrible* nice, & make lots of fuss over it. . . .

**General Court Martial Rooms,
Helena, Ark., June 29, 1863.**

. . . .

Capt. C. C. White is commissioned Major, of which you are doubtless aware. It is not the fair thing & we captains here know it. I think it probable that some of the Captains will resign — I don't know as I shall — but I may. While the conflict continues I wish to be doing *something,* but I am not satisfied *here,* (in the 28th) Do you blame me? I really stand no chance.

Yesterday was so very hot that I could hardly live — much more write letters. It was absolutely *terrible.* Today is not much better, though there is some air stirring. The news of the blowing up of one of the rebel forts at Vicksburg by our men is confirmed by arrivals from below. I hope they will do what they seem confident of doing — celebrate the Fourth of July in that City.

Gen Prentiss has rec'd notice from up river that Price & Marmaduke are massing their forces again for an attack upon this place. He thinks they cannot raise more than 9000 to 10,000 men, & that we can hold Helena against that number. I think so — and I don't believe they will ever attack us here.
. . . .

I believe my men *are* ready to follow me anywhere, and I sometimes wish I could have a chance to lead them into danger to see what they are made of & if *I* would run. Not that we have not been in dangerous positions, but we never have been under an infantry fire of any account, or charged by cavalry.
. . . .

Helena, Ark., July 1, 1863. 5 A.M.

How the months roll around — how swiftly they pass — and yet *how long* they are.

It hardly seems as if I had been almost a year in the service, and yet it does seem almost an age since I left you, darling. Time — days & hours seem so long without seeing the dear faces of *my* Carrie & *our* little ones.

I have been very busy for the past few days. Yesterday was muster day, and I had to prepare the *muster rolls;* which is a long, dry job. Then, too, it was the close of the Quarter, and I had to make a *quarterly return Monthly Report* &c., and now I have yet to make my *quarterly reports* of Clothing, Camp and Garrison Equipage, — of Ordnance & Ordnance stores — besides a yearly Inventory of the latter, besides the usual every day business, and attending Court Martial.

The appointment of Capt. White to the Majorship don't go down here at all. The officers had a meeting on Monday, the day we rec'd the news, and passed resolutions; among which was one that we would *resign*.

The resolutions are signed by 20 line officers, being all that are here except Capt White's 2 lieutenants, and by the Adjutant, and what is more, nearly all of the 21 have already handed in their resignations — *myself* among the number.

Whether they will be accepted or not is a question. They have to be forwarded to Gen. Grant, and the matter then rests with him. One thing is certain — we don't wish to remain in the regiment under White if *we can help it* — & we *wont* if we can get out *honorably*.

It is kicking up a big row here, and we are agreed in the matter. We all feel that we are slighted & insulted by the appointment. Copies of our resolutions are being sent to Capt. White & to the Governor. Let the wolf howl. ——

. . . .

Helena, Ark., July 1, 1863. 2 P.M.

. . . .

Instead of looking out upon pleasant fields covered with waving grain & flocks, I see everywhere about me frowning battlements from whence look down the "grim dogs of war" — I see each plain & hillside covered with snow-white tents — bristling bayonets glistening in the sun by day, and by moon light these pleasant nights as sentinels pace their monotonous "beat" upon the walls of the forts, or upon the lines of the camps.

And all this I have become so accustomed to that any other scenes would seem almost unreal — a dream — a vision. I see a steamboat coming down the river. Does she carry a burden of produce or merchandize seeking a market? No. Hers is a cargo of armed men, and from her sides look out the death dealing cannon, while bristling bayonets are stacked upon her decks. Once all this would have seemed strange — passing strange — to me; but now it seems to me only a matter of course ——

July 3, 1863.

Yesterday 5 reg'ts of rebels were reported as being 12 miles out from here, marching on us. We were ordered up about 3 this morning, and are ready for an attack, though I hardly expect one. We intend to celebrate the *Fourth* tomorrow. I suppose this will find you at Columbus.

All well. No news of importance.

. . . .

Helena, Ark. July 4/63 5 ½ P.M.

We fought from 4 to 11 A.M. today, when we repulsed the rebels.

Our reg't lost 9 men. My Company lost *none*. All well. I write you more fully directing to Columbus, where I presume you are. Love & kisses to you all.

The attack may be renewed at any moment.

Helena, Ark., July 6th, 1863

I have already dropped you a few lines in relation to the novel and most exciting celebration of the "glorious Fourth" at Helena, and now as I am getting partially over the fatigue incident to fifty hours in the trenches, a portion of the time in one of Arkansas' heaviest rain storms, with soft mud for a couch, I will try & give you a more detailed account of the affair, as I know it will not be uninteresting to you & my friends & the friends of my company.

Time and again for the past few weeks we have had rumors of the advance of a large rebel force against this post, and although they had not appeared to attack us, Gen. Salomon who has of late been in command of the post has been at work strengthening the works for the defense of the place. On the first day of this month the Generals here received information of the near approach of the enemy, & the forces here were ordered to be in readiness to resist them at a moments notice. To this end we were called out & formed in line in our company streets at about 3 ½ o'clock in the morning, as it was reasonable to presume that the attack would be made at about daylight. A grand celebration of the Fourth of July had been talked of, but on the 3rd the different regiments were notified that it would not take place, but that each regiment might celebrate the day in its own camp as it saw fit, only that the firing of guns was prohibited except a salute from Fort Curtiss. Accordingly a committee of the officers of the *Twenty eighth* "got up" a *programme* very like unto those we have so often followed at home, & preparation was made to celebrate — a reader having been selected for the immortal "Declaration of Independence," as well as an orator for the occasion, but

"The best laid schemes of mice & men
Gang aft aglei —"

And so it was upon this occasion. Instead of the eloquent lips of Adjutant *Savage* it was the mouth of the cannon from which came the "address," directed more particularly to the foes than the friends of our country. The whistling of shot & shell took the place of our national airs. In fact it was found necessary to adopt an entirely different "bill of fare." On Friday evening the near approach of the enemy made our commanding General suspect that they might attempt to *celebrate* with us, and soon after 3 o'clock in the morning of the fourth our companies fell into line at the tap of the drum. Half an hour later the alarm gun was fired from Fort Curtiss, and we march[ed] promptly to the positions assigned us. A few minutes later our pickets were seen falling back on the right and left before the advancing foe. Our batteries opened upon the rebels with shot & shell, but they continued to advance. Their attack was directed against our positions upon the flat next the river, both above and below the town, and batteries "C" & "D", the first near the center of our line — the latter a few hundred yards to the left. To the 28th was assigned the duty of supporting battery "B", (some 400 yards to the right of battery C,) against which it was supposed a strong assailing force would be sent. It happened, however, that none were sent in that direction, so that we had an opportunity of witnessing some portion of the battle at the other points on our line, and directing our fire against the assailants of battery "C".

The batteries here are situated upon a series of broken ridges in rear of the town, between which are deep and winding ravines. The positions upon the river were not visible from our position, but the different batteries & their approaches were plainly to be seen from our breastworks. Emerging from the woods, the enemy sent a force down a ravine lying between batteries "C" & "B" to approach "C" upon the right while another force attacked in front. As they advanced a galling fire from its guns and the infantry supporting it, was poured into them; but they faltered not. In numbers they had the greatest advantage, and battalion after battalion swarmed from the woods and moved on, exhibiting the most daring bravery — charged up the steep [slope] with fixed bayonets, sprung into the works with exulting yells & drove our men from the guns — not however until the pieces were spiked — hauled down our flag and raised in its place the emblem of their treason. That was an exciting and terribly interesting scene. The rebels were defiant and outnumbered us four to one. It seemed then that for us the day was lost. Our men fled down the declivity opposite where the rebels had entered, towards the town, followed by a host of the enemy. But the tide soon turned. Fort Curtiss & the different batteries had opened upon them in the meantime with terrible effect; and the infantry from different positions added to the storm of death. The hillside was literally piled with their dead & wounded. They halted — endeavored to form behind a negro church — but grape & spherical case shot crashing through the building drove them from that shelter & they retreated to the battery, under a terrible fire. Our men reformed, were reinforced, charged back up the hill, and after a desperate conflict were once more in possession of the works. Battery "D" had been assaulted in the meantime, but here the rebels were repulsed with great loss. The battle raged from 4 to 11 o'clock A.M. — seven hours — when the enemy withdrew terribly cut to pieces. The fight was going on along the line on the right & left at the same time, but as my observation was mostly confined to the points mentioned I cannot give particulars.

I went over the field about batteries "C" & "D" in the afternoon. It was a sickening sight. The ridges & ravines were thickly strewn with ghastly corpses covered with gore — heads, arms, legs shot away — mutilated in almost every manner by the shot & shell — while the groans of the severely wounded could be heard on every side. It was a bloody fight. On one spot of ground less than a rod square lay *nine* dead bodies. Under every bush, alongside every log & stump were the wounded. The slightly wounded mostly escaped from the field, but a great many were afterward captured — and others came in & gave themselves up.

The loss of the enemy in killed, wounded and prisoners foots up to about *3,000*. They probably had about 15,000 men. We had only 3,800 effective men, including Cavalry, Artillery & Infantry. Our loss is only about 200. It was a signal and disastrous defeat for them. It has been one of the bloodiest battles of the war, and our loss is singularly small considering the punishment we inflicted upon the enemy. We have shown

their wounded every possible attention, and many of them
have already been sent north to hospitals. I hear that we have
prisoners from 33 different regiments.

They were led by Lt. Gen. Holmes, Maj. Gen. Price, Brig.
Gens. Marmaduke, McCrea, Parons, Frost, Fagan & perhaps
one or two others.[8] Gens. McCrea & Fagan are reported
killed. Three of their colonels & *lots* of minor officers were
either killed or captured. Our victory was complete.

The twenty eight lost six men wounded (2 mortally) and five
missing — eleven in all. We were less exposed than most of
the other regiments. Every man found himself a "brave boy!"
Even the sick came out & handled their rifles with good effect.

We laid in the trenches all the time (except 4 or 5 hours
Sunday afternoon) (5th) from 4 A.M. on the 4th till 6 ½ A.M.
on the 6th as it was apprehended that they would return &
renew the conflict. But they were too badly whipped — they
could not have been hired or driven to return — in fact they
were completely routed. It rained horribly Sunday night, giving us a good wetting, and we spread our rubber blankets in
about two inches of mud & slept what we could, as we had
been out long enough to be tired. The sun fairly broiled us
during the two days. Every man of us was anxious to have
them renew the attack on (this) Monday morning, but they are
"skedaddling" at the top of their speed. We were reinforced
by two regiments of Infantry Sunday night, but we had no
need of them & they have returned to Memphis.

We have news this morning — official — of the fall of
Vicksburg. There we have 22,700 prisoners. They surrendered
on the 4th too, at 10 A.M. We have an impression here that the
"Fourth of July" is a great day. Hurrah for the day! Three
cheers in honor of its victories!

One word in relation to our Generals.

Major General Prentiss who commands the Department of
Eastern Arkansas, with his headquarters here, will doubtless
be credited highly on account of our successes. He is a brave

soldier, and I would not wish that one leaf be plucked from his wreath of laurels — but to Brig. Gen. F. Salomon, of Wisconsin, who commands this post and the troops here, belongs the honors of our successful defense. He has kept large parties of the soldiers here at work almost constantly for several weeks past digging rifle pits, building Batteries & other defenses, and now we appreciate his sagacity. Without them Helena would doubtless be held now by the rebel army, & we prisoners in their hands, if not sacrificed in opposing them.

I shall write you hereafter of many incidents of the battle for which I have no time now. We feel no apprehension of the return of the enemy. Our cavalry force went out about 10 miles yesterday & encountered no force except what appeared to be a rear guard of Cavalry, & they scattered in the woods at the approach of our scouts. They found a large house with about 100 of the rebels wounded.

As all of our folks & perhaps some of my friends would like to hear from me, and as I cannot well write long letters to all of them, you will please let them read this. You will doubtless see accounts of the affair more in detail in the newspapers, if the great victory at Vicksburg does now swallow up entirely our at Helena. I picked up several articles upon the battle field, one of which — a secesh cartridge box — I will send home by Q. M. Sergeant Hawks if he gets away in a day or two as he is endeavoring to do. I have also a cap box, canteen &c. from the same source. Nearly all of the men have trophies from the field won by us upon the 87th Anniversary of the natal day of the Republic.

. . . .

Helena, Ark., July 10, 1863.

Yours of the 2nd is just received, & though it is so hot that I can't write much, or think either, I will send a line to let you know that I'm well. We have had no more battles here since the 4th, though we have had a few alarms. This morning about 5 ½ o'clock our pickets were driven in on the right of the line, but after a little picket firing the rebel skirmishers fell back. We were in the trenches an hour or two & then came back to camp. My company was placed in the rifle pit immediately under the guns of battery "B", where they would fire right over our heads.

A force of Cavalry is now passing through our camp on their way out scouting. Gen. Ross has returned to Helena. I am making an effort once more to get Marshall Nelson sent home. He has been sick three months, but I have been unable to get him off. I got mad day before yesterday about it, & gave the Col. (Gray) a left handed blessing, as well as some of the other officers. It all depends on whether an officer is a *favorite* or not. If he is not his sick men must suffer for it unless the man happens to have an influential friend somewhere about. Two men (1 well & the other only slightly ill) had just gone home, when I renewed my application for Nelson's furlough. I then got a Surgeon's certificate of disability, but I couldn't get the furlough — so I'm trying to get him discharged. We hear that Gen. Meade has routed Lee in Penn. I hope it so.

. . . .

P.S. 8 ½ P.M. I just hear that there is a prospect of our being ordered out to chase the *rebs* today.

Helena, Ark., July 11, 1863.

Yours inclosing a piece of Lulu's dress is received. I think it is very pretty. Won't she look nice in it? I wish I could see her with it on. She must not get too proud of *fine clothes*, though. Lots of dangers of that I guess. I guess you had *not* better pay any more on the house at present. We may need it for something else. I don't like to let Frank have the money to use, — he is, as you say, "so careless." And I don't want it put in the bank just now. I don't know what to say about it. Frank is always ready to accommodate, but first he knows he will be over head and ears in debt & can't raise the money if it is any large amount. I don't want it to be where any one will be slapping on to it for my debts — I owe a little yet, but can't pay it just now — till I get a little more ahead. If you keep it by you, get it into large bills — $100.s or $50.s & it will occupy but little space & you can carry it almost anywhere — but be careful of it. I know I needn't say *that,* but you know *we* can't afford to lose it. Perhaps your father would keep it for us. Don't he want to use it, or a part of it for a while? If he does, let him. It will be *safe* there I *know.*

. . . .

I will *think* about getting some photographs. They cost $6. pr Dozen here or $4. for ½ dozen. They won't make less than ½ dozen — a common melainotype costs $1. *without* a case. Perhaps I'll get one of some kind. Yes, dearest, I want baby's picture, but I'm afraid I shall keep it when I get it — if it is a good one. Hadn't I better? —

I have sent Leander Christy's things to Mrs. Christy by Express. I was afraid we would be ordered to move from here, and as I couldn't very well carry them about I thought I'd better send them & not risk it, as they might get lost. I sent the clothing in a box, & the Watch, money &c in a small package. I could not have sold his clothes for much of anything now, as the boys are out of money. I disposed of his hat & threw in the boots, as they were poor & the box would not hold them.

. . . .

Helena, Ark., July 15, 1863.

. . . .

We are still safe here from the *rebs,* though some of them are prowling about yet. A squad of them came up in front of one of our picket posts yesterday twice. I was brigade officer of the day yesterday, & had to visit the chain guard & cavalry outposts after midnight. The cavalry are posted on the roads about a mile outside the chain guard. It is a lonely ride in the night with only one man for an escort. It was a dark foggy night & we could see but a little ways in advance, but I got around all right just at daylight, well tired out. . . .

We have no reinforcements here yet, but probably will have soon. It is surmised that the rebels meditate another attack here with a stronger force than before. If they come we will try & give them a reception similar to our fourth of July affair, but, though we can whip a pile of them as we are, we ought to have a few more men here in case of attack by 20,000. Gen. Salomon says that if they come their force will be large enough so that *we* can *take 10,000 prisoners.*

. . . .

Head Quarters Co. C. 28th Wis. Inf'ty Vols.
Helena, Arkansas, July 16, 1863.

Once again it seems probable that the enemy of our free government is about to attack us here. Kirby Smith is reported to have crossed the White river, and has doubtless formed a junction with the defeated forces of Holmes ere this.[9] If so they must have from 20,000 to 25,000 men, as Smith is said to have had at least 12,000 with him. There is some apprehension of an attack within 24 hours, and tonight I am ordered out with my company to guard a ravine leading into town from the west between batteries "A" & "B". I hardly think the attack will be made as soon as tomorrow — I *hope* not, for *Friday* you remember is my *unlucky day* — but we must be on the alert as our force here is small. It probably numbers full 500 less then it did on the 4th when we whipped them so badly. We lost then 231. Some are absent on furlough, and two companies of the 1st Ind. Cavalry have been mustered out & gone home, their time having expired. They were nine months men. Then too, a good many of our men are sick from exposure during the late battle & succeeding day, & from hard work & the effect of the hot weather &c. Our men have been over worked here this summer. There has been a great amount of work on the fortifications & but few to do it. Then there has been picket & guard duty to do keeping men out nights as well as days. All this & in this very unhealthy place has reduced our effective force terribly. Some are detailed as hospital & ambulance attendants, ambulance drivers & teamsters & artificers, clerks &c., so that I can report but about 38 men for duty — that is, to carry muskets. We ought to have reinforcements — perhaps we will before the attack takes place — but help or not we shall *fight* before we are *beaten*. If they come now it will be a desperate fight. I have escaped sickness & the bullet this summer beyond my most sanguine expectations — we will hope that the same Hand that has shielded me heretofore will protect me in the coming strife. I fear not, — but harm *may* come even to me. If it should, be my own brave wife still, heroic & patriotic — for woman as well as man may & does sacrifice upon her country's altar.

If the enemy appears tomorrow, it is uncertain when I can write you again, but my thoughts will often be with you, my Carrie, and our little Lulu & Mary. God bless you all my own darlings. You will think, I know, of your absent loved ones. I send all my love & kisses to you & the babies. The drum beats. I must go.

Helena, Ark., July 17, 1863.

We are safe still. I went out last night just after sundown, chose a position where we could give an enemy a raking fire in case he attempted to enter town by the ravine which I was to guard, posted my company, put out videttes, ascertained the whereabouts of the cavalry picket & chain guard just outside of my position, so as not to fire upon them, assured Col. Gray by messenger of my favorable position, spread my blanket on the grass & laid down beneath the stars — Long time I gazed on the stars & though perhaps you might be looking upon them too, and thinking of me, as I did of *you* & *ours*. At last I slept, soundly too, though I often woke during the night, for I held a responsible position, and that kept my thoughts busy. I was visited by the commanding officer & two of his staff during the night, who complimented me upon the excellent position I had chosen.

Morning came, but no attack. We were on the alert & ready. At 5 o'clock we were relieved, picked up our blankets & marched back to camp. You wouldn't have believed once that I could lie out of nights in this way without injury. I positively feel better than yesterday. O, I'm a tough one now!

. . . .

Everything is quiet here this morning. I don't think we will be disturbed today — no telling though. *Major* White appeared before us in all the glory of a new double breasted coat and a major's straps last night for the first time. He seemed to fell out of place, I thought. We do not hear from our resignations. Gen. Salomon detained them here several days, which he had no right to do.

. . . .

10 A.M. 17th July.

. . . . I just heard that our boxes have arrived, & have sent Lieut Alvord & some men with a team for them. Am glad they have arrived. Now won't Co. C. have lots of good things?

No further news from the rebs. It is reported in camp that a boat brought us reinforcements this morning. I hope it is true.

. . . .

Helena, Ark., July 19, 1863.

I have but a few minutes to write and scarcely a word of news. I am getting ready to go out on outpost for 24 hours. Six companies of the reg't with detachments of other regiments have gone on a scout into the country today some 12 or 15 miles. Their force is small, and I'm half inclined to think that it is a wild move on the part of some one — that it wouldn't take a large or a smart party of the enemy to "gobble" them.

Our sick men are all better, but we have a host of sick ones. I can only report 29 men for duty after deducting details &c. I dread the next two months here. I believe it will be terrible upon us. I am glad that I am in good health myself, so as to be able to see after, if I can do but little, for my ailing men. If I can help them & save the life of *one* soldier, I shall have done something for my country.

Yours of the 12th & 13th was rec'd this morning. You must have rec'd my letters ere this. No fight since the 4th, & the danger is not considered as imminent as it was a few days ago.

We have been overworked here. Not less than 10,000 men should have been here to do the work which we have done with 4,000 this hot summer — now we are suffering the consequences in having our men sick & dying around us by scores, & still a host of work to do. This duty day & night has worn them out. For this, if for no other reason, I hope we may be reinforced.

Our boxes have been rec'd. I rec'd my coat, a towel 15 collars, 1 bot. wine, 1 package currants, the sausage, (thank Mrs. Kreeger for me,) 3 prs socks & some horse radish. Thank you, love & all who have remembered me with these offerings.

. . . .

[Helena, July 20, 1863]

. . . .

It happened to be Capt. Enos who went north with prisoners instead of Capt. Stevens. I don't toady to officers sufficiently to secure such chances — and I *won't do it* — that's flat! If I can't have an equal chance with others of my rank without *that,* I'll quietly try & do without. ——

Am sorry you got excited. My turn may come by and by, then you & Lulu will be *so* happy, & myself too. Do just as you think best about paying up for the house. If you think best you can *pay it all up* and get a *deed* of the place. I wish I was there to see to it, for I'm afraid the description in the papers does not define the boundaries of the lot *exactly* as it should be — that it varies a few inches. If you do it, have it surveyed, (at Mr. Kreeger's expense it should be) & take no less front on the street than the bond calls for.

5 P.M. It has been raining & the air feels a little cooler. I suppose my company will be one of two to lie in the rifle pits tonight. I hear that the 25th & 27th Wis. & one or two other regiments have arrived here, & that our force is to be increased to 10,000 men immediately. If it is, an expedition will probably be sent out from here to take Little Rock and drive the rebels from this state. In that case our reg't. will probably be one to go on the *tramp.*

. . . .

Helena, Ark., July 22, 1863.

. . . . Our boys are all out of hospital, & those who were sick in their own tents are nearly all better. Rumor says that Charleston is ours. May it prove true. The advance of Rosecrans' Army into secessia seems to be a success. Morgan, we hope, is surely cut off from escape by this time. The rebels have left this section — that is, most of them. I think there is no large force this side of Jacksonport, on White river. We have received some guns — (artillery) — here, but no reinforcements of infantry of any account.

. . . .

P.S. I have a *shell* which I picked up on the battlefield, from which I have removed the powder — (it had not exploded.) will send it home the first chance I have.

P.S. No. 2 — 9 A.M. 22nd — The box has just come. The jar

is broken all to pieces — butter run all over the fruit &c — Part of the cherries will be good. The butter is about spoiled — too bad.

Head Quarters Co. C, 28th Wis. Vols.,
Helena, Arkansas, July 24, 1863, 9 P.M.

Once more I write you, *apparently* on the eve of a battle. We may be deceived, but the indications are that we will be attacked soon — perhaps before another sun shall rise on us. The enemy is reported at or near La Grange, which is but 12 or 15 miles from here — his force is said to be larger than before — but we still think we can hold Helena against him with our brave little army. It seems to me that we are strangely neglected here — no reinforcements sent us — and this an important post upon the great Mississippi.

The only addition to our force since July 4th is a few guns. The Infantry force which is always sent us when we have no use for it has left again. If we are attacked tomorrow we will be reinforced Sunday evening — too late to be of any use.

Well, we shall all go into the fight with confidence in ourselves — ready, yes anxious to meet the *traitor* foe. God grant that foe may fall beneath the strong, earnest blows we are anxious to deal in defense of Liberty & Right. We feel that the loved ones at home look with pride upon those they have sent out to redeem the country from dishonor, — that they think of us — & that knowledge lightens our hearts while it gives weight to the blows we strike for the honor of the *good old flag*.

I am on duty tonight. At 3 o'clock tomorrow morning we are to be under arms — *ready* in case the attack shall come. We are anxious but very hopeful. The moon which looks down tonight upon quiet scenes here — comparatively quiet — may tomorrow night light up the hard cold bed of the wounded & dying, & the gory resting place of the ghastly, mangled dead.

Whether or no we fight — whether or now we succeed, may it be well with our country & the dear ones at home.

. . . .

Helena, Ark., July 24, 1863.

Yours of the 17th — the first I have rec'd from there — was just rec'd. I am *on duty* again, and have hardly time to answer. Nothing has happened since my last writing that would be interesting to you. A scout went out two or three days ago, but returned without finding an enemy.

We have rec'd quite a number of pieces of artillery, and they are being placed in position. A rumor is current this morning that General Price is again within 25 miles of us, and making this way. I hardly believe he will attack us again, but he may. . . . .

Our resignations are not heard from yet. I think we will be paid off within 10 days — hope so. The weather here is terribly hot & sultry. It makes me feel perfectly *shiftless*. Haven't the energy or will enough to do anything hardly, except what I am obliged to. None of my men are sick so but they keep about — but some are unfit for duty. Perkins, Plympton, Tucker, Kimball, Lewis, Ward, & Glamm are *ailing*. I believe all the rest are returned to duty. Lt. Alvord is not very well. I'm afraid the next two months will try us all if we stay in this unhealthy place.

. . . .

I have got a negro cooking & working for me. I like him first rate, & hope to keep him. I can while here, but if we leave here he may want to stay here, as his family is here. He is a contraband. His master lived in Mississippi, opposite the mouth of White river. He *had* over 300 slaves. 140 of them *left* in a heap, my *"Fred"* among them.

. . . .

Helena, Ark., July 26, 1863.

Sunday morning has come again, bright and hot. The mail is not yet up from the boat, but probably will be within an hour, when I hope to hear again from you.

Col. Lewis, Q. M. Wylie, Brick & Nickles arrived here by the boat this morning. The boys are looking very well indeed. I have not seen the Colonel. The box of paper collars & the two H'kd'fs are all right. Thank you, dearest, for them. Tell Lulu that papa thanks her for the handkerchief she sent me, and sends her a kiss for it. Frank sent me a quarter ream of note paper, marked $2.50 pr Ream. You will please settle with him for it, as well as for the other things he sends me.

. . . .

We continue to receive information of the presence of the enemy in our vicinity, but have not been attacked again. We may be very soon — but hope to whip him.

Yesterday we were paid off for the months of May & June. I shall probably send to you about $200. Do as you think about paying something on the house — or all of it.

. . . .

Our fight did not come off yesterday. We have to be up at ½ past 2 every morning & fall into line by company ready for whatever comes along. It is reported that Price has attempted to cross the river below here, and been repulsed — he had but a small part of his force there I hear. His main force is in this vicinity, or was at last accounts. Lt. Gen. Holmes is said to have been removed from command. I rec'd by the last mail another package of the Christian Banner. It is the 3rd or 4th I have rec'd. I presume they are sent monthly, but do not come. This package was directed *"via Nashville,* Tenn." Should be *"via* Cairo" or "Helena, Ark."

Our wounded are all doing well. I now report about 40 men for duty — about as many as any company in the regiment.

Have you rec'd the cartridge box I sent by Hawks? & the
Package I sent by Jenkinson?
[missing second sheet of letter]

Helena, Ark., July 27, 1863.

Herewith I send you $270. in Treasury notes. Times are so
risky here (Price may come in & want to borrow our money,
you know!) that I send it all along, & will write for it if I want
& can't borrow.

All well. I was out with my company all night last night.
P.S. I shall probably write to you to pay out a part of this to
some of the friends of my men.

Helena, Arkansas, July 29th 1863.

. . . .

I can form no opinion, dearest, as to the probability of our
resignations being accepted, nor as to when I can come home
to stay with my loved ones. Col. Lewis has returned, and, of
course, sides with *White* & against the rest of us. We knew he
would, as there is no doubt that he advised & urged his appointment. Perhaps he will make himself by putting himself up
against us for his own personal aggrandizement, and to favor a
political friend, for political reasons alone. He tries to make us
think it is all right, & wants us to withdraw our papers. We
coolly tell him *we won't do it* unless we see reasons for it
which we do not now. Col. Lewis proposes to *run* the regiment
for *his own* benefit — we intend to claim our rights — *if we
have any* — he says in effect that we have *none*. If that is so,
then we don't want to remain here, & we will tell him so. He
came & talked with me 2 hours and tried his best to win me
over & then to *bluff* me. Hope he went away satisfied. I hope
the "immortal 20" will all stick to their text. He will then have
a few of his puppies left who are always fawning about him —
let them stay.

I keep well as usual. A great many of the men are sick. I think Corporal Perkins will have to go home if I can get a furlough for him. I wish 4 or 5 of our sick men could go. We now have reinforcements here, but they are not yet reported for duty, & three of the regiments here have gone out on a scout, so that we have more picket duty to do than ever. Gen. Davidson is said to be approaching Helena from the North, Gen Blunt from the North-west — both driving the rebels before them — so that Arkansas will be relieved of the presence of a traitor army pretty soon, I hope.[10]

I sent you $270. on the 27th by express, in a package of $744. sent to Frank to be delivered.

If you go to keeping house you must keep a girl — you can't get along alone *and must not try.*

I don't know how you would like it at Baker's. I'd rather you would stay in Oconomowoc than Summit if you are in either, *other things being equal,* but if you would be more comfortably or more pleasantly situated there I want you to go there. I am sorry you have to be tumbled around from one place to another so often. Perhaps it would be better to get some help and keep house. I think of you so often, and of the unpleasant times you are experiencing while I am away. It is too bad. May it end soon. I have no news. Companies "A" & "K" have been added to the detail for Provost Guard in the city, so we have only 6 companies in camp now. Kindest regards to all & write soon. I send love & kisses to Carrie, Lulu & Mary — my sweet loved ones. O, if I could but see them!

Helena, Arkansas, July 31, 1863.

. . . .

Nothing new here since my last. I sent the shell by Corporal Perkins. He said he would call and leave it with you. The powder is removed, so you can handle and examine it without danger of an explosion. Isn't it a pretty thing for men to throw at each other. When it explodes it might wound a score of men, as the outside iron shell or case breaks all to pieces, and the leaden bullets imbedded in rosin with which it is filled fly in all directions.

I hear that Col. Lewis has been appointed Provost Marshall in place of Capt. Townsend of Co. B., and that our regiment will all be detailed as Provost Guard. If so we will have no picket duty to do, (except the captains as brigade officers of the day) but I can't say that the change suits me.

Some of the men continue sick, but I have none in hospital now, except those who have gone up the river. I have 51 men in Helena, but 6 of them are detached from the company on other duty.

I keep perfectly well. I expected after having such a sickness last winter that every little exposure or exertion, especially in hot weather, would be followed by an attack of diarrhea — but I have nothing of the kind.

Our resignations have not been heard from yet. It is the opinion of many that they will be accepted, or we *dismissed* from the service. Well, I had about as soon it were so, as to remain under officers whose only object is to advance their own personal ends — who *run* the regiment for their *personal aggrandizement.*

. . . .

Provost Marshall's Office,
Helena, Ark., Aug. 2, 1863.

My letter of Friday was too late for the boat, so that I am enabled to add this little to it, though it is but little news that I can write. Our army here is now 8,000 men to 10,000 strong I suppose, so that there is no danger of an attack here. An expedition will probably be sent out from here shortly, which is expected to find its way into Texas. The 28th probably will not accompany it, as Col. Lewis has been appointed Provost Marshall, and our regiment is detailed upon Provost duty. I had rather we would go than stay, as we have been here altogether too long to suit me. I want a change. To be sure there would be some drawbacks — for instance our mails would be irregular, and I could not hear from you so often — and I should miss your dear letters so much. I think it would be better for our men than the duty they have been performing for the last three or four months here — besides which we could take a look at the country, & I could pick out my plantation, you know.

. . . .

Helena, Ark., Aug. 4, 1863.

. . . .

I sometimes wish I were *more* patriotic — not *less* so — that I might endure any treatment, do anything for the sake of the service. I had rather endure much than make trouble, as you know, but there is a limit to endurance of slights, neglects & almost open insults from those who have pretended to be ones friends, and who have ever been treated with all the respect due them as such, as well as superior officers. At present I shall remain with the regiment — but I cannot & will not endure everything. I have never been treated fairly by some officers of the regiment, and never expect to be — but while here I shall endeavor to do my duty uncomplainingly, & *outwardly* respect those who are placed above me in the service — in some cases it will be *lip-service*, I'm afraid, in which the heart has no place. It would not do for me to write all I know & feel. Aside from this I get along as pleasantly as I could expect, changing as I did from one of the quietest of boys to the responsible position of leader of nearly 100 men.

I rejoice, love, that you keep up so brave a heart. It makes me proud of my little wife to know that she endures so cheer-

fully for my sake, that I may, cheerfully too, do something for
our country. Continue thus, dearest, and know that it makes
me happier. When I asked you to be mine — when I took you
to my heart and called you "wife," we little dreamed that we
would ever be so long separated, & from such a cause — but
we may not see all that is in store for us. Here we are, and we
must make the best of it, loving each other none the less, but
rather the more. If I may only keep well, & my life be spared
that I may return to your arms when this war is over, we will
then be happy. May it be soon, for I am very anxious to see
you and our little darlings. You ask me how much I owe. I owe
Pierce Bros & Flanders of Boston on note about $140. &
Interest from about Oct. 1857. To — Andrus of Grand de Tour,
Ill. about $100 & a years interest on note — To David Stevens
$100. & interest from fall of 1856, — amounting in all to
about $450. or $500. When I can I wish it all paid, but not now
when I am away and with the uncertainty of my return which
we must think of in such matters. I sent you a day or two ago
some secesh money & c. in a large envelope — also letters,
receipts, &c. written by rebels here & elsewhere, before our
arms had triumphed along the Mississippi. I'll send a few
more letters in this I think.

I have just been told that our reg't. has orders to march.
Whether it is for a long march or only a scout I don't know, but
will try & find out before I close this letter. Should it be for a
long march to Little Rock & Texas you must make up your
mind not to hear from me so often as now, for it will be
impossible — but you must write often still, and I shall improve every opportunity to write you. I keep well yet, & shall
try and be careful of myself for your sake & that of our little
ones.

. . . .

I have just been down to learn what I could about the regiment leaving here. An expedition is to leave for Little Rock,
and our brigade is set down as a part of it, but an effort is being

made by some of the parties interested to have the 28th left here, and I think it will succeed. It may be some days before we know, as some time will elapse before the army leaves. As for me I care but little wether [*sic*] we go or stay. We have been here a long time, and here I have buried a dozen of my men — less one. I have seen so many sicken & die here that it seems that *any* change from this sickly place would be welcome. I think the chances for life & health would be quite as good elsewhere. But I could not hear from home as often if we should go in that direction (towards Little Rock,) and other drawbacks would doubtless present themselves. It would be hot weather for a march at this time, but we would make short marches — probably not exceeding 6 or 8 miles per day.

The rebel Lieut. Gen. Holmes, who was in command of the secesh here on the fourth of July, is reported to have since died at Little Rock. I think the informations is reliable. I saw a man from the country 75 miles from here yesterday, (living near *Des Arcs*, Prairie Co.) who said that the information is perfectly reliable. I am not certain whether Holmes was wounded in the fight here or not. He makes *three* at least of their Generals who were leading them here just one month ago today, who will lead them no more — the halter is cheated of its dues by their death.[11] We are glad to hear that Morgan & his guerrilla gang have been finished. If they had been permitted to escape, Indiana & Ohio were deserving of eternal infamy. Have not the last five weeks been laden with good tidings for those who love liberty & their country? May it still continue till once more peace may spread her wings over a united country. We hope to hear soon that Charleston is ours. Mobile will probably be attempted soon. Let us get our seacost, & then we are ready for our perfidious English & French friends to show their hands if they want war.

[missing page]

Helena, Ark., Aug 6/63

. . . .

Yesterday the officers of the command were invited to call at
Major General Prentiss' quarters on the wharf boat at the levee.
I went down at 5 o'clock P.M. I had no idea what was the
occasion, or that so many would be present. The tables were
filled with drinks — iced lemonades — iced punches — wines
& liquors. A party of 150 to 200 shoulderstrapped gentry were
present, ranging from the double-starred Maj. Generals Prentiss & Steele, down through all the different grades to the
barless second lieutenant.[12] Gen. Prentiss made a short address, alluding favorably to our doings here upon all occasions
& especially on the 4th of July last, & stated that he was about
to leave us — that his baggage was aboard the "Connir,"
which would leave in a few minutes. — He then introduced
Maj. Gen. Steele who made a short speech to us, when Gen.
Prentiss took him by the arm and led him down the cabin to the
table & proposed that they set us an example, which they
immediately did by taking a drink & inviting us all to do the
same — using whichever we saw fit of the beverages present
— which of course we did, and the tables were soon lighter by
a couple of hundred drinks or so. Gen. Prentiss then led off in
singing the "Battle Cry of Freedom" which was done with a
will. After a few minutes further of social intercourse Gen. P.
bade us good bye, adding "God bless every many who helped
me here on the 4th of July!" went on board the boat, and left
for Memphis with the cheers of the assembled crowd ringing
over the great river. I understand he will remain at Memphis
for the present. Gen. Steele will probably assume command of
this District (East Ark.). The Expedition for the west & south
is fitting out. 1100 mules were bro't down by the "Imperial"
night before last, and a pile of waggons, harness &c. We do
not know whether we will go or not, but I think not. I presume
it will be 2 or 3 weeks before we know whether we go or not

— It will take about that time for them to get ready, & changes will be made till they start, probably.

. . . .

Helena, Arkansas, Aug. 10, 1863.

We are finally under orders to march at 6 o'clock tomorrow morning, and are all in confusion getting ready for the tramp — turning over our tents &c., which we leave here. We shall be in a muddle now till we get off — no time to think or write hardly. We take five days rations from here. At the White river we will meet a steamboat and take supplies to last us to Little Rock I suppose. How many of our men will leave here I don't know yet. Shall doubtless leave some.

I hope we will get a mail before leaving here in the morning, for it may be weeks before I can hear from you again. I just had to buy me a pair of boots — paid $10. for them. Newspapers cost us 10 to 15 cents — two Chicago, Cin. or St. Louis papers 2 for 25¢.

I have been down town and "got my picture drawed!" How do you like it? I was all dirt and sweat, tired &c. This is the only thing I can think of or get to send to little Mary. I think she ought to have this but she will let you *look at* it once in a while.

11th 7 A.M.

We will not probably get away before noon, or about that time. We are all "in a suds" yet. No news. I don't know whether we will get a mail this morning or not. I am afraid not.

Well, darling, good bye. Don't worry about me. I know you will be anxious, but don't be too anxious. As often as I can I will let you hear from me. Lulu & Mary, good bye, be good girls, & papa will love you. I send love & kisses to you all. Remember me to all friends. If you have not paid Kreeger any more, do not at present.

Our desks &c have got to go aboard now. We slept without

tents last night. It looks like rain. Again, good bye, my darling loved ones.

Diary of March from Helena, Ark., *towards* Little Rock, Ark.

Helena, Aug. 11. Tuesday. Struck tents yesterday, & were to leave at 6 A.M. today, but were delayed till afternoon. Fell into line about 2 P.M. and marched just below the "Hiredman House" where we were halted and waited till nearly night for the balance of the Division, Wagons &c to pass us. Got in motion again about dark. It was dark as pitch & raining before we had gone a mile. The wagon train was detained, & we got behind the balance of the column, as we were the rear guard. Tried to march after dark, but it was slow getting along. I fell from the end of a bridge and bruised myself somewhat, but was able to keep along. Maj White's horse fell from another bridge into a ravine & could not get up. Found a piece of candle & a match, & finally got the horse up. Marched a little further by the light of the candle — couldn't catch up, so we halted about ½ past 8 for the night. The officers baggage &c is ahead, so we are without blankets — laid down in our wet clothes & tried to rest a little in the rain.

Aug. 12th. At 1 o'clock A.M. were ordered forward to take the advance during the day. Has cleared off finely. Caught up with the advance about ½ past 3. Rested awhile and marched about ½ past 4. Were on the road with occasional rests till 5 P.M., when we halted for the night, as there was a bridge to build before we could go any further. Camped in a little grove, cooked our supper, spread our blankets & laid down for the night. This has been a very hot day. The men carry their knapsacks, and it wears hard on them. Several had to give it up. Knapsacks, blankets, portfolios, shirts, clothing of all kinds, bibles & Testaments &c., &c., lie scattered all along the road, thrown away by the soldiers rather than carry them. Unless the teams can carry the knapsacks tomorrow, lots more of them will be thrown away. Very warm this evening — my clothing is completely saturated with perspiration — coat & all — Can hardly endure a blanket — laid a long while looking at the stars through the leaves overhead, & thinking of home & the dear ones there. Would I could see them all.

Thursday, Aug. 13. The drum called us up about 4 o'clock this morning. Got our breakfasts & are waiting for the completion of the bridge. We are probably from 15 to 18 miles from Helena. Sergt. Olson, Corp. Ludington, Batchelder, Byam, Breck, Briggs & Evenson sick.

Noon — The bridge is done and we are off on our tramp. Peaches & apples along the road, which the men *will* have. Passing along with the reg't this P.M. a club thrown by a man to knock off pears from a tree fell upon my head & knocked my down, raised a big *welt* on my head & made it ache for the rest of the day & night, worse than ever. The heat of the sun & the march had made it bad enough before. Camped about ½ past 4.

Aug. 14. Called up at 3 A.M. Marched about 4, & kept it up with frequent intermissions till 4 ½ P.M. — marched 15 miles. This has been a terrible hard day for us who go on foot — the dust, the hot sun & sweltering heat — it was *rough*. The men fell out by scores. We are marched too far for men in our condition, & at this time of year in Arkansas, half the time without water. Last night a guard was placed over the wells to prevent our men from getting water! Today we are forbidden to take peaches & other fruit along the road! Thank the boys the order is not obeyed by them all. Commanders often act like *fools* — I can use no milder form. They talk about the *policy* of *letting the peaches alone* as we march along using *kindness* & all that sort of thing to *turn Arkansas back to the Union*. What mocking is this! I don't believe in pilfering & destroying property without an object, but such things as these the men should have — & *will have I hope*.

15th Up at 3 A.M., but did not get more than a mile from our camp till 10 A.M. being delayed by the pontoon wagons

Dear Carrie

&c. ahead. Had a hard march today in the hot sun & blinding, choking dust, of about 15 or 16 miles, reaching Clarendon about ½ past 4 P.M. & got into our camp below town soon after dark.

> **Head Qr's 28th Wis. Vol Inf'ty.**
> **2nd Brigade, 3rd Div. Ark. Expedition.**
> **Clarendon, Ark., Aug. 16, 1863.**
> **Sunday, 10 A.M.**

We arrived here last night, footsore and tired, and as I hear that a mail will go down today I improve the opportunity to write you, writing on my knee, setting on my blankets. I have stood the march finely so far, though I have been as near *bushed* as I could well be when night come, marching in the sun & dust. My men who started all came through, though several of them had to ride a good share of the way. The men I left at Helena we found here upon our arrival, having been sent around by boat, except two (H. Evenson & Bare) who are left at H. They are all unfit to march, & will, I think, have to be left here. I think from what I see & hear that we will remain here from 4 to 6 days before marching on Little Rock. Our gunboats captured two rebel transports above here on the 14th or 15th, & destroyed their pontoon bridge over the river. The enemy are in force near here. They are fortifying 25 miles from here on the road to Little Rock — we will probably have a fight there. Plympton, Lewis, Leavitt & in fact all the boys who came up on the boat, except Clark, are better.

We are to change our camp this P.M. so as to be nearer the river. There is quite a force here now, and more to arrive. I think a regular post will be established here.

. . . .

> **Clarendon, Ark., Aug. 18, 1863. 10 A.M.**

We are still here, but expecting orders to cross the river at any moment. The other divisions are crossing now — & have been since yesterday forenoon. When we get across I suppose we shall be where we shall have to be continually on the alert — shall doubtless be continually annoyed by guerrillas, if not by strong parties of the rebels' regular forces. The boys are writing home, fixing up their duds, and preparing generally for a hard tramp. We have no mail yet, hope we will have soon.

Some of the boys have been buying supplies of tobacco at $2. pr pound! & Whiskey at the moderate price of $1. per pint! Think of that — $8. per gallon for the same that would cost 40¢ pr gallon at home! We only allow them to get it in very small quantities, for medicinal purposes.

I leave 11 sick men here — viz:
Sergeant F. W. Plympton,
Corporal H. M. Ward,
   " John D. Zimmerman,
Privates
   " Benj. F. Baker,
   " Loren Byam,
   " Thomas Carr,
   " M. D. Clark,
   " H. C. Holcomb
   " Iver Iverson
   " H. S. Lewis
   " Christian Zabel
At Helena are left
James Bare & Hans Evenson.

The regiment leaves about 87 men here, I think. There may be more by the time we leave, & some of these may possibly be able to go, if we should stay a few days longer. Briggs has also got the ague, & Breck is not feeling very well. Chaffee, Thompson, Ludington, & all the rest of the "Conie" boys are well I believe. Ed. Olson has had the ague, but is getting better. The march may bring it on again.

Carrie, I shall want a couple of flannel shirts if you can get some made for me and send the first opportunity. Please have them made large and longer [than] the others — they are now altogether too small for me, & the sleeves are nearly as tight as my skin. I suppose they have not been washed properly for one things. Get some *plain, neat color* — I go without a coat a great deal of the time. I can hardly carry what clothes I need, & presume I shall throw away some on the march, though I have nothing here that I do not need. But if necessary they shall go, & I can go without . . . .

18th 1 P.M. I have just learned from pretty good authority that we will leave here day after tomorrow. If we are here till then I shall probably have time to write again, though I have a great deal to do. I have just made out descriptive rolls for my thirteen sick men — a good deal of a job. I have some other writing to do as well. I think our first pitched battle will be at or near Bayou Metoc, just this side of Little Rock — perhaps another at Little Rock.[13] They will strive hard to beat us this side of Arckadelphia, on the Washita river, some 60 or 70 miles south west from Little Rock, for there the greater part of the supplies for their army west of the Mississippi are manufactured, as I learn. It is in Clark County. I shall keep you advised as to our movements as often as possible.
. . . .

Clarendon, Ark, Aug. 18, 1863.
7 ½ o'clock P.M.

I am aware I am writing often these days, but you will, perhaps, excuse it when you remember that I was unable to mail any letters for five days, and it may be twice that length of time before I can send one after tomorrow. I have been up town to see the sick boys this afternoon. I intended to have given a statement of the disease of each one as far as I was able in my letter today, and left a blank for that purpose, but did not get time to fill it up. I'll get at it as near as I can on next page, though I may get some of them wrong, as I am not much of a *doctor,* & have had no chance to consult with the surgeon in relation to them. Here they are — *to be left at Clarendon.*

Serg't. Plympton - Debility - not recovered from fever.
Corp'l Ward - Debility & "Common Fever."
Corp'l Zimmerman - Debility & prostration following fev.
~~Benj. F. Baker~~ - ~~Don't know~~ - *think he shirks*. (goes with us.)
Loren Byam - Intermittant Fever.
~~Thomas Carr~~ - ~~Chill fever~~. goes with us.
Martin D. Clark - Congestive fever. Seriously ill.
Hiram C. Holcomb - Debility.
Iver Iverson - Pulmonary disease (following fever.)
Horatio S. Lewis - Weakness of lungs & debility
Christian Zabel - Billious fever. - seriously ill.
   Left at Helena,
James Bare - Chronic Diarrhea.
Hans Evenson - Billious fever.
Lewis is not doing as well as he was. I have made repeated efforts to get him home on furlough, but cannot succeed. He is not in a serious situation, but is weak & unfit for duty. Sergeant Plympton is weak & don't gain much. Carr is not badly off — but has *shakes*. Zabel is quite ill with fever, and having always been tough it takes hold of him. They have had no care since we left Helena, for which we may thank the surgeon in whose charge they were left at that place. They ought not to have been sent here for some time yet. Three of the twelve they sent here will try & go with us, & even they are hardly fit, but is decided that they go, & they are anxious to do so.
   I have just been in the river with several of the officers. It is very nice to bathe in, but bad getting out — we get our feet all clay. I feel so much refreshed after a swim. The boys enjoy it, I assure you.
   Tomorrow morning Maj. White & myself are to go up town to make some arrangement for the better care of the sick men to be left here by the regiment. It is not our fault that they have not been attended to, as we have been making a hard march, got tired out, & have been at work under orders since arriving

here preparing to move forward again toward the Capital of the State, & I for one have been unable to do but little. I venture to express the opinion that the medical department of our army is very poorly managed in many instances — & this is an instance to the point. Jealousy among the Surgeons has much to do with it — and for that reason the poor soldiers, who risk their lives for their country, have to suffer. How long shall these things be? O, Lord, how long?

If we can get time Capt. Williams & myself intend to get up a complete statement of the deaths, discharges, desertions &c., as well as the names of those now absent from each Waukesha Co. Company, sick, where they are & their diseases as near as we can ascertain. I expect to be very busy tomorrow, so I must to bed & to sleep, so with a kiss for you lips, two for the babies, & love for you all, I'll bid you good night & lie down thinking of you as I look up at the stars & spat the musketoes & bugs — & *scratch.*

. . . .

Clarendon, Ark., Aug. 20, 1863.

We are here yet, though our time here will doubtless be short. Gen. Rice told me this morning that he expected orders to move his division across the river today, but I hardly think we will get off before tomorrow, as there is a large wagon train to cross ahead of us, and it takes time to ferry them over.[14]

Gen. Rice was Col. of the 33rd Iowa Vols., & received his commission as Brig. Gen. after our arrival here. He commands our division.

. . . .

I am Brigade Officer of the Day today. I have been up town to see my sick men this forenoon. Sergeant Pympton is not as well. I'm afraid he is going to be very sick. I do wish I could send him home, he is such a good man. I think a great deal of him — he has been a great help to me in taking care of the sick as much as he has. Am very sorry that I must leave him behind. Lewis is doing well, as near as I can see. Carr is back with the Co. Col. Lewis is trying to go home again, I hear. He has been sick for some days. We all wish that Lt. Col. Gray was here.

Wherever the army goes, it marks its way with the graves of our noble "citizen soldiers." Going up town today I passed the new graves of five of our freemen in one place — all from our division I presume. Our regiment has lost none here yet. We think we are fortunate — but we are leaving nearly or quite 100 men here, and no doubt some of them will find here their last resting place on earth. How sad it seems that they must die so far away from home and friends — here in the wilds of Arkansas. Would that *I* could send them home to the tender care of wives, mothers, & sisters, where many a life might be saved which will now be lost, and where those who *must* die might find a smoother path to tread adown the slope that leads to the tomb — to the river of death. May that river prove to them to be the *river of life* — that tomb, the gate to the City whose "shining towers" we may not yet see — even *heaven*.

The campaign ahead of us will be one of hardship & suffering. We have before us much to encounter — much to endure. The bones of many of us may sleep upon the prairies of Arkansas ere the war shall end, but we will all endeavor to "suffer and be strong." When we think of the cause for which we fight, we are *willing* to suffer if we may but assist in saving the government & our native land.

I wish, dearest, that you could see how we live — and yet I *don't*, for I know you would worry so much about it. You ought to see some of the dishes we get up — hard bread *stewed, fried* &c. Cold water pancakes when the boys are so *unlucky* as to draw flour. Fried *bacon* & *raw* bacon — but one thing — our tea & coffee is very good, and that helps the rest along wonderfully.

Notwithstanding all their sufferings & hardships, the "brave soldier boys'' have a "heap" of fun, and though many of them would jump at the chance to go home, I believe that more than half would be homesick, in less than a month, and anxious to get back again. There is no end to their facetious remarks about their "grub" & their duties. If I hadn't a home & family this life would fascinate me, I do believe.

. . . .

Aug. 21. 5 A.M. Good morning, dearest. We have our baggage all aboard the wagons ready for moving, except our blankets, so that we shall cross the river today, probably. I went down town again last night to see the boys. I found Serg't Plympton much worse. The Chill fever & diarrhea is reducing him very fast. He is so weak that he can hardly get about. I'm really afraid he is not going to get well. I would give anything if I could get him home. He is too good a soldier — too good a man to be left to die here. He does not wish his wife to know how bad he is, & did not wish me to write to her but I think I shall, for she would rather know just how he is than have him die here & she be ignorant of his illnesses. It seems to me I never saw a man run down so fast as he did yesterday. He is always very quiet & unobtrusive, doing everything & anything for all of us; giving every attention to the sick which he possibly could — if we lost him we shall miss him very much — no one knows *how* much.

It is thought Col. Lewis will go home again. Some of us here think he had better *resign,* though it does not seem likely that he will. He isn't the man to do that when getting good pay. He says he feels no regret at leaving his regiment, as he leaves it in command of an excellent officer (Maj. White!) I say "good officer!" He can't handle a regiment at all. Every one to his taste. White has no command over the regiment scarcely. But very few respect him.

I'm sorry I do not hear from you before leaving. Well, the letters will be good & welcome when they *do* come. Haven't I "done well for a boy" since we have been here. Have written every day I think — though I'm sure the letters can't amount to much; but then my "handwrite" may do you good, even if I write but little sense & much nonsense. I know you will be glad to get them, though I expect you'll get 3 or 4 at a time. It may be several days, — perhaps *weeks* before I can write you again — so don't worry if you don't hear from me right away, for I am perfectly well & able to do my regular duty.

21st 10 P.M. I have been up again to see the sick men. Serg't Plympton appears a little better this morning. He did not wish me to write to his wife, but I thought I ought to do so. You can read it, & if you think she should have it please forward it to her. He said he would try & write today. I don't think we will cross the river before night.

I have heard that Col. Lewis can only get leave of absence to go to Memphis, but if he gets that far he will go home I think. Our reg't leaves 106 here sick, I believe — a very large number. A great part of them will probably be able to join us in a week or two. Some ought to go north & I hope they will. . . .

3 ½ P.M. The drum has beat for us to fall in, so we are off. Presume we will have to wait on the bank of the river 3 or 4 hours. Ludington, L. C. Evenson & Briggs, will, I think, have to be left here — making 12 of C. Co.

Duval's Bluff, Ark., Aug. 24, 1863.

We arrived here at dark last after marching hard all day after 10 o'clock — through all the heat of the day. I found much to my surprise that all the sick had been sent up here from Clarendon by boat. I went down to the boat as soon as I could, though all tired out, & found Serg't Plympton much worse & entirely delirious. He did not recognize me except for a moment. He died about daylight this morning. It is a sad loss to our Company — a much sadder one to his wife & family. I am well. Our sick are suffering a great deal for want of care,

accommodations & medicines. Don't know how long we may
be here. The mail leaves immediately. Will write more today if
I can, but must sent this to the boat *now*. . . .

Duval's Bluff, Ark., Aug. 26, 1863.

I believe I gave you the particulars of our march up to the
crossing of the pontoon bridge this side of the White river. We
laid in camp near there the next day, & hoped to rest there over
Sunday, but about 9 o'clock A.M. we rec'd orders to prepare
to march, and at 10 o'clock fell in and left for this place,
marching through all the heat of the day, without halting long
enough for the men to boil their coffee. It was a hard tiresome
march, & some of the boys were nearly "played out" long
before night. I carried one man's gun nearly all day & wished I
could carry half a dozen more. We reached here about dark,
having marched about 13 miles as near as I could calculate.
Arriving here we found that all the sick left at Clarendon had
been sent here by boat. I immediately went down to the landing to look after my sick. I found them all doing pretty well
except Sergeant Plympton, who had failed very fast, and who
was entirely delirious. He did not recognize me until just as I
was going away, when he knew me for a moment only. He had
been delirious since the night that we left Clarendon; had been
very wild much of the time. He imagined that he was in his old
home in Mass., sometimes — at other times he wanted to go
and see his family; had tried to jump overboard several times.
His eyes were sunken, & he was considerably emaciated. Poor
fellow! I saw then that there was no hope — that he must die. I
left him late in the evening & returned to camp. At about
daylight next morning he died, having been restless & wild
nearly all night. Several men had died on the boats during the
day and night, and not a coffin was to be had — hardly a
board. I finally managed to procure some heavy, dirty, plank,
& with an old saw & a hatchet had a rude box made for a

coffin, and at 4 o'clock P.M. we gave him to his rest upon a ridge of land about 15 rods from the steamboat landing, near the White river. I learn that he expressed a wish to be buried at home, but it was impossible to forward the remains. He will sleep sweetly in these wilds of Arkansas. He was an excellent man — one of the *best* — a faithful soldier — a true practical Christian. What a sad loss to his bereaved wife & family. We shall miss him very much from our company — he was always so attentive to the sick — so kind & obliging to all. May he rest in peace. I went yesterday & got a board, upon which I cut with a pocket knife his name, rank, company & regiment, & the date of his death, and helped to place it at the head of his grave. Many have been buried without coffins — merely wrapped in their blankets. We have 700 or 800 sick men here, & very inadquate provision for their comfort. It seems hard to see so much misery which we cannot relieve. I think Serg't Plympton is the only one from our reg't. who has died here. My men are all with the company now, but I shall have to leave about a dozen here. They will be examined today by a medical board who are to decide who are to remain here. I think we will leave here about tomorrow, though I have rec'd no orders. Col. Lewis, Chaplain Peake & Luther Feller left yesterday morning — for Memphis I suppose. The 27th Wisconsin which is with the expedition has only about 100 men for duty. I hear that they left over 400 sick at Helena! They have been at Vicksburg. I keep well. Have had diarrhea for a couple of days, but am about over it. Sergeant Olson is not very well, but says he will not be left behind the company. Most of our sick men are doing pretty well.

Davidson's Cavalry has been in advance of us. They sent in about 30 prisoners last night. A boat came up last night, but I cannot learn as it brought any mail for us. I do so wish I could hear from you, dearest. We are now having rather a rough time of it — no tents — no shelter but bushes & our blankets — but we have no fighting yet. I think there is no doubt but Price has

a force 11 miles this side of Little Rock. Duval's Bluff contains a house or two at present. The balance has been burned.
There is a rail road from here to Little Rock — don't know
anything about the cars & engines, but presume they have
some at the other end of the road. Darling, we all think of
home, and wish we could see our loved ones. But we must
wait patiently & hope to be with you by & by. Then we will be
happy, won't we, my own?

Last night was very cold — I could hardly keep warm. I
suppose we will march as soon as it gets *hot* again.

   . . . .

Oconomowoc, Wis. Sept. 4, /63

Capt. T. N. Stevens,
Dear Sir,

Your letter bearing date Aug 24, was received Sept. 2,
announcing the death of my dear husband. Another letter of
yours dated 21 of Aug. giving me an account of his severe
illness was rec'd the next day Sept. 3. You can only imagine
how unexpected the intelligence was when I tell you we received a letter from him dated Aug. 15, stating that they had
arrived at Clarendon and his health was restored — the next
news that reached us was his death —

How true it is that in the midst of life we are in *death*. I gave
him as a sacrifice upon the altar of his country and God has
seen fit to accept it, and taken him to himself and I can only
say "His will be done."

We thank you for your promptness in writing us and for you
manifold kindness towards him, and your memory will ever be
held in grateful remembrance by us all. If there are any other
particulars in regard to his death we should like to hear them,
and also of his funeral and where he was buried. It would be a
great consolation to have had his body sent home but we
supposed it would be an impossibility. Please extend my sin-

cere thanks to Mr Byam for his unwearied care and kindness to my dear Husband, and for the facts contained in his letter to us, received at the same time as yours, and I will reply as early as possible.

May *you* if called to lay down your life for your country leave behind the testimony to be transmitted to mourning wife and friends "that you have never been ashamed to own yourself a christian."

I am most respectfully yours,

Jennie Plympton

Duval's Bluff, Arkansas, August 28, 1863.

My own Carrie:

Yesterday we remained in camp. I spent most of the day at work at the Company Muster rolls, preparatory to muster on the 31st inst. It was a dirty, dusty time, but we got through with it after a fashion. Last night in the night a rainstorm came up & gave us a wetting. Our bough houses most of them were blown down, & though the rubber blankets helped to keep off the rain, we nearly all got soaked more or less. Some of the men were completely drenched. Lt. Alvord & I had to change the location of our *tent,* (made by putting our rubber blankets up over poles) on account of the wet. We have it now in a more comfortable position; have cut brush for a bed and are now "comfortably situated." You'd think so if you could see us, with blankets, coats &c., out to dry, the boys cleaning their guns &c. Well, it's only a part of a soldier's life, and if we have nothing worse than this, I think I can get along after a fashion, for I feel well, and have a ravenous appetite. We really got a barrel of potatoes yesterday, & what is more, they only cost us $2.25. They taste good I assure you. We get fresh beef often, & plenty of hard bread at present.

We hear this morning that Price has abandoned his position 11 miles this side of Little Rock, and has retreated to Archidelphia. I don't know whether the report is reliable or not, but it is said to come from Gen. Davidson. If it is true we shall probably occupy Little Rock without a fight. It is said that our division may be sent up the river to *Des Arcs,* about 15 miles by land, where Marmaduke is said to have a force of about 2000 men. Des Arcs is a town of some 1,500 inhabitants I think from what I hear. I am detailed to take charge of ordnance again today. It is a disagreeable job, & I hope to get through with it soon. Since the rain the sun shines out warmly, & the mud will soon dry off. Can't hear when we are to start again on the march, but presume it will be managed so that we will start again on *Sunday,* about the middle of the forenoon, & march all the rest of the day without rest. That is about the style in which things are done here on this expedition. The Generals don't seem to have common sense, — but all these things are military, & I have no right to complain I suppose — though complain I will if it can do any good. I hope we will have a mail again soon, & that I may hear from you, love. The long, weary weeks of absence seem longer when I cannot hear from home & wifey & babies.

If we do not meet the rebels this side of Archidelphia it will be some time before we have a fight, very likely. If we fight there I hope we may be successful — may not be compelled to retreat — though I heard a Corporal *quoting Scripture* the other evening like unto this — Said he — the Bible says — That "he who fights & runs away, May live to fight another day," which is, I think, decidedly original! Did you ever discover the couplet in your bible? *I* cannot find it.[15]

Lt. Alvord is well, & all the Oconomowoc boys are so so. Frank Ludington is not very well. Ed. Olson ditto.

The regiment is not very well suited with its commandant — Maj. White. We hope to see Lt. Col. Gray back here soon. He is the only one of the field officers who commands our respect (Lieut.)[*sic*]

. . . .

Seven miles west of Duval's Bluff, Arkansas, August 31st 1863. Just at sunset

We left our camp at Duval's Bluff at half past ten this morning and marched to this place, where we found water, & camped for the night. It was a short march, & an easy one, compared with the marching we have heretofore done. On such marches the men will feel well and get fat. We crossed a small prairie today extending nearly as far as our days journey. Are camped tonight in a pleasant spot in the woods. Have been here since about 3 P.M. I have 44 men with me. Reports today say that Price has about 20,000 men at "Bayou Metoc," or some such name, between here & Little Rock, so we may have an "affair" before reaching the state capital. I hope we shall not have hard marches to make, it is so fatiguing for the men. I stand marching first rate myself. Have walked all the way from Helena thus far.

How happy I would be if I could only call in & see my little family at home tonight — my own wife & darling children — I know they would be as happy to see the absent husband & father. In the years agone we never dreamed that we would be separated so long in this life — nor from such a cause. We never dreamed that such as I would be called upon the draw the sword to protect those liberties of which we supposed our-selves so surely possessed. But so it is — and for many long months I have been wandering from place to place with our glorious army, with freedom's banner floating above me — far from my dear loved ones.

When will this end? Soon, I hope, with the army of the republic victorious over all its foes — with the good old flag streaming over every state of the Union. Then will the spared ones return to our homes.

Well, our "traps" must be loaded tonight, & I must stop writing. . . . .

3 miles S.E. from Brownsville, Ark.,
Tuesday evening, Sept. 1, 1863

We were up at 3 ½ this morning, & started at 5, with our canteens filled with the muddy water we found at our last night's camp, as we had a march of 20 miles before us for today — to Brownsville — & no water on the route. We had a hard march of it, all the way over the prairie. Brownsville lies in the opening just off from the prairie. We reached there soon after 2 o'clock P.M., tired and thirsty. There we halted but for a few moments, & then pushed on three miles further into the woods to a spot where we have to bring water *only half a mile!* Here we camped for the night. It was a *choking* march — 23 miles with nothing like a supply of water! I hope we will not have to march as far again very soon, on one canteen full. I had my sword, revolver, cartridge box, canteen of water & haversack with rations to carry, beside which I carried a gun for Zabel, who is sick, from 8 o'clock till the end of the march, which was after 4 P.M. I am footsore & weary tonight — lame & dirty — *not used up,* for a nights rest will set me right again. I expect to have to go on picket tonight, but, luckily for me, was not called upon.

Several of my men gave out, but will all be up on the ambulances & wagons I think. It has been quite a good day for marching — though a hot sun was shining, we had a little breeze nearly all day on the prairie, which kept us alive. Gen Davidsons Cavalry division is in this vicinity — They have had a skirmish or two with the rebs. We are to move forward seven miles further tomorrow, where water is said to be more plenty — & so are rebels, probably. We are now about 24 miles from Little Rock, so the cavalry say. It may be further — *cavalry miles* are sometimes *long* ones. Brownsville is a town a little larger than Fall River — perhaps *twice* as large in *peace* times — & has several fine buildings — that is, *good ones for this country.* We slept in the open air last night. Tonight Alvord & I have a *roof* to sleep under, consisting of *one oil cloth poncho.* Isn't that a shelter? We had no time to eat while on the road, except to take a bite from our haversacks while resting — I'm off to supper — so you'll excuse me for closing now. . . . .

Head Qr's 28th Wis. Inf'ty.
Camp near Brownville, Ark., Sept. 5, 1863.

We are in camp again, and I hasten to improve the opportunity to write you. On Thursday morning the 3rd, we left here (our whole division) & marched in the direction of Little Rock. We left Camp at 6 A.M. & marched till 3 P.M. when we came upon an old rebel camp, with a long line of brestworks, which had been abandoned by the enemy. This was near "Bayou Metoe." We had marched about 15 miles. We camped here for the night. It was a splendid place for a camp, & clean as pleasant. The cavalry was out in advance, & shelled the woods to see if any *rebs* were there — but none appeared.

Gen. Davidsons Cavalry had in the mean time gone some 12 or 15 miles above with the intention of crossing the Arkansas above Little Rock, while our force was to engage the rebels in our vicinity. They found, however, that the river was not fordable, & were obliged to return. We had marched with only blankets & two days rations, leaving a few sick in camp, a guard &c. Our train was to have come on yesterday, but when morning came we rec'd orders to return here to our old camp; so at 9 ½ A.M. we started, reaching here at 6 ½ P.M. It was hot & dusty — water was scarce again, as usual in this country. We got well tired out Thursday. I think I should have been obliged to "give out" yesterday, but soon after starting I was detailed as "brigade officer of the day," & furnished with a horse, so I came through first rate. I was very tired though last night — but am partly rested this morning. Ed. Kinne is quite sick — has been having chills & fever for several days. . . .

When we left here Thursday morning we fully expected to have a "scrimmage" with the rebels before this — & we more certainly expected it when we heard the booming of the guns with the Cavalry when they were shelling the woods. Our men growled at having to come back yesterday. Nine out of ten would much rather have gone forward to a fight — they hate to march so far for nothing, over these dusty prairies, half choked with thirst.

. . . .

Head Quarters 28th Wis. Inf'ty.
Camp near Brownville, Ark., Sept. 5th, 1863.

. . . .

Our Expedition is under command of Maj. Gen. Steele. I can't say that he looks to me like much of a General, though I have seen him but two or three times. In fact I can't *brag* on any of our commanding officers from Gen. Steele down to Maj. White who commands the 28th. Col. Lewis came out in command of our brigade, but went back from Duval's Bluff, sick. I presume he will get home, though I heard that he only got leave of absence to go to Memphis. We are expecting Lt. Col. Gray every day. I hope he will come soon — he will be glad to see him in the regiment — & we *need* him here. Maj. White has had no experience scarcely, not even in command of his company, having been away from it & the regiment almost all the time since we left Wisconsin last December.

. . . .

Camp 28th Wis. Infty,
Near Arkansas river, about 10 miles from
Little Rock, Ark.,
Monday eve'g, Sept. 7, 1863.

Yesterday morning before 1 o'clock I was disturbed by the Adjutant who informed me that we would march at 4 ½ A.M. leaving the sick & taking everything else.

We did not get away till near 6 o'clock. Ed. Kinne, Stock. Lewis & 6 others (Lillie, Nelson, Iverson, Breck, O'Neil, & Robinson) we left in hospital. Kinne is quite ill.

We marched about 10 miles yesterday, making rather an easy march, though a slow one, as the roads were bad a part of the way & we did not get into camp till after dark. Starting again at 7 this morning we have marched 8 or 10 miles further, & are now further from Brownville than we were last Thursday night. The cavalry in advance had a skirmish with the rebels & had some men wounded. I have not heard of any being killed. They also captured Col. Dobyns' Adjutant & some important information was obtained from his papers. We also learned that Marmaduke & Walker of the rebel service have fought a duel & Walker was killed. Marmaduke was wounded & is disabled for some time.[16]

At one time today we expected to see a fight within an hour, but here we are & none yet. I think we are bound to have one but it may not be for some days & may be before sunrise tomorrow. I have only 32 men here besides teamsters, hospital & ambulance attendants &c. My company is about like the rest in that respect.

I felt rather unwell this morning, but am well tonight. Have had fried pork, pancake, sweet potatoes & coffee for supper, & am "full as a flea."

. . . .

Head Qr's. 28th Wis. Inf'ty.
10 miles from Little Rock, Ark., Sept. 10, 1863

We are still in camp here, where we have been since Monday evening. Yesterday morning I was detailed to take charge of a foraging party of 75 men from the brigade & go into the country for vegetables &c. for the brigade. We took 4 six-mule teams — went out into rebel territory 3 or 4 miles from camp, but found no *armed* rebels. Dug potatoes all day & got back to camp at 6 P.M. We got nothing scarcely except sweet potatoes & a few chickens — not enough of either to pay for going out. A party of cavalry was seen a mile or so off, but they were on the opposite side of the bayou & could not have got to us if they had tried, & then our 75 muskets would have cleaned them out. I had a horse for the day, as I was in charge of the whole & had a great deal of running around to do. Came back tired, got my supper, & slept soundly through the night, and am up this morning enjoying the best of health.

We have just rec'd marching orders. We are to have everything loaded at 7.15 & start at 8 o'clock. It is now half past 6 & I only just rec'd the order. I presume we will not move far today — some think we will get into a fight today. We are to cross the "Bayou" I am told. Well, if we fight, we will trust that it will result in a victory for the right, & that my usual good luck will attend me. Remember, darling, that though engaged in a dangerous work, it is the cause of right & liberty, & if the worst comes, it is no more than some must expect & meet. I shall remember you, my darling wife, and our loved little ones in the midst of every danger. Kiss for me dear Lulu and our baby Mary. So she can say "pa" — the sweet little darling. I do wish I could see her & you all. I must close, dearest. Good bye to you all til I can write again.

**Camp 28th Wis. Inf'ty.
Little Rock, Ark., Sept. 11, 1863.**

Another is added to the list of victories for the Union. We left our camp at 9 45 yesterday morning for this place, expecting to go into a fight before noon, as we could hear cannonading in advance even then. As we moved forward the artillery seemed to do the same. A division of infantry was in advance of us, as well as the cavalry & most of the artillery. A part of the cavalry crossed the river 7 miles below here, as well as a part of the artillery. They were attacked & lost some men, but repulsed the enemy.

The rebels had their most extensive fortifications on the left bank of the river, expecting we would attempt to do the fighting here; but they made a slight mistake in their calculations. We bridged the river, upon learning which they took all the guns from the batteries on the left bank & crossed the river, leaving us free to come in on this side, with nothing to annoy us but the batteries across the river. Our reg't was so far in the rear that we saw nothing scarcely of the fight, & stood in no danger from the rebs. We camped at an hour after dark, opposite the city, Price & Co having *skedaddled*. What the loss is upon either side I cannot learn, though it cannot be large. I have seen but one wounded man, & he was accidentally shot in his own regiment. We left our train behind us; it will be up with us today probably. Our sick from Brownville are also expected today. We expected a severe engagement, but we have easily taken the capital of the State of Arkansas. The rebels burnt a train of cars, an iron clad gun boat, and several buildings &c. There are two engines & several platform cars left — also 2 small steamboats which will be useful when the water in the river is higher. It is very low now. A man or a horse can wade it.

How long we will remain here is to be seen. I hope we will follow Price to Archidelphia as soon as our supplies come up, before they have time to fortify much more there.

I have not been into the city yet but from this side the river it seems a very pleasant place, with some pretty good buildings. I shall try & go over today or tomorrow if we stay here so long.

We hear a cannon ahead occasionally this morning. I suppose Davidson is following up Price, & will make an effort to cut off his supply train. I hope he will succeed.

Yesterday was a very hot day. We carried 2 days rations & all our traps. My heavy clothing was completely saturated with perspiration — I could wring it from my handkerchief any time during the day. It bids fair to be about as hot today.

. . . .

We get occasionally a little fresh beef, but live mostly on hard bread & bacon & pork. I can't eat bacon very well, but manage to eat pork once or twice a day with a relish. We also have tea or coffee. We have very heavy dews. Get up in the morning & find our blankets wet wherever the rubbers do not cover them.

. . . .

Little Rock, Ark., Sept. 12, 1863.

I have just been told that the mail will probably go out tomorrow, so I'll attempt another short letter, as I desire to have you hear from me as often as possible, knowing how anxious you are to hear from me, the more especially *now* while I am with one of the victorious armies which are invading the country, which has been held by the enemy from the beginning of the present war.

Our expedition thus far has been a success, though our sick have been poorly cared for — almost *inhumanely* treated. Clarendon & Duval's Bluff, the important points on the White river, are ours. Little Rock, the Capital of Arkansas, is ours.

The White River is navigable at all seasons of the year, & the rail road from Duval's Bluff to this place can easily be opened, though it will require something of a force to guard it. The Arkansas river is navigable only a portion of the year. At present the water is very low.

Our loss at the taking of Little Rock was only about 60 killed & wounded. The loss of the enemy I have not learned. It is reported that Gen. Davidson, who is following Price, has captured a portion of his train, & that Price is burning the balance.

Hurrah! Since I commenced writing Lt. Col. Gray has arrived in camp. We are glad to see him. He brings us no news of any importance. I don't know whether he has any late papers or not. Wish I had one — *or a dozen.*

We expect to move camp tomorrow, so I suppose *this day* must be *Saturday.* A heavy thunder-storm is promised for tonight, for which we are not very well prepared. We have been lying in a naked field, exposed to a burning sun for two days. I hope our next camp will be *shaded* at least.

We have heard a great deal at the north about *starving out* the rebels. It is all nonsense to think of such a thing, if I may judge by the crops in that part of this state which we have passed through. Miles on miles of corn fields are seen in every direction, ready to be plucked. As a gentleman expressed himself to me, they had to plant corn or *swing from a limb.* He afterwards qualified it by saying they had to go to prison if they failed to plant corn, & await trial & an unknown punishment. Beef Cattle are also plenty. I send some seeds of the pawpaw. I don't know but you have seen them before, but they are new to me.

. . . .

Little Rock, Ark., Sept. 13, 1863.

. . . .

I was very glad to hear from you, darling; that you are all feeling so well, and that you are so happy with our little ones. So you are going to Mr. Faurot's to board. I do hope it will be pleasant there — that it will be a *home* to you & the babies till I return to you. The price ($3 pr week,) is very reasonable. . . .

By the way, Lt. Col. Gray informs me that all letters sent from our army must be endorsed by a commissioned officer, or they will be opened at Helena or Memphis, before being sent forward. Very likely some that I have sent during the last few weeks may come under the restriction, of which I have known nothing till now, but there is nothing in them "out of the way"

I believe. You need not be surprised to find some letters opened. I suppose you are all looking in this direction for stirring news. Well, you will soon be gratified in a day or two from now probably to know that Little Rock is ours. As to anything further I can say nothing. I hope we shall follow up the flying forces of Price — drive them from the state, and keep on wherever needed. Let us keep the ball rolling until this cursed rebellion of a cursed slaveholding aristocracy is crushed. I am longing to see the end of the war, but while it lasts *am not sick* of it. I am enduring more than I supposed I could — am willing to endure, so the government be sustained, and the Union still live. And when peace shall come, I hope to return to enjoy the quiet home life as of old.

Lt. Alvord & I have each hired a colored boy to wait on us. Mine is named Jordan, 21 years old — His is William, 15 yrs old. I think they will be good boys for us — at least I hope so, for I need some help, especially when on a hard march or after it. . . .

Little Rock, Ark., Sept. 14, 1863.

. . . . I think we'll not pay any more on the house & lot — at least not till next pay-day.

One thing you *may* do *immediately* — send me a draft on Chicago or St. Louis for $50. I sent home about all my money last time, & have had to borrow some since. I want to pay up & have a little on hand. . . . Yes, dear, I got the box of paper collars, as well as the linen ones. The latter I find to be of but little use, as I can't get them half washed except once in a while. The paper ones I can use & throw away. I don't wear any at present, it is so very warm & dusty, except when I'm on duty as officer of the day, or some such time.

. . . .

So you think that picture is a good one, do you? Don't I look dirty in it? I sat down in my fatigue suit just as I had been at

work, my face streaked with sweat & dust, for I wanted you to
see me just as I look when in camp. I wish I could have had it
taken *full length — big boots & all!* Will try to next time. I
wear the linen coat considerably when in camp — it is so much
cooler & more comfortable than the others. I have had on my
dress coat but once or twice since leaving Helena, & have seen
my "gorilla" of a face in a glass but once in that time — 5
weeks ago tomorrow.

We have not crossed the river yet. A part of the pontoon
bridge has sunk, & we will have to wait till it is repaired. I
intend to try & get leave to go over this afternoon. We had —
what do you think? — for dinner today. A boiled pudding with
dried apples in it, with sauce! Aren't we extravagant? Lt. Col.
Gray messes with us now. It is very hot. "They say" a steamboat is in sight, coming up the river. She cannot be from the
mouth of the river, I think, as guerrillas would not permit an
unarmed transport to come up — & gun boats can not run in
the shallow water — nothing but small wooden boats. We will
see by & by what she is. I asked the price of milk at a house
near camp the other day. The reply was two "bitts" (25¢) for
buttermilk or four "bitts" for sweet milk! A pretty round
price. I didn't buy — though have seen the time when I would.
I can think of no nonsense, but may be able to pick up some
thing before I close this. Do you think there will be any chance
to send me a pair of shirts by & by? I will wait awhile and see
before buying. A good shirt costs $5. down here. I could get it
by mail for less than that if we should remain here. I wish I
could be in Milwaukee about the middle of October long
enough to get me a dress suit. I am getting decidedly
"shabby," "seedy" or something of that sort. I hear that Col.
Lewis has gone home from Memphis. Well — perhaps I'd
better not say what I think *now.* I am glad to hear that J. T.
Lewis is nominated for Governor, in place of Salomon.[17] We
don't think here that Governor Salomon has used us just as he
ought.

. . . . I see no prospect of our leaving here at present. A good many wounded men have, I hear, been brought in from Davidson's cavalry who went out in pursuit of Price & his flying army. *Poor* Price got outgeneraled here. The story of the duel between Walker & Marmaduke turns out to be *a true one*. Walker is buried here. The rebels are losing a great many of their Generals lately — may they lose more of them! Lewis is quite unwell. I wish I could have him go home for a while, but its no use to try.

. . . .

Little Rock, Ark., Sept. 14, 1863.
5 o'clock P.M.

I have just returned from a short stroll about Little Rock. I have only been around a very little, and can give no idea of the place, except that it seems to be regularly laid out, and would be, in times of peace & business, a pleasant, lively town. The state-house is a large, but not very commodious building situated in a small park. It is at present filled with soldiers & secesh prisoners. I found at the post office some old Confederate postage stamps, which I will inclose herewith. Also an old letter with an entirely original 10 cent stamp affixed. I obtained a copy of C. S. Army Regulations, which I shall try to carry or send home, & a small secesh work on drill.

. . . .

Little Rock, Ark., Sept. 16th, 1863.

. . . .

Yesterday morning I was again ordered to take command of a foraging party from the brigade, of about 60 men & two teams and go for potatotes for the brigade. I had to go out about 6 miles from camp, and though on dangerous ground on account of guerrillas, met with no adventure. At 2 ½ P.M. I had my wagons loaded and started for camp. About 4 o'clock a furious thunder storm came up, preceded by a terrible wind, which caused a commotion among the timber through which we were travelling. Several large dry trees came down with a crash, shaking the very earth; one near us by the side of the road — another a short distance ahead of us directly across the road, — but none injured us. We got pretty well soaked with rain, &, when we got back to camp, found that the regiment had been ordered to move at 7 o'clock that morning, (I left at 6) across the river & back to our present camp. The storm had cast loose a boat in the river, which the wind had driven through the pontoon bridge, rendering it impassable, & had also broken up the bridge below town, so that we could not cross with our loaded wagons. I left a guard with the wagons, & told them to remain till today. The balance of the party pulled off their clothes & forded the river, while I got across on horseback without difficulty. The bridge was repaired so that the wagons got over about noon today.

Our new camp will be pleasant, I think, when we get it cleared up. It is now full of small bushes, stumps &c. My men whom I left at Brownville all arrived here yesterday except one — Geo. Lillie — he is still there, somewhat ill. Kinne is not at all well, but is better than when I left him there. Lewis & Byam are in hospital here. I will try & write to Mr. Lewis tonight or tomorrow. I do wish I could get Stockton home on furlough, but am unable so far. Kinne lost his blankets & knapsack — in fact nearly all his things, while he was sick at Brownville, and there are no more to be had till we can get them from Helena, which will be 3 weeks probably. My new waiter — "Jordan" — is going to be a good, useful "boy," I think. I like him well so far, & he is intelligent. Lt. Alvord has his brother for his waiter — a smart young boy. Jordan went out with me yesterday, foraging, and, as it happened, we went to his "old Master's" plantation — though neither he nor I knew we were going there when we started. I bought three chickens for $1.20. Could get butter for 40¢ & Eggs for two "bitts."

We have good water in our new camp — better than we often get. We had dress parade tonight for the first time in several weeks — since some time before leaving Helena. I *really had my boots blacked,* my dress coat & sash on, and was generally brushed up, though I forgot to put on a *collar.* Today we have been busy in camp, though I don't see as I have accomplished much yet. We hope to have our tents &c. here by & by. I learn that a man will be sent for them soon. I wouldn't wonder if we remain here some time. I expect to hear from you all by next mail. . . . .

Little Rock, Ark., Sept. 18th, 1863.

I was awakened about 3 ½ A.M. yesterday by the rolling thunder & the howling wind. I waked up Lt. Alvord, and we just had time to dress & roll up our blankets, when the rain came pouring down in torrents, drenching our poor shelters of boughs completely. We found our rubber blankets useful about that time. My "rain coat" came in play that time, and saved me from absorbing more of the liquid than I required. We had only to sit and wait for daylight, shivering with cold. It continued to rain till long after breakfast time, so hard, too, that it was almost impossible to light fires, and consequently I had to go on picket, (having been detailed as officer of the picket guard) without my breakfast, but as I have a "darkey" now, I did not have to go hungry, as he could bring me my rations when they were cooked. It cleared off for two or three hours towards noon, but rained again during the afternoon, making it very disagreeable. At night it ceased raining again, & became quite cold, so much so that I felt it severely, though I had taken my overcoat with me. I got through the night "after a fashion," & was relieved soon after 7 o'clock this morning, when

I came into camp & made a breakfast upon sweet potatoes, fried ham, *biscuit* (of flour & Indian meal) & coffee with milk which cost *only* 20¢ per quart. Today Lt. Alvord & I have been at work on a *schebang* (of *brush!*) for our own quarters. It *looks* quite comfortable *now,* but the first rain that comes pouring through our roof will *change the complexion* materially. However we have rubber blankets over our bed, so that we can keep *that* nearly dry. Our bed — or "bunk" is built of poles laid upon "crotches" about two feet from the ground, & covered with *pine twigs,* which make a very comfortable bed while they remain green. We hope to have our tents here in three or four weeks at the longest. Our men have their "cribs" built much as we have ours, and appear quite comfortable *considering,* though their shelters are none too warm for a cold night.

. . . .

One fifth of the Commissioned Officers of companies who were mustered with me at Milwaukee on the 13th of Oct. last are dead — and not one ever received a scratch from the enemy. Disease has carried them off. Eight others have resigned, been promoted, or mustered out, leaving 16 of the original 30 who hold commissions in their companies. Of that 16 only 9 are on duty with the regiment — the others being on special duty out of the reg't, sick & absent. How we are scattered. We have had a dreadful climate to live in, have been exposed to cold & storms — I sometimes wonder that *so many* are left. What will the record of the next year be? We can only wait and see, hoping always for the best. I am detailed as brigade officer of the day for tomorrow — am on duty every day now a days — so I must to bed & sleep. . . . .

Little Rock, Sept. 20th, 1863.

This is a beautiful sabbath day, as bright and pleasant as one could well wish for, even in the sunny south. The nights and mornings are cold now, but the days are "splendid."

Yesterday I was "brigade officer of the day," and beside my other duties acted as Marshall at the burial of our late associate — Capt. Morton. He was buried in a field which has been used by the rebels for a cemetery, but which is now used by our army here for the same purpose. A space has been left between the graves of our men & the rebels. They have about 1100 buried there. In another place they have 400 buried, & in another 600. Suggestive, is it not, of the suffering which an army has to endure. Our Chaplain — Mr. Peake — arrived here soon after noon yesterday — just in time to attend the service. He left the Col. at Memphis I believe. The Sutler left Duval's Bluff in the same train with him, but is not here yet. Presume he will make his appearance in a day or two. Lillie, who was left at Brownville, sick, & Kimmerly, who was at Helena, both arrived here yesterday.

This morning I obtained a pass and went down town to church. I hunted up the Presbyterian church — & heard a very good sermon, though a rather long one. The text was Psalms (CXLX:96). There was a full attendance, the large church being crowded so much that they had to bring seats into the aisles. About two thirds of the congregation were officers & soldiers. There were probably 60 or 70 of the *shoulder strapped* "persuasion." There was a "smart" sprinkling of ladies present. They were all well dressed — some of them richly dressed, & in excellent taste — so you see silks & satins, laces & fringes are not entirely gone yet in Arkansas. After church I went down & took dinner with Capt Redington, who is quartered in town, and afterwards took a walk about town. The streets on which the residences are situated are finely shaded, and are very pleasant. With the addition of sidewalks, they would be equal to almost any I have seen anywhere — far ahead of anything I have seen in the south. I think this would be a capital place for a residence. I'm half inclined to "locate" here. What do you say? I understand that the rail road from here to White river will be in running order

in a day or two, with only platform cars, however, the passenger cars having all been burned by the *secesh*. That will help our communications with "the states" considerably. We had a very small mail this morning, but there was nothing for me. I have seen northern papers as late as the 8th. A correspondent says that the stories of extreme suffering by our sick are *lies*. I say that our sick have been treated inhumanely — have suffered extremely, and for several days received no attention such as sick men are entitled to. The fault may not lie with the Medical gentlemen accompanying the expedition, but when so many sick men are sent along to follow up such an expedition they cannot help but suffer, — especially when an entirely inadequate supply of medical stores are taken along, as was the case in this instance, as I am informed. The sick should not have been sent on — or at least not at that time.

Our men are now suffering somewhat at night for the want of their blankets & overcoats. The over coats were all left behind, as they could not be carried, & some of the blankets were thrown away upon the march, during the hot weather, by the men, who did it rather than carry them. A supply has been sent for, and will, I hope, arrive before long, though I presume it will be weeks. I get along comfortably — am entirely well. I wish I could have gone to church with you today, and had a good *visit at home* with you & the *darlings*. To you all I send warmest love & kisses. How do you all get along. I wrote you a while ago for a $50 draft. If you have not sent it, please do so, as I am short of money. I hope the paymaster will get along soon. . . . .

**Head Quarters "C" Co., 28th Wis. Inf'ty Vols.
Little Rock, Ark., Sept. 24, 1863.**

Dear Sister:

Here I am, dating my letter from this, one of the earliest of the seceding states.[18] We arrived here & occupied Little Rock on the 10th after a brisk little fight here, in which the cavalry & artillery played the most conspicuous part. Our division did not get in range of a single rebel bullet, though we were *ready*. We were one month on the way from Helena here, including stoppages — having left there Aug. 11th. During that time we have seen something of privation & suffering, but no fighting — that is — we — the 28th — have done none. We have lost some men from disease. One of mine — Sergeant F. W. Plympton, a most excellent man & soldier, is among the number. He died at Duval's Bluff, Aug. 24th. I have a few sick here — two are quite so — J. W. Robinson of Summit, & Isaac L. Bogart of Monterey. Lewis, Leavitt, Ward & Byam are unfit for duty, but able to be about camp. I have 45 men with me. Little Rock is the most pleasant place I have yet seen in rebeldom. I am half in love with it, & feel almost like locating here — that is if a nice square in the city can be held under the "homestead bill." We took several hundred prisoners here, and more are being brought in daily. There is a rebel hospital here, containing some 400 to 500 sick rebels. There are about 2100 rebel soldiers graves in & about Little Rock — now an addition of graves of union soldiers is being made.

. . . .

    As to how long we will remain here I will not try to guess. It may be 10 days — it may be all winter — & is about as likely to be the one as the other. From the time we left Helena I did not sleep in a tent or house till night before last, sleeping under my blankets, bushes & trees, or in the open air with only the stars above me for 43 nights — & some of them rainy ones. My health never was better. I have been hard at work putting a floor in my tent today. The boards cost me $2. (100 feet) The weather is delightful, though the nights are quite cold.

    We passed some very large fields of corn on our way here, some of them extending for miles. Don't talk of *starving* the south. The rail road from here to Duval's Bluff on White river is now in running order, though we have no passenger cars. Some of the platform cars have been sided up with boiler iron, making them bullet proof, and are used for passengers.

Our loss at the taking of Little Rock is said to have been only about 60 killed & wounded. The place was well fortified upon the right bank of the river, but Gen. Steele bridged the river 7 miles below & sent cavalry & artillery across, thus flanking Price & compelling him to abandon the strong works he had spent so much time & labor in building.

. . . .

Head Q'rs "C" Co., 28th Wis. Inf'ty Vols.
Little Rock, Ark., Sept. 24, 1863.
7 o'clock, P.M.

My darling:

. . . . Yesterday & today I have been "off duty" except drilling the company in the morning, & attending to the usual routine of camp duties. So I have improved the time assisting Lt. Alvord to "fix up." I have finally obtained a wall tent for him & myself, & we have been getting ready to "live" in it. Yesterday I bought 100 feet of boards for a floor, for which I paid $2.00, sent into the woods & got some "sleepers", & today as Lt. Alvord was absent on duty, I have scored & hewed the timbers & laid the floor — *alone*. I feel proud of the achievement. Our "bunk" is a curiosity in its way. "The boys" say it is *a straw tick filled with hickory poles!* Well, as Lt. Col. Gray says, "it is good enough for a do-r-g!" & I know it. I slept in a tent for the first time since leaving Helena, night before last — had slept in the open air, or under trees, bushes or rubber blankets for 43 nights. If we stay here this winter, & get our tents from Helena, we can "fix up" very comfortably. We (officers) are getting a pretty fair supply of eatables now. Hard bread, pork, sweet potatotes, white fish, dried apples, coffee, tea & sugar, — & we really had a loaf of *soft bread* today. A bakery is rapidly approaching completion in our camp, so we hope to have plenty of bread soon — though some are inclined to think it a sign of our hasty departure, as all our others have been. There is a rumor that we are to leave for Texas in 10 days or so, but it is *only* a rumor, upon which no dependence can be placed. A little newspaper is being started here. — The first number was issued last Saturday, but I was not able to obtain a copy. I will try & get one this week & send to you. . . .

I had the honor of commanding at dress parade this evening, in the temporary absence of the Lt. Col. *Maj. White* is on duty down town away from the regiment, *as usual. Capt. Meyer ditto.*

We have very few officers here for duty. Only *nine* company (commissioned) officers are reported as "present for duty." Quartermaster Wylie is very low again with diarrhea, & has handed in his resignation. I hope it may be accepted, though I dislike to part with so genial a companion as he. We have had no mail since Sunday (20th) I hope to hear again soon from home.

Whe have very pleasant weather yet, but rather cool nights. We have heard that Gilmore occupies Morris Island & that Chattenooga is ours. Hurrah! I hope our victories may continue till this rebellion is ended. . . .

P.S. The cars are now running from here to Duval's Bluff.

Little Rock, Arkansas, Sept. 27th, 1863.

Again has returned the Sabbath evening, and again I am seated to write you, my own dear wife. This has been another pleasant day, bright and beautiful like those we have so often read of as pervading the "sunny south." I attended Presbyterian church again this morning, in the city, and this afternoon we had service in camp.

The mail arrived this morning, and I was pleased to receive

a letter from you, one from Lavantia, & one from Homer. I also rec'd one from Mrs. Plympton & one from Mrs. Gilmore, mother of the Lieutenant. I am glad to hear again that you are usually well and that the horrors of moving are safely passed. I hope you may find pleasant at Mr. Faurot's—I *think* you will—and that you will not have to move again right away.

. . . .

Little Rock, Arkansas, Sept. 28th 1863, 11 P.M.

At midnight I have to start on my rounds as "brigade officer of the day." I have to visit one post on the "up river road," about four miles from here, and one on the junction of the Manmelle and Archidelphia roads, so that I have some 10 miles to ride beside the length of our brigade line. I have been over it twice today. In going from one road to other I have to go though a piece of woods, and also through fields grown up to brush & tall weeds, where it will be hard work to find my way through by night I presume. It is also rather an exposed situation, where bush-whackers might operate, though they have not attempted it along that line yet as I am aware of. I shall get back just before daylight, tired & sleepy I presume.

It is rumored that a paymaster is on the way hither with money to pay off our army. I hope it may prove true, but presume it is only one of our *camp rumors*. A little money would be acceptable to almost any of us just now. We are all speculating upon the chances of our leaving here this fall, but of course cannot form much of an opinion upon the subject, though it seems to be a general impression that we will not remain here during the winter. I think Little Rock is altogether too pleasant a place for the 28th at least.

I wish you could look in and see my tent. One third of it is occupied by the bed, under which are thrown in admirable confusion our valises, boots, slips, dirty clothes &c. At the foot and around the walls of the tent are hung coats, pants, swords, belts, sashes, towels, brushes, looking-glasses & a *boot-jack!* the latter manufactured on the spot by *"our special artist,"* as is also the *bunk* on which we sleep. On the bed is a paper of candles, an overcoat, my revolver, books &c. Opposite the bed stand my field-desk, & Lt. Alvord's table on which I am now writing. I am seated upon a bench or stool which is also a product of Lt. Alvord's labor & ingenuity. The floor — of boards — I laid myself. Our eating house is close by — *a brush shanty.* So you see we live in elegant style. I forgot to say that I have obtained a small pile of broom corn of which to have some brooms made to *sweep out* with. It lies at the foot of the bed on the floor. I have also manufactured a wash-stand. It is out of doors. It consists of a stake driven into the ground with a short piece of board, large enough to set a wash basin on, nailed on the end. It is *elegant,* though not very expensive. There is a hole in the top of my tent about 14 inches long & 8 wide, but I don't see it does any harm as long as we have dry, warm weather. The floor is rough & covered with "silvers," but it keeps us off the ground. My candle stick consists of a cover of a blacking box nailed onto a piece of board, with four nails which stand about an inch high, forming the socket for the candle. The cover serves to catch the melted tallow which will run down sometimes, especially in windy weather. How do you like our house? Well, if you can't stay, call again & bring the children next time. "Run in at any time." Good bye!

Little Rock, Arkansas, October 9th, 1863.

I have been hard at work today, and am somewhat tired, but have taken a good wash all over, changed my clothes, & feel better. We have received most of our tents & got them up, so that we have quite comfortable quarters. We have no stoves for our wall tents, but expect them soon.

Did I tell you of my "adventure" the other day? I was

"officer of the day" in camp. At two o'clock in the morning firing was heard in the direction of the outpost on the Arkadelphia road. I was immediately ordered to go and ascertain the occasion of it — so I mounted "old Cream" and set out. After riding about half a mile the outpost was reached, where I learned that the firing was outside the lines. I rode out in the direction given me by the pickets, through the openings, & soon discovered a fire. Riding up toward it I discovered several soldiers around it, most of whom "send" into the brush upon seeing me, but I succeeded in arresting four & brought them into camp. They were men from our army who had procured a jug of whiskey & gone out for a "spree." A portion of them were armed, & had got to fooling with their arms, causing the alarm. If they had been a little more or less sober I might have had trouble with them. Col. Gray thought I did a "big thing" going *alone* two or three miles out from camp and bringing in four men — a part of whom were armed. I was complimented several times for it.

Gen. Salomon has arrived here & is assigned to the command of our (the 3rd) Division. Gen. Rice will now command our brigade.

I yesterday mailed you a copy of the "National Democrat," published here, containing a notice of our brigade.

Our men are improving in health — only three of my company attended "Surgeons call" this morning.

A report is in circulation to the effect that Gen's. Holmes & Price, (rebels) fought a duel at Arkadelphia the other day, in which Holmes was killed.[19] I do not know how true it may be, but think it not improbable. Lt. Alvord & most of the boys from O- are well. Jas Hall has chills & fever, as have a few others. We have a nice camp here — & *nice clear water.* I am very well indeed. Yesterday I weighed 146 in light coat & shoes, with no vest.

. . . .

Little Rock, Arkansas, October 12th 1863, 6 P.M.

Again I have time to write a word, & as Lt. Wylie has not
yet gone I hope to send this by him. He is waiting for the
Paymaster who is expected here to pay us off tomorrow or next
day. He is now in town, & if the papers are all right will pay us
tomorrow. If the draft is sent I can return it, & the expense will
be small. How much was the cost? I shall probably send you
some money by Lt. Wylie, though I can't tell yet how much it
will be, as I have got to keep enough for some clothes. My suit,
now a year old, is getting to be decidedly "seedy." I was fairly
ashamed of my dress coat the other day when at Gen. Rice's
headquarters on duty — it was badly torn under the arms &c. I
had it repaired a day or two since, & it *passes,* though much
soiled. My pants are about the same, & the vest I cannot wear
with comfort it is so small, having been washed — & *shrunk* —
& my coat would be too small over it. I have worn no vest this
summer. Others have spread themselves on their fancy, white &
buff vests, but I *saved* my five to eight dollars. A good coat &
straps will cost me about $45 here — Pants $15 to $18. & other
things in proportion. I think I will try & make my dress pants do
for this winter, as I have got a coarse pair of private's pants for
every day wear. I wear the same that I had in Milwaukee over a
year ago. I have only one woolen shirt left fit to wear. I think I
have written enough about my *old clothes!* Capt. Kenyon will
probably go home with Lt. Wylie.

1st Sergeant Magill of "D" Co. was today promoted to
Sergeant Major of the Regiment, in place of Albert S. Ken-
drick promoted to Adjutant. Sergeant Browne of my company
was a candidate for the place & ought to have got it, but failed.

Today we have been having a brick fireplace built in our
tent. It will probably be finished by noon tomorrow, & then I
can keep warm when the cold, rainy days come on, I *guess.*

We have no further news here. Everything is quiet, & the
indications are that we will winter here. If we could move to

any advantage I would be very glad if we could go on and finish up our work. Our men are now healthier generally than they have been at any time since leaving the State. Our work here is light just at present, but I expect it will soon be heavy enough, especially if General Salomon goes to fortifying here as he did at Helena. It was necessary there, & it may be here, but we have more troops here to do it.

.   .   .   .

Little Rock, Ark., October 13th, 1863.

We were fortunate enough to be visited today by a regular live paymaster with a supply of "greenbacks" for Uncle Samuels happy, innocent boys. As most of us had already emptied our pockets to supply the necessary food & clothing which our poor bodies demand, he was "hailed with delight,"—and we eagerly fobbed the amounts which he dealt out to us. We are this time paid up to August 31st.

But while we remember *ourselves*, we also bear in mind the dear ones we have left behind us, and from our company we have already forwarded $718. to our families & friends. One package goes to Oconomowoc containing $626, of which amount $160 is addressed to "Mrs. Carrie E. Stevens," sent to here by her truant Captain. Isn't it a great consolation, seeing I am away, that I am able to send these "pretty pcitures" once in a while? *I think it must be!* Ain't it next to seeing me?

Seriously, dearest, I am glad to be able to send you enough to keep you from want while I am away, & hope I may continue to be able to do so. If I could not do this I should certainly be miserable—thinking of your privations. It is bad enough for you to be thus left alone—but it might be worse.

Lt. Wylie will take the package to Elkhorn & express it from there to Oconomowoc. It is directed to Frank, & he will deliver the different packages. I had no time to write a line or a word with the packages, as I had to put them right up in order to send by the Lieutenant. I trust the money will arrive safe. Ask Frank what the charges on the entire packages are, and pay him the amount. It will be but little—probably less than $1. Some of the boys might & ought to have sent more, but as a general thing they have done pretty well.

Can't you send the shirts — one at a time — by mail? I think they can be done up with strong paper, or in a pasteboard box so as to come safely, & if the postage is not more than $1. or $1.25 it will then be less than I would have to pay for poorer shirts. You may possibly have a chance to forward them. I begin to need them.

I will try & write Frank tomorrow in relation to delivering the money. I had no time to do it & send with the package tonight.

. . . .

Little Rock, Arkansas, Friday, October 16th, 1863.

. . . .

I am ordered again to be ready to leave for Duval's Bluff & Helena any day, to look up the property of the regiment. The order may come at any time for me to start, — and it may be countermanded, as the other was. I hope it will, for I do not want to go. It will be hard work & will cost me at least $1.50 per day more than to stay here. My transportation would be furnished, but I have to board myself — and it *costs* on steamboats in this section, as well as at Helena boarding houses & Hotels. I hope some one else will go. My men continue to improve in health, generally. Serg't Brown has been sick a couple of days, but is better this morning. Robinson is out of hospital, but is very weak. Kinne & the rest are better.

My company now consists of 60 men beside Lt. Alvord & myself. Forty nine of the sixty are here at Little Rock & vicinity — two have gone to Memphis with prisoners, — leaving nine scattered from Helena to Madison — all sick I suppose.

Knox & Perkins are at Madison. —
Waller, Rugg & Weaver at Keokuk. —
Borron at St. Louis. —
Hans Evenson at Memphis, &
Hinkley at Helena.
I expect some of them will be returned to the regiment soon.

. . . .

I wish you could see some of the darkies down here —
especially the women. Aren't they vain? They don't dress as
gaily as at Helena, on account, I suppose of the scarcity of
finery in this rebel city. They beat *all* at Helena.

Price's army is in very bad condition. Price is said to have
been removed from command & "Granny Holmes" (Lt. Gen.)
put in his place.[20] Arkansas & Missouri troops are very much
dissatisfied with this. Desertions from the rebel army are of
frequent occurrence. Quite a number of prisoners — members
of guerrilla gangs — have been taken & brought in lately — 23
were in one body. Dobyns & his command narrowly escaped
capture the other day.

We get no important news. We are glad to hear that our
army in Tennessee is safe. . . .

Little Rock, Arkansas, Sunday, Oct. 18th 1863.

Night before last I received the detail ordering me to go to
Helena to look up the property of the regiment, which was left
behind, a great deal of which has not been forwarded to us. It
was too late for me to get my "passes" & "transportation"
that night so as to leave on the Saturday morning train. Yesterday I went to the Provost Marshall and got my pass to Helena,
to the Chief Quartermaster of the Army of Arkansas & got my
order for transporation — reported to Gen. Salomon who had
some orders for me — packed my carpet bag — or rather Lt.
Col. Gray's! — & prepared to leave by today's train if it
brought word that a boat was at the Bluff ready to leave.

This morning came, but last nights train from Duval's Bluff had not arrived; and a few hours later a mounted messenger reached here stating that the engine had broken down a few miles this side of the Bluff, & could come no further till another engine is sent from here. One was immediately dispatched, and will probably arrive here this evening with the train. I wish it would arrive soon enough so that I could get my mail before leaving, but don't expect that it will — consequently I shall not probably hear from you till I return to Little Rock — some two weeks from now. If the train brings news tonight that a boat is up for Helena, I shall leave in the morning. It will be a long, dreary journey — one which I dread — and the presence of dismal Helena will counterbalance all pleasure I might derive from being so much nearer you — even if I would not be deprived of my letters from you for two weeks longer — as I expect to be. It is about 320 miles from here to Helena by way of the Bluff & the rivers — with nothing of interest on the route unless it be the ruins of St. Charles, to which place we made a "pilgrimage" last winter. We will pass some other small towns upon the river, but the monotony of wild, wooded, tangled, lifeless banks for 250 miles will hardly be broken, unless it be by an attack by guerrillas — some of whom are along the river & sometimes annoy boats, especially when they are not convoyed by gunboats. I do not, however, apprehend any danger from them.

If I could have been ordered to return by way of Milwaukee & Oconomowoc, the trip would prove quite agreeable — but now I had much rather remain in camp and do my share of lighter duty — such as drilling, officer of the day &c. I want to get back here by the 31st — *muster day* — but don't suppose that I can.

The transportation is furnished me, as I go on public business, but I have to pay my own board, which on steamboats & at hotels will cost me from $1.50 to $2. per day. If I can suit myself I may buy me a new uniform — or a part of one at

Helena. I need it sadly — especially if I am to "keep up style." I have lots of errands for officers here.

Yesterday I had to buy me a new haversack, which cost me $3.50 & a *money belt,* costing $1.50.

The weather still continues fine, though rain has been threatened for two or three days. It has now cleared off beautifully. A little rain would make it much more pleasant in some respects, as the roads are now very dusty. The nights are very cold.

This forenoon I attended the Episcopal Church in Little Rock, at which our Chaplain, the Rev. E. Steele Peake, regularly officiates. Sergeant Joseph G. Robinson of my company acts in the capacity of organist — and a very good one he is too. The church building is quite a pleasant one. I noticed that the congregation, — ladies & all — responded audibly to the prayers for "the President of the United States" — a hopeful sign of rebeldom. There was not a very full attendance. The rebel ladies stay away, I presume, as there was not an excessive display of finery, though some were well dressed. Mr. Peake has charge of a sabbath school at the church. He is but little with the regiment, but may be doing quite as much good as if he were here.

. . . .

On board Steamboat Lebanon.
White River, Arkansas, Oct. 21, 1863.

The train arriving at Little Rock on Monday evening brought news of the arrival at Duval's Bluff of two steamboats, but *no mail.* I immediately got ready for my journey, and at 7 o'clock yesterday morning left by the train, which consisted of some half dozen *platform* cars, drawn by a poor little locomotive. There was not even a box car for passengers — only some boards up at the sides of one or two and I believe one board put up for a seat. There was quite a number of passengers; among them Brig. Gen. Davidson & his staff.

Escaping all guerrillas along the road, we reached the Bluff at 11 o'clock A.M., and immediately went on board the boat, as we were told that it would start immediately. Had I known that I could have had time I would have visited poor Sergeant Plymptons grave — but as it was I did not dare run the risk. We finally got off about 3 o'clock P.M., our fleet consisting of three steamboats — "Lebanon," "T. J. Pattin" & "Saline," convoyed by a "tin-clad" gunboat as the muskets fleet is sometimes called to distinguish it from the heavy iron clad-boats. We run till dark last night, when we tied up a short distance above Clarendon, which place we passed early this morning — before this lazy soldier was up. It rained hard through the night & this forenoon & the indications are that it will continue to do till we get mud enough to make up for the dust which we have of late been afflicted with.

The distance from Little Rock to Duval's Bluff is something over 50 miles. From the Bluff to the mouth of White river is about 180 miles — & from there to Helena is 90 or 100 miles — making a distance of 320 miles — so that I shall have travelled 640 miles when I reach my regiment again. It is very dull on board the boat — We have the poorest of accommodations & almost nothing to eat at 50 cents per meal.

The berths are very poor, consisting of a dirty mattress & 1 poor, small quilt.

. . . .

Helena, Oct. 24, 9 A.M.

Just arrived here. Cold — Cold — froze hard last night. Had a long, tedious trip from Mouth of White river. Our boat towed a heavy barge up from there & had a head wind to run against, as well as the current. Have been ever since daylight yesterday morning coming up. Will write more as soon as I can. Hurrah for the good Election news from Ohio, Penn, Iowa & Ind! I hope Vallandigham is satisfied now that *the people* are not all traitors like himself.[21] The soldiers vote right.

. . . .

Helena, Arkansas, Sunday eve, Oct. 25th, 1863.

I arrived here safely at about 9 A.M. yesterday. At the mouth of White river, where we laid up on Thursday night, I met Capt. Townsend & Lieut. Tichenor, who were on their way down from Wisconsin, and spent the evening with them on board the "Des Moines City." Our boat had a heavy barge to tow up the river and was from daylight Friday morning running up here. I went to the Post Office, where a boy from Co. "A" is clerk, and got him to open the packages for our regiment, & got a letter from you, dated Oct. 15. I had not heard from you in a long time, though I suppose there are two or three letters at Little Rock for me. I hunted up the sick men of the regiment the first thing, after getting a sick Captain from Chicago aboard the Memphis packet. I forgot to send along my letter by him.

. . . .

I came from Little Rock & left my over coat, and have needed it on my journey. Capt. Townsend kindly lent me a cape, which makes me quite comfortable. It is very cold here, though very pleasant just now. It rained a great deal during my journey here. Tomorrow I shall go to work in earnest, I have got a job before me. A part of the "traps" have been sent on, but I have got enough to do to find out what is left, besides making a heap of purchases for the officers & myself. I shall try to get a pass from the Provost Marshall & go to Memphis to do my trading. I do not, however, suppose I can "get to go there," as southerners say. I think I can do better there than here. I will write you what I buy for myself. I hope to hear from you again in a day or two. I think I will. I bought a St. Louis "Democrat" of the 20th yesterday. It cost *only 15 cents, which I really thought quite cheap, since I have paid a quarter* for them at Little Rock. Here a watch glass costs only 50¢. There it would be 75¢. I break too many of them. I have a good notion to buy a good hunting-case & save glasses. I think I will *when I get rich,* & can spare $35. or $40. as well as not.

Dearest Carrie, you must not dress so poorly as to make people think I am mean. I'm coming home by & by to *dress you up in style!* Don't you want me to come?

. . . .

The wind has been blowing cold all day so I could hardly bear to be out, but did run about some. I got my hair cut, which cost me 35¢ *only.* Two apples 10¢. My board is $2. to $2.50 per day. Verily it *costs* to *live* here, & we live poor enough at that — all of us. I will write often, darling, & tell you all about my doings. . . . .

On board Steam "Leonora",
Helena, Ark., Oct. 30, 1863.

I reached Memphis about 9 A.M. Wednesday. I hurried about and did my trading, only in time to take the "Igo" back to Helena. I was afraid to stay another day for fear I would miss a boat for White river, so I did not have time to hunt up Hans Everson who is sick at one of the hospitals there. I bought for myself 1 Dress coat $35. Straps for same $8. 1 pr Pants $15. 1 ruling pen $1. and about $125. worth of articles for others.

We reached Helena Thursday morning about 2 o'clock, escaping attack from guerrillas. A boat, the "Adriatic" which arrived here from Memphis a few hours later was fired into 30 miles above here by a large party of guerrillas, who wounded three men & one woman. The boat on which I came near taking passage from the mouth of White river to this place last week, was fired into a few miles below here, and one man was killed. He was Sutler of one of the Ill. regiments — the 18th I think.

Yesterday morning a wagon train went out for fire wood from here. A short distance outside our pickets they were attacked & "gobbled" by guerrillas. A scout of cavalry was sent out to hunt them up, but I don't know with what success.

Guerrillas are becoming very plenty about here again. Gen. Buford has today issued a General Order cutting off all trade with citizens outside the lines until they organize & drive the bushwhackers from Phillips County — a sensible order if lived up to.[22]

I had an adventure this afternoon. Gen. Buford requires all officers arriving here to report to him at once. I did not "report" when I came, as I did not know that it was necessary — I had however *called at his adjutant's office & shown my orders*. I called there today to see about some tents belonging to the 28th which I had found in the contraband camp. The Gen. was in & inquired who I was. I told him, & also how long I had been here. He immediately pitched into me with his tongue — would hear no explanation — said he would at once report me to Gen. Steele for staying here so long doing nothing, & not reporting to him, & ended by ordering me to my quarters — which was equivalent to placing me in arrest. I went away & immediately addressed a letter to him stating all the facts in the case, & that there had been no boat up White river since Sunday &c., &c. I was bound if I was to be placed in arrest to have the matter appear in its true light. I sent the line to him — he immediately sent for me & apologized to me handsomely for his rudeness — & said that he wished to send some dispatches by me to Gen. Steele, but added *that he should not mention my case*. He then talked to me for some time very pleasantly, apologized again, & when I left asked me to call upon him again before I left — which I shall certainly do. Yesterday & today have been very rainy, cold & disagreeable. I think we will start tomorrow sometime, & will leave the mouth of White river Monday morning. I am anxious to get back, for it is costing me a heap to live here, & am out of money. I hope to get a letter from you tomorrow.

. . . .

Little Rock, Ark., Nov. 6, 1863. 10 P.M.

I arrived here safely last night. Have been very busy today, and just at dark we received orders to march for Pine Bluff at Daylight tomorrow morning. I rather think we are to remain there for some time, as we take our tents — or rather a part of them, along. I will write from there as soon as I can. I have got to work a good share of the night tonight to get ready to move.

I found 15 letters here for me when I got here — *6 from you* — and rec'd four more today — one of the 18th from you. It is quite cold tonight, though it was warm today. I left my new haversack on the boat at Duval's Bluff by mistake. It had in it a towel, a map, & more than all the rest my *diary for 1863.* — a good one for which I paid $2.00. I am sorry to lose it. I have sent to see if I can't get it, but hardly expect to be able to.

. . . .

Head Qrs 28th Wis. Inf'ty, Pine Bluff, Ark., Nov. 11, 1863.

I arrived safely at Little Rock on Thursday evening Nov. 5th. The next day I was very busy, & was out to drill in the afternoon. About sundown we rec'd orders to march next morning for this place. We left Little Rock about noon on Saturday and arrived here yesterday, crossing the river soon after 11 A.M. We had an ammunition train along, and the wagons frequently got stuck in the mud, delaying us considerably. We crossed the river at Little Rock, & came down on the east side, as the road is better that way. The distance is about 65 miles I believe. We brought a part of our tents, & will probably have more soon. We all stood the march first rate. I left two men sick at Little Rock — Sergt. Brown & Iverson.

We have cold nights for lying out on a march. I had a tent to sleep in, & then suffered with the cold. The day we started was very warm. The balance of the time we had good weather for marching.

Pine Bluff is a larger town than Helena — has had some 3,000 inhabitants, I am told. Two weeks ago last Sunday the rebels attacked our small force here but got licked. The 5th Kansas Cavalry & 1st Indiana Cavalry was about all we had here. The rebels were much stronger. I am told that the negroes took hold & worked well. The town shows marks of a hard fight, many of the houses being riddled with shot. A part of the town was burnt.

We are fixing up our camp today. We came on short notice & I had no time to provide myself with eatables. We can get some things quite cheap here — beef steak for 7¢ chickens 15¢. I am sitting on a box, writing this upon my knee. Don't know when I shall have any better accommodations.

I found 15 letters for me when I arrived at Little Rock — 6 from you. I rec'd the $50. draft. Thank you. I also rec'd Lulu's measure. How she has grown, the dear darling.

I was sorry not to be back to camp in time to vote — my company voted 34 for Lewis — for Palmer none! Good. I have not ascertained how large a majority Lewis had in the regiment. I trust he is elected — and by a handsome majority. . . .

Camp 28th Wis. Inf'ty,
Pine Bluff, Ark., Nov. 13, 1863.

. . . .

We are here, busy at work trying to "fix up." We have to move camp so often and leave all our little "extras" which we buy or make that it is "up hill business" sometimes to "fix up." We may pay out $5 or $20 for floors, chairs, tables, &c., or lumber to build them of, — and for building chimnies & fire places &c., and then get up & leave them in a day, a week or a

month. And then we never can carry them, & have no time to
sell them, so they are a dead loss unless we burn or break them
up!

At Little Rock Alvord & I had floored both our tents, made
tables & a bunk, built a fire place & Chimney, & fixed up
generally, at a considerable cost — it is all gone. I have already expended some money here for such purposes, but don't
intend it shall be much.

We have drawn a few new tents, but are going to work
immediately to build log barracks for winter quarters. I think
we shall stay here until spring.

. . . .

Of the 39 men I have here now, not one is reported "sick"
— of which fact I am proud.

I have slept on the ground ever since leaving Little Rock,
but shall have a bunk tonight. Have also got a table today to eat
from.

I had to leave "Jordan," my contraband, sick at the Rock. I
have "accumulated" another here, named Nathan. He was
"run off" from here to Texas by the rebs, but escaped and
came back. On the way he was caught & put in jail, but broke
out & reached here about the time we did. He was raised in
Tennessee.

Have you or any of your friends any butter milk for sale? It
is worth 10 cents per quart in Arkansas. Sweet milk is 15 to 25
cts. Irish potatoes are $1.50 pr. bush. Sweet potatoes 50¢.

It is warm tonight, & has just commenced to rain, & is
thundering "right smart." I wonder how you all are tonight.
All well, I trust. I sent a Cavalry Sabre home by Ed. Olson. I
don't know whether he will be able to get it through or not, I
hope he will. It is one that "Jordan" picked up on the battle
field at Little Rock, after the fight there. He says it belonged to
a *"Seceshioner."* Let me know if you get it or not. It is now
after 9 o'clock P.M. I must close & go to bed, for I'm
tired. . . .

Camp 28th Wis. Inf'ty Vols.,
Pine Bluff, Arkansas, Nov. 20th, 1863.

. . . .

There are rumors in town tonight of the presence in our vicinity of a large force of the enemy. Some suppose that they are on their way to attack us here. We are ordered to have everything in readiness to move inside the fortifications at short notice — & see that our men are all armed properly, and furnished with a full supply (40 rounds each) of ammunition.

I shall pack my valise tonight, so as to be ready in case of emergency. Lt. Col. Gray seems to think we will have a fight in the morning. I do not think we shall. If we do we shall fight them hard. We have had a force of negroes at work on the fortifications all the week, & have a large number of cotton bales to use for breastworks. Nearly 100 of our men arrived today with the train, so we have some more help than if the fight had been today. If we fight I hope to do my whole duty. At Helena I think I did it — & hope I may always be ready to do so while my country needs me.

. . . .

P.S. All the men of my company who are here are well, except 3 or 4 who have chills & fever a little. 6 arrived today. I have now 45 men here. Lt. Alvord is well. . . . The latest paper I have seen is the Chicago Tribune of the 6th. I see that Lewis is elected Governor by a fair majority. Good! Long live the Union!

Pine Bluff, Arkansas, Sunday morning,
Nov. 22, 1863. 7 A.M.

Yesterday morning came & went, but the attack of the enemy which we expected to encounter has not come. During Friday night a large force of negroes (some 200) were kept at work all night on the earthworks defending the town. Lt.

Alvord was up in charge of them till 1 o'clock A.M., when he was relieved by another officer, and the work went on.

Yesterday was a bright, pleasant day, after the storm of Friday. We were up & had inspection of arms at 4 A.M. The day passed without any further alarm. The work continues upon the works, and if the rebels see fit to come here, they will meet with a warm reception.

We were up again & in line of battle by company at 4 ½ A.M. this morning, waiting again; but I don't fancy that Price or Marmaduke will visit us at present.

. . . .

Yesterday, darling, I received the shirts. They are beauties I assure you — and I was much in want of them. I have not yet had a chance to try them on, but I think they will fit if not too large in the neck. If they are, I can get them fixed, as I have a tailor in my company. Mary's picture also came safely through, as well as the candies which dear Lulu sent to her papa. Thank you & Lulu & Mary for them all . . . .

Pine Bluff, Arkansas, November 27th., 1863.

. . . .

Do what you please with the money, my darling. I'll risk it with you. I've a great mind to have you pay for the house & lot now. What do you think of it. Do as you think about it. I guess we will not want the money right away — and then perhaps we can sell the house if we wish to.

We were paid off yesterday. I shall send $200 home this time. I put it up to send by the paymaster who is to start for St. Louis tomorrow, but it rains so hard and is so muddy that I shall not carry it over to him tonight if it don't go in a month. I have also several hundred dollars to send for the company. Should have more yet to send for them, but the clothing accounts were settled this pay day, & nearly all were owing the Government for extra clothing drawn. The pay received this time is up to Oct. 31st (for Sept. & Oct.)

I was on picket again day before yesterday. It was *very* cold. I did not lie down at all & slept none from Wednesday morning about 4 o'clock till after dark last night, except about 15 minutes yesterday. I had just got to sleep when I was called to go to the pay table. Yesterday was thanksgiving. I succeeded in getting nothing for dinner better than bread & beef, with pickles, "Krout," (my favorite you know,) & coffee. What did you have? I had a pleasant day on picket, but a cold night. We have two officers on picket each day, and 38 men.

. . . .

Camp 28th Wis. Inf'ty.
Pine Bluff, Ark., Dec. 1, 1863.

. . . .

We are still busy building log barracks. Co. "C" has theirs up. They are built of logs, & are about 22 feet wide by 32 feet long for each company. The will be much more comfortable at the chimney tomorrow. The roof is covered with *"shakes"* split from Pine logs. I shall probably live in my tent this winter, as I have a nice little fireplace built. We had a terrible rain last Friday night. It has been pleasant, but cold, since Saturday. Ice froze from 1 ½ to 2 inches in thickness. Citizens here say that it has not been cold here for years.

We get but little or no news here.

I send you a copy of the "Pine Bluff Express" of this date, *printed on wrapping paper*. I paid *10 cents* for it.

I am to go on picket tomorrow. I attended the concert last Saturday evening. It was rather a poor affair — most of it. The Pine Bluff ladies are poor singers if we heard a fair specimen of them at that time. I think our "Soldier Boys" will do better tomorrow night, and am sorry I cannot attend — but picket must be attended to. I come regularly once a week now. Lt. Alvord & most of the boys are well. I sent you last Saturday an Express package containing $632 — $200 of which was mine

— the balance to be left with Frank for delivery — being sent by the men of my company. I see that Oconomowoc went *"Union"* at the late election. Hurrah! Lewis is elected of course.

I have enlisted two darkies in my company for "under cooks" for the company, under a late order of the War Department — so you see I'm *commanding niggers!*

Most of the companies have negro cooks now. They are mustered like other Volunteers, & get $10 pr. month, $3. of which *may be* in clothing.

. . . .

Camp 28th Wis. Inf'ty.
Pine Bluff, Ark., Dec. 4, 1863.

Dear Father:

. . . . I left Little Rock Oct 20th and returned from Memphis Nov 5th, just in time to march here with my company. We have pretty hard picket duty to do here, and have built log barracks for the men, so that we have been busy since coming here. We are, however, relieved from heavy fatigue duty, such as building fortifications. Negroes are employed on that work. Our men have worked at it but one day — that was when we were hourly expecting an attack from Marmaduke. I think that danger is past now, though all such matters are uncertain in our line of business. He may happen around again any day, as he did on the 25th of Oct.

This section of country is rich — the most so of any part of Arkansas I have yet visited. I am half inclined to settle here "when this cruel war is over" and things become settled again. Many Arkansians are becoming sick of the war *for their rights*. Wonder how the rights which they have secured suit them! Some are joining the Union army — many more are deserting Jeff. Davis & Co. I believe that this state will soon be back again under the old flag.

Is Sergeant Olson doing anything at recruiting? I hope he will get enough to fill up the company, but do not expect it. I think some of the lucky ones, whose names have been *lifted* will have to go into the service. I wish some of the Copperhead fraternity could be *compelled* to come. It would do them good. I have now no idea of my being able to come home for some time. I don't seem to be a favorite with commanding officers — probably one reason is that I don't buy and *absorb* a sufficient quantity of bogus wine and commissary whisky — and *perhaps* I sometimes speak my mind too freely in the regiment for my own good, in regard to the conduct & actions of superior officers. So mote it be!

. . . .

Camp 28th Wis. Inf'ty Vols.,
Pine Bluff, Ark., Dec. 6, 1863.

My own dear Carrie:

It is Sunday again, and as I cannot spend the day with you as I did 52 weeks ago today, I will converse again with you through the medium of the pen.

Has it been a long year to you since I left you? I know it has been, my own dear wife — and yet it hardly seems that a year could have passed since then, though I have been through more hardship and seen more of life and the world than in many years before. But, darling I have indeed missed you very much, and the weeks and months have been very, very long since I said "good bye" to you, received your embrace and your parting kiss.

I have been setting and thinking today of the past — of the days when, so free from care, I first knew you as a friend — of the deep regard I felt then for you, which, long ere I told it, ripened into the deepest love. How I feared you would not — could not, regard me as more than a friend.

I remember when I ventured to intrude upon you — of the

time when we used to part at your father's door. Do you remember the Sunday we spent with Jennie & Mr._____ in
Elba? or the ride *from* Camp-meeting one beautiful moonlight
evening? I was so happy to be with you, but dared not tell you
that I loved you — and *you knew* I did. I remember when first I
wrote you from O——c, and how eagerly looked, how
warmly welcomed were the first letters which I rec'd from you
— as a *friend* only, — for I did not dream you could regard me
as anything more.

But, dearest, when you told me that you would *"try"* to love
me always — then I was happy. Do you remember the time,
my own, my love? How sweet was then the kiss which sealed
your promise to be *mine — only mine*! The many happy hours
I spent with you ere the earthly form was complied with — we
both remember them well. And the months passed by and I
was permitted to fold you to my breast as my own dear wife.
Darling love how swiftly have passed the years since then —
and their footsteps are not unmarked upon us — but the deep
love we cherished then for each other burns but the brighter
and warmer in our hearts. Grief as well as joy has been ours
since then, but by sharing grief it has been lightened on each
our hearts, while our joys by the same means have been
doubled.

Little ones have been given us — one is ready to welcome
us above — our darling Lulu you have placed in my arms —
and baby Mary, dear pet bird that she is, waits to have papa
come home to see her sweet face. Poverty and privation have
been ours, but have we not been happy?

Duty has called me from you, my Carrie, and for long,
weary months I have been from thy side, but each day my
heart, my thoughts, have been with you and the dear ones —
our children. I know you suffer much, endure much, while I
am away. You will patiently endure for my sake — any by and
by I will come home to your arms, my darling. Then the

sufferings we have both endured will seem light beside our heightened joys.

How I would love to kiss you and our little girls today — to fold you all to my heart, and be with you at home. Indeed, my joy would be full. But we must bide our time.

You know, darling wife, I came not out at the call of our country for help from her sons, because I wished to leave home. I felt that I owed my services to my native land in her need — I give them, and my life if need be for her — but when the day shall come when I *may*, how gladly will I fly to my little home, to meet the dear ones who await my coming, though the service I like quite as well — *better* than I antici-pated. When my work here is done, what a sweet resting place will be they dear bosom — *my home*.

How strange it seems that a little one whom I have never seen is there — almost able to run alone now — a beautiful little household pet. How I long to see her and hold her in my arms. Will she be afraid of me do you think? I hope not. I want her to spring delighted to papa's arms. How glad I am that dear Lu. remembers me so well. I hope she will know me when I come home — the loved one.

I have pictures of you all before me as I write. How glad am I that I have them — but how much rather had I look upon your living faces.

. . . .

Camp 28th Wis. Inf'ty Vols.
Pine Bluff, Ark., Sunday, Dec 20/63.

One year ago today the 28th left Wisconsin for *"Dixie"* — strong in numbers, strong in the faith that we could and would do much toward putting down this infernal rebellion — each man almost, strong in muscle and in limb. Today we are still in Secessia — the rebellion still existing, though weakened we hope *and know* by the blows inflicted upon it by the armies of freedom & right. But we, too, are weakened. How have our numbers diminished! Disease and death have called away many an one, many of our best, our noblest, men.

It is fitting that now, a year from the day we left our Wisconsin homes, with our proud banner floating above us, we should think of what we were then as a regiment, and what we now are. Look at my own company. *Fifteen* of those who on the 20th of Dec., 1863, composed my little command are gone, forever gone from the earth! gone from the homes, the hearts of those who loved them; from those who with weeping eyes then bade them *good bye*, and waited and watched again for their coming. Brave men and patriots as they were, we will ever remember them, and proudly, too.

All the companies have not suffered so severely — some have fared even worse — but from this statement you may judge what loss of men the Regiment has endured.

But, we are doubtless stronger now in ability to endure fatigue, to encounter the varied hardships to which we are as soldiers exposed, than a twelve-month ago. If we should now be called to fight an enemy, we are stronger *to do and to suffer*, than then. We have many of us become somewhat acclimated — we have been under fire, and assisted in driving before us an enemy who attacked us confident of an easy victory, but who was compelled to fly in inglorious haste, utterly defeated. This has given us a confidence in our own abilities which makes us stronger than ever.

We have been for long, weary months exposed to storms & disease upon the crowded decks of steamboats — for more long months kept in unhealthy localities. But for a time those sufferings and exposures seem to be over to some extent. At Little Rock we were excellently situated — and Pine Bluff is, I believe, much more healthy than Helena or the Tallahatchie bottoms.

There our sick men were numbered by the dozen in each

company — now they are hardly sufficient for couples. May we never see such times again as in our first nine months in the "sunny south." Our prospect for remaining here until the opening of the spring campaign, seems to be good. It is well! . . . . I have as yet, seen not a word in relation to the battle in which Bragg is said to have been whipped near Chattenooga.[23] One of the first things I must do when I get home will be to get a History of the Rebellion and read it. You people at home know ten times as much of the situation of affairs as *we* do in the field. We get a few papers, dated days and weeks apart, and are left *entirely ignorant* of what has transpired in the mean time. I wish I *could* get papers regularly, I would subscribe for one or two.

. . . .

Pine Bluff, Dec. 20, 1863.

. . . .

My Haversack and Diary were received yesterday. The charges on them were only 50¢. I wouldn't have lost them & the contents for $20. I'll *see about* sending the Diary *sometime*. You have already in my letters more of a Diary of my last year than *it* contains.

. . . .

I was at Church again this morning — heard another dry sermon, founded on Luke XIIII, 25. The congregation consisted mostly of Soldiers. The church was very cold, but the coldest part of it seemed to me to be *the pulpit*.

. . . .

Camp 28th Wis. Vols.,
Pine Bluff, Arkansas, December 25th, 1863.

"A Merry Christmas" to you my Carrie, and to our little darlings — to bright-eyed Lulu and baby Mary. O, that I could be with you today to visit with you through this pleasant holiday — & *the next seven*. Would it not be a pleasant Christmas? For me it would, and I'm sure 'twould be for you. But we cannot be together today, so we will each think of the other and thus spend the day as happily as we may. Did you ask what I had good for dinner? I had stewed potatoes, bread and coffee. I think that was all. The bacon which was cooked with the potatoes I couldn't eat. Somehow I can't swallow it & feel comfortable. Beef we couldn't get. It is getting scarce here. We had a couple of chickens yesterday, but *we never keep good victuals*, for fear we won't get a chance to eat them. Procrastination is a terrible thief you remember, and I wouldn't wonder if he *steals eatables* sometimes. At any rate we won't trust him.

There was a dance in town last at which the beauty of Pine Bluff & Uncle Sam's blue-coated chivalry were well represented, it is said. I didn't attend, so I have to take *hearsay* for it.

Today I am at work a part of the time, and loafing about Camp the rest. No more mail yet. We have no news here. Everything is about as dull as can be, except work — plenty of that. We have to drill 2 ½ hours every forenoon, beside our other work.

My eyes are quite bad yet, and picket duty almost uses them up. Hope they will be better soon. I have my monthly and quarterly reports to make up, so that I have to write a good deal just now. The men are all well — none of C. Co. reported sick today, though one or two are rather unwell, though not really sick.

I hope, dearest wife, that by the next Christmas I may be at home, to leave you no more.

I am sorry I could send you nothing for the holidays, but there is nothing to be had here.

Col. Lewis & Major White are still at Little Rock, leaving Lt. Col. Gray in command of the 28th.

We have been on short rations here lately. The boat brought some provisions down the other day, but a large portion of them were damaged and were condemned. I managed to get a bbl of flour for $6.50, & bbl of Potatoes $2.55. Today I bought 20 bushels of sweet Potatoes, for which I paid $15. or 75 cents per bushel. Most of them were for the company.

The weather has not been very severe lately, but is colder tonight. I suppose you are having frigid weather in Wisconsin. How cold it must be for you to get up and build fires. I hope you have some one to help you before this.

Again, A Merry Christmas and a Happy New Year for my darlings. . .

Pine Bluff, Dec. 26/63
12 M.

The steamboat "Alamo" arrived from Little Rock an hour ago, bringing a mail. I rec'd your letters of Dec 6th & 9th, and am so glad to hear that you get along so nicely — that you are happier than when boarding. I hope that you will not work *too* hard for the happiness, and make yourself sick.

. . . .

I am glad you got the sabres. Lieut. Alvord wishes his given to his father. Mine you may put away and keep for me. They are cavalry sabres, and *secesh* at that — that is they were carried by *secesh* at the battle of Little Rock, and picked up on the field after the fight by "Jordon," the darky I had.

. . . .

Capitol House, Madison, Wis., Mch 17, 1864.

I expected to be home today but cannot. If possible I will be there tomorrow. If not you may meet me in Milwaukee on Saturday. Go in on the morning train, and I will meet you at the depot.

The 16th arrived last night & had a reception this morning.

You remember Lt. Curtiss of My Co. He is now here. He is Major of the 1st D. C. Cavalry. He is here with authority to raise a reg't. of Cavalry & is to be Lt. Col. I am well. Some of my recruits are sick. . . . .

Madison, May, 3, 1864.

Isn't this a nice, pleasant day? I have been very busy, but have got nearly through my hurry for today. I mailed the letter for you on the cars, and asked the Mail Agent to leave it at the Junction; so if the cars connect there to-night you will get it. I sent $250. to Pa Silsbee and told him to invest $200. of it in 10-40 Bonds if he thought it a good investment. I thought the $50. had better be where you can get it any time you may need it, as it is uncertain when we will be paid again. I may get some money at St. Louis or Chicago. If so I shall send home from $200. to $250 — to Columbus.

. . . .

I take with me about $100. beside the $100. of the Company money which I have. It will probably cost about $30 or $40 to get to the Reg't. Shall make it cost me as little as possible.

How lonesome I felt last night — and I *know you* did. It will be a long, dreary time to us both while I am gone, but life will be sweet when we met [*sic*] again, will it not my own darling Carrie? How short has seemed the 14 seeks I have been at home. It hardly seems that it can have been so long. But —

"Softly falls the foot of time
That only treads on flowers!"

. . . .

Cairo, Ill., May 9, 1864.

We reached here about 10 last night. Took my men to the Soldiers Home & went to the "St. Charles" Hotel myself, where after some difficulty I found room to sleep with another

Capt. of the 8th Wis. for which & a poor breakfast I paid only
$1.75.

. . . .

The J. C. Swan is a fine boat and sets a splendid table —
better than almost any hotel in our northern cities. We had a
pleasant trip down.

The "Naval Depot" left here this morning. It is a building 2
stories high & larger than the "LaBelle House," built upon a
flat boat, so that she can be towed from one point to another.
Three large steamers had her in tow. It contains public offices
& storage room for supplies — a "big thing."

. . . .

The war has made a busy place of Cairo. Being at the
confluence of the Mississippi & Ohio Rivers, it becomes a
great central point for supplies &c. The R.R. trains & boats
come loaded from both ways, & are constantly arriving.

I expect to leave here on the "Mollie Abel" at 7 A.M.
tomorrow. She is a splendid new boat. I have now 35 men & 1
captain under my charge.

. . . .

"On Board Illinois Central Railroad Packet Line"
"Passenger Steamer Mollie Able"
Cairo, Ill., May 10th., 1864.

I came on board this boat yesterday P.M. with my men,
after getting Reports made here, & drawing rations to last
from here to Memphis, after which I had time to run about
some. . . .

This boat is a fine, new one. In one corner of the forward
cabin is a nice writing desk, for the accommodation of passengers, which I am now using. Opposite to it is a news office
where, Books, Periodicals, & the latest papers are sold. Daily
Papers sell here for a dime. The main and ladies cabins are
nicely furnished and well lighted. The state rooms are larger

than on most boats, & furnished with wash bowls & pitchers, Towels, Looking glasses &c., as well as nice clean spring beds, and *linen* sheets.

She also carries a great amount of freight, and is heavily loaded. She is, I hear, to start immediately upon the arrival of the train from Chicago this morning. The report that Pine Bluff had fallen into the hands of rebels turns out to be false. Steele met with severe losses, but got back to Little Rock with a heavy rebel force turned loose against him. I feared he would be cut up when I heard of the disaster to the Red river expedition. It seems he lost his wagon train & a good many men.[24]

Gen. Rice, our brigade commander was wounded slightly, a piece of canister or shell furrowing his scalp. The rebels may have attacked Pine Bluff ere this — if they do with a strong force they may take it, but they will have to fight if they do. Behind their works our men can ship a much greater number than they can muster themselves.

It rained hard yesterday afternoon, and very hard last night. It rains a little this morning. Am glad I am on the boat, and not out in the *Cairo mud.* I got enough of *that* yesterday. Hope it will be pleasant again before we reach Memphis.

Below Cairo, May 10, 1864.
2 P.M.

We left Cairo about 9 A.M., after taking on a regiment of Veterans (Indiana) returning to the front, and ran down the river 8 or 10 miles, where the boat stopped for wood. Has put on a big pile, and as I write the bell sounds to start again.

How eager were all to learn the latest news from Grant's army when the train arrived this morning. Newspapers were in great demand, and the Chicago, Cincinnati & St. Louis dailies were sold — hundreds of them — as fast as they could be handed out by the newsboys. This is probably the latest news I shall hear before I reach Little Rock, unless I should be detained a day at Memphis. I do hope Grant will whip Lee now, for it would be a terrible blow to the rebellion.[25]

We had a capital dinner on board today, with lots of delicacies & luxuries — fresh green peas, tomatoes &c. — puddings 2 kinds — 3 or 4 kinds of pies — 5 or 6 kinds of cakes, fish, roast & boiled meats, tongue, turkey, chicken, salads &c. &c. I wish you could have had some of it.

We are now moving down the river. There are 3 Colonels & lots of other officers on board. It has been pleasant since 9 A.M., but is now getting ready to rain again. It is so cloudy as to be quite dark in the cabin — I can hardly see to write — have to strain my eyes too much — so I'll close.

. . . .

Worsham House, Memphis, Tenn., May 11/64.

We reached here about noon today — have been busy since then reporting to Gens. Washburne & Buckland, drawing rations again, & getting transportation for myself & men.[26]

But, darling, what do you think? I am ordered to go from here to Vicksburgh, New Orleans, & Fort Jackson below N.O. with my squads of recruits for the 11th, 23rd, & 29th Inf'ty, 4th Cav. & 1st Wis. Heavy Artillery. It was unexpected by me, and will cost me something for board &c., but transportation is furnished me, and I can have a chance to see the sights at those places. However I shall be a long time getting to the regiment, & shall not hear from you for some time. As soon as you get this, please write me at Vicksburg, Miss. Direct to Capt. T. N. Stevens, Vicksburg, Miss., and add on the lower corner "If not called for in 10 days, forward to 28th Wis. Inf., Pine Bluff, Ark."

The Trunks &c. I have sent on to the boys by Capt. Redington. He & our boys left here at 5 this P.M. I shall probably get off tomorrow. I have got no pay yet, but may get some tomorrow. If I do I shall send some to Columbus — $200 or $250. . . .

What is the news from Richmond, I wonder? I hope Grant & his army are winning or have a victory. How anxious all are down here to hear from him. When boats arrive, papers are anxiously called for. Well, the suspense will *sometime* be over. . . . .

Steamer Mississippi, Miss River, May 14, 1864.

. . . .

This boat was to leave Memphis at 2 P.M. yesterday, but was detained till 5. We passed Helena in the night, & were at Mouth of White River about 10 A.M. today. Below there I had never been, and the scenery is entirely new to me — though there is but little to see a great deal of the way. We have just passed Greenville, Miss. (5 P.M.) which is 257 miles below Memphis & 136 above Vicksburg. We shall be at Vicksburg by 8 or 9 o'clock tomorrow, probably.

I had to pay $3.00 pr. day for board, at Memphis, which with porterage &c. made it cost me about $4. pr day. It costs $1.50 to board on the boat. I shall be glad when the trip is over, for *it costs* — though I shall see a great deal that is new.

A man who came from Memphis with us yesterday, got drunk last night & walked off the boat & was drowned, as it was very dark & nothing could be done. He was a respectable looking, well dressed man. Another victim to whiskey!

The Mississippi is a fine boat, & they live nearly as well on board as on the "Mollie Able."

From Vicksburg to New Orleans is about 335 miles. I expect to have to stop at Vicksburg 1 day.

How far it is from N.O. to Fort Jackson I don't know. Hope it won't take me long to go. We have just passed some very pleasant plantations on the river banks — at least they appear pleasant from the boat. There are quite a large number of passengers on board, as there are on nearly all boats either way now a days.

Our news yesterday (by St. Louis papers of the 12th) from Grant's army seemed quite favorable. I hope the next may be equally so. May he take Richmond & destroy Lee's Army! I expect Pine Bluff will be attacked — perhaps captured — before I reach there, though I hope not. This morning & half the forenoon was quite cold — warmer now, though growing cooler this evening.

Some of the negro waiters on the boat are very good musicians — 4 of them played last night for us — 2 on the violin, 1 on the Bass Viol & 1 on the bugle — they made good music, & afterwards one of them danced for the amusement of the crowd, after which he "passed the hat" as they do at — *other places*!

We have passed several gunboats today, stationed along the river for the protection of river trade & navigation. They nearly all send out boats, when we do not land, for papers, being anxious for the latest news.

I have been out again viewing plantations along the river through my glass — I think I told you I bought one in St. Louis. We had a magnificent sunset. The wind is blowing cold, so that I find it convenient to come inside.

. . . .

Steamer Mississippi, Below Port Hudson,
Monday, May 16, 1864
9 o'clock, A.M.

We left Vicksburg about 1 P.M. yesterday, and had a fine run during the afternoon, as the boat left a large amount of freight there so that she ran lighter. It was a pleasant afternoon, and a delightful evening we had last night, the moon shining brightly. Vicksburg presents a formidable appearance from the river. The heavy guns bristling from the bluffs look as if they were enough for any foe.

We had some time to look about town there. The bluffs are

dug full of caves which the rebels & citizens made and used
for shelter during the siege. I entered one of them. The entrance was narrow, & I had to stoop going in; but once inside I
found quite a room, with a smooth ground floor. Quite a curiosity I thought.

We reached Natchez at 9 ½ last evening — unloaded a lot of
freight & left there about midnight I believe, though I was
abed & asleep before we left there.

Fired upon!

I awoke about 5 o'clock this morning, looked at my watch,
& turned over for another nap. Was just getting asleep when I
heard the report of fire arms, jumped out of bed, pulled on my
pants & boots, seized my revolver & went out. The rebels had
planted a battery near the head of "Tunica Island," a short
distance below the mouth of Red river, and had opened upon
us. They apparently had 2 or 3 guns — probably 6 & 12
pounders, & a quantity of small arms. They were firing briskly
at us when I went out. The musket balls did not reach us, but
the[y] put 10 or 12 solid shot & shell through our boat. One
shell exploded on board. Strangely enough not a soul of animal on board was injured, though the missiles passed through
the texas, cabin, state rooms, barroom, barber shop, & all
about the boat, fragments & splinters flying in all directions.
We have some 200 persons on board, & lots of cattle, &
hundreds of chickens, turkeys, geese & ducks, but nothing
having life was touched. The lady passengers, of whom there
are several, were badly frightened. One shell passed through
the cabin & fell upon the pantry floor. A darkey waiter picked
it up & threw it overboard before it exploded. The wife & child
of the rebel general Schuyler were on board — she was
awfully scared. The negro cooks were so scared that they
spoiled our breakfast. A gun boat laid a short distance above
there, & two a few miles below. One of them reached the spot
before we got out of sight & commenced firing, but the rebels
had probably skedaddled before then. We kept on down the

river without stopping, merely stating the case as we passed
the gunboats. It was an exciting time, but we all object to
being waked up so early another time. There are some ugly
looking holes in the boat.

We passed Port Hudson about 8 o'clock this morning, stopping only a few minutes.

It is a pleasant morning, & bids fair to be very warm today.
We shall probably meet with no more adventure this side of
New Orleans, which place we will probably reach late tonight
or early tomorrow morning. We are now within a few miles of
Baton Rouge, the Capitol of La., where I leave a portion of my
men, who belong to the 4th Cavalry. . . .

Monday 16th 3 P.M.

We reached Baton Rouge at about half past 9 this morning. I
went to the camp of the 4th Cavalry. . . . Left Baton Rouge at
10. Since passing there the country has put on a delightful
appearance. The land is all low, but looks so green and fresh.
There are many large plantations along the river, some of them
having buildings for 1000 negroes or more, making quite a
village. In fact it seems almost like a continuous village for
many, many miles. We have passed Plaquemine & Donaldson-
ville — it is now some 80 miles to New Orleans. It is a
delightful day, though rather warm; but sitting on the forward
deck we get a breeze which makes it quite comfortable. We
live high here. Radishes, lettuce, asparagus, green corn, (last
years) Oranges, nuts, figs, raisins, strawberry pie, peach pie,
blackberry and raspberry pie, chickens, eggs, veal, mutton,
pig, ham, turkey, 6 or 8 kinds of cake, tarts, 3 kinds of jellies,
custard, & lots of other things for dinner, including ice cream.
Army fare will be *coarse* when I get down to it, I dare say. We
have had no more trouble from "Johnny Reb." I forgot to say
that the secesh made a "raid" on Port Hudson yesterday,
burning a saw-mill and capturing 2 of our guns. They are

giving us some trouble on the river since the disastrous defeat which Banks experienced on Red river. That has proved a hard affair for us. We are all wondering what can be the news from Grant. We hope for the best. At Natchez we were told last night that the "secesh" citizens had rec'd some news which they were *glum* over. It was thought they had news from Richmond, — as there is a rebel telegraph within some 30 miles of Natchez, as I was told, and rebel sympathizers may have brought news from there. I shall look anxiously for the next papers from the north. May they come soon and bring good news for Unionists.

. . . .

St. Charles Hotel, New Orleans, La., May 17, 1864.

We reached this city about 10 o'clock last night. I did not come on shore till this morning. Today I have been running nearly all day and am very tired. It has been very warm here — so much so that my clothing has been saturated with perspiration all day. It has been hard work to get my business done, but done it is. I shall not go to Fort Jackson, as another officer is going down from here, and will take the men. I can't say that I am sorry — I had rather dreaded that part of the trip. Shall probably leave here on the Steamer "Mississippi" at 5 P.M. tomorrow — if she gets off as soon as that — she is advertised to leave at that time. I was up to the market this P.M. They have vegetables & fruits in profusion here already. I saw onions, turnips, radishes, ripe blackberries, oranges, a kind of plum, & lots of things. I took a plate of blackberries with sugar & milk — cost 15¢. I had a dish of ripe strawberries at Memphis — did I tell you? They cost 50¢ per dish, but I didn't pay for them — I will go without such luxuries rather than pay such prices. At Memphis I went in to get my photograph taken, but they asked me $6. pr dozen — I have had it taken today, to be finished tomorrow noon, at $3. pr. dozen. I will mail them or have them mailed to you.

New Orleans must have been a busy place in former years, judging from its present appearance. Many goods are cheaper here than at Memphis & Cairo. I met here this evening a couple of Captains (of the 7th Vt.) who went up from Memphis to Cairo on the boat with me last winter. They have just arrived here by way of N.Y. & the gulf. Had a pleasant chat with them.

I'm tired, and my eyes ache, so I'll close by sending you many kisses, & wishing you a pleasant good night.

Gayoso House, Memphis, Tenn., Tuesday, May 24, 1864 6 A.M.

We arrived at Memphis at about 10 o'clock last evening, and as the Worsham House, where I stopped when I went down, is a dirty place for a first class hotel, I made a change of it for this time, & concluded to try the Gayoso. One thing is sure — I had a good, clean bed, and one free from *bugs* last night — & that is more than I can say for the Worsham. I had a very pleasant trip from N. O., though the weather was very warm some days. We all hoped to get some news here of Lee's defeat by Grant — but will have to wait, it seems.

I must go out this morning and see if there are any boats for the White or Arkansas rivers. I am getting anxious to get to the 28th — not only because I am wanting to be with the boys, but it is confounded expensive to be running about on such duty as I have been on the last 3 weeks. I have tried to be careful, but it has cost me a great deal of money since leaving home — board is $3. pr day here — at N. O. it was from that *up*. I bought me a pair of shoes in N. O., got my pictures taken &c. I might have got along without, I suppose. I should not have bought my field glass if I had though of having to pay out half as much as I have, for *we* can not afford it — *I ought* not, when you are doing without so many needed things at home. Well, I shall get to my reg't. soon, & then my expenses will be less. I wish

I could come home, though! I do miss you and the children so much, dear Carrie. What a happy visit I have had with you the past winter. . . .

Steamer "Empress" Miss. River. May 25, 1864.

I got left yesterday through the stupidity or worse of a negro porter, and my baggage went off down the river on the "White Cloud", on which I intended to have taken passage. My only alternative was to wait for another boat & follow my valise & other "traps." The "White Cloud" is bound for Duvalls Bluff, so I hope to find my things there if I do not overtake her this side of that point. My detention enabled me to visit with my old friend Butler again. I waited up till about 11 o'clock last night hoping a boat would come along — and then went to bed. Got up at 4 this morning, as boats were expected down every hour. At a little before 6 the "Empress" and "Leviathan", both large boats for N. O. hove in sight. The Empress being the first to leave, I took passage on her. Shall leave her at Helena if I find the "White Cloud" there — if not shall go to Mouth of White river on her. We left Memphis about 9 this morning. The boat is heavily laden, so that she will get along slowly I suppose.

As my valise is gone I have not a rag of clothing except what I have on — hope I shall find it for I'll need some clothes by & by. Our news from Grants Army is not all we hoped for, — but we have been hoping for too much I suppose. He has a great task before him — a powerful foe to fight. I hope he may be equal to the task, & fight the enemy only to whip him.

. . . .

DuVall's Bluff, Ark., May 28th 1864.

We reached here about 6 o'clock this morning. The first train was just leaving for Little Rock, so I have to wait till 2 o'clock this P.M. Am glad I have to wait no longer, for this is a poor place to stay. The trip up has been a tedious one, though not as bad as the ones I made last fall and winter. I have been among strangers — I seem to hardly ever meet old acquaintances when travelling, as some people do. We had a little excitement yesterday. The pilot never had been up the White river before, and by mistake run the boat up a "bayou" called "Indian Bay." We had gone 4 or 5 miles before the mistake was discovered, and about that time we discovered some mounted rebels on the shore, a little distance off. The men on board (cavalry) were immediately ordered under arms, and we expected an attack. The boat was put about, and off we went down stream. Why the rebs did not attack us is a mystery — they may have not had quite force enough. Situated as we were 50 well armed men could have "gobbled" our boat & all on board (300 Cavalry.) But we got off safely. No other excitement on the way up.

I am still quite well.

Darling, I have been terribly lonesome lately. How I have longed to see my own wife and our little ones — and how much they have wanted to see me! Have you not my own loved ones? I heard at Helena that Lieut. Alvord had gone home on furlough, about the time that I left home. Also that Capt. Townsend of our Reg't. who was on Gen Rice's Staff, was killed during the late campaign in which our army was forced to fall back to Little Rock. Capt. Noble, A.Q.M. at Helena, told me this. Capt Townsend was a pleasant good natured man — I regret to hear of his death. He is the first of our officers who has ever been killed by the enemy. His father was with him & was taken prisoner. He has been exchanged I hear.

I will write you again from Little Rock if I get time . . . .

P.S. I have just been ashore. I had on my best pants, run on to a nail & tore one of the legs nearly off. Am getting them mended. Expect it will almost entirely spoil them. If they look too bad when mended, I shall write you to have Jones make me a pair. He has my measure, & you can send them to me by mail or express if you have no other chance.

Camp 28th Wis. Inf.,
Pine Bluff, Ark., June 3, 1864.

. . . .
I am boarding at $4. pr week. It is the best I can do now, for I can't get a servant, and our dishes & things are all — nearly all — gone.

Our regiment is just being furnished with new arms — the new Springfield rifle Musket. I rec'd them for my company on the first & turned over my old ones today. When will Lt. Alvord return?

The rebels are hanging about here, but don't attack us.

When does Alvord return? Has he gone to Canada?

. . . .

Pine Bluff, June 10, 1864.

. . . .
I do not know as there are any certain indications of an advance of the rebel army upon this post, though it seems probable, from what we hear, that Price is preparing to attack some point which we occupy on the line of Arkansas, and it seems more than likely that this will be the one — though I hardly think we shall receive a visit from them.[27]

Quite extensive earthworks have been erected here since I left last winter, consisting of a line of breastworks around the town, with embrasures in several places for cannon, which can be so placed as to sweep the roads & all approaches to the town. This line is outside of the line erected last fall, so that in case of attack if we were driven from the outer works, we would still have the inner ones, from behind which we could send terrible havoc into the ranks of a storming party. We have some 20 pieces of artillery here, including the cavalry (mountain) howitzers. The force here consists of the 28th Wis., 3rd Min. & 62d Ill. Infty, 1st Ind. 5th Kan. & 7th Mo. Cav. and some detachments of Artillery. . . .

The boys here, men I should say if I spoke of their size & age have great times playing *marbles*. Almost every one in the regiment has marbles, and it seems a little funny to see men 35 years old, with boys of 16 or less playing at the juvenile game. They all seem to enjoy it hugely. My supper bell (a *cow-bell* by the way!) is ringing — so I'll quit a little while.

. . . .

Head Qr's 28th Wis. Inf. Vols., Pine Bluff, Ark., June 16th, 1864.

I have not written you for several days — first, because I have been very busy, — and, second, because there has been no boat here to carry away our mail.

Lt. Col. Gray is very sick, and I have been this week in command of the regiment. I have had but little to do as regimental commander, but my company business got so far behind in my absence that I have had a large amount of writing to do — and it is not all done yet. I am getting tired of so much work of this kind — had rather be doing more active, out door work. Our men are at work still strengthening our line of fortifications — some 80 are detailed each day from the 28th for that purpose, beside which we have heavy details for picket, guard &c., and 1 company is detached, acting as Provost Guard (Co. E.) Lt. Bingham, (Co. E.) & Lt. Syke, (Co. F.) are both quite ill.

. . . .

June 17th

I was interrupted yesterday by the sound of fire arms on our picket line. A party of some 400 rebel cavalry drove in one of our outposts, and there was a sharp firing along one picket line for an hour. The 28th was ordered out to the position on the right of our line of breastworks, a portion of it supporting two batteries. There seemed a right smart chance for a fight for a while. Being in command of the regiment I straddled a steed and took the boys out to our position, assigning the companies their several places. We remained there an hour or two, but no enemy appeared on our part of the line. A portion of the 62d Ill. had a skirmish with the enemy, and had 2 men killed. The rebels soon left. They were only a scouting party it is thought, though a deserter who came in yesterday states that the rebels have a force of 7,000 men this side the Saline river. If that is so, it looks like a raid upon us — but we don't anticipate an attack. Our boys went out feeling well yesterday, and felt disappointed at not having a *"scrimmage"* with the *"butternuts."*

. . . .

Pine Bluff, Ark., June 17, 1864.

. . . . Lieut Alvord reached here last Saturday (11th). I rec'd by him your letter containing the neck tie, and the 4 pairs of stockings — they are *first rate* — thank you, dear Carrie, for them. Lt. Alvord & I are boarding ourselves now — commenced last Tuesday morning. His darky is a pretty good cook, and so far we have got along first rate, though we are short of *furniture*. My pail of butter & jug of horse radish is first rate — aint they good though?!

. . . .

I am glad you have got your room fixed up so nicely. Is it plastered? I hope you will take a great deal of comfort there, & that by & by I may enjoy being with you there. I am glad you had the lower rooms painted. Hadn't you better have the rooms up stairs served the same? It would not cost so much. Am glad you have got a strawberry bed, though I don't want you to work to take care of them — you have too much to do without that.

. . . .

I have no idea that the 28th will leave this Division — this summer at least. More troops are needed here instead of fewer.

My stockings fit nicely, though if I have any more I would like them to have longer legs. Don't *you* knit me any. Some heavy cotton ones would be nice for winter.

I have not yet sent the balance of my pictures. Several of the officers wish to exchange photographs, so I'll have to keep these or have some more taken. . . . I wish you could have a cistern built — have it so it can be covered so as not to freeze, and, darling, don't leave it open so that the children can fall in. I don't suppose you would, but I am so afraid something of the kind will happen. I'm afraid of that hole in the back end of the garden. Is there any water in it this summer?. . . .

Pine Bluff, Ark., June 27, 1864

Well, we had our drill on Saturday in presence of Col. Clayton, and still survive. It was a terribly hot day, and we were out from 8 o'clock A.M. till nearly noon. I for one came very nearly burning up. My uniform cap left my neck and ears exposed to the scorching sun, and yesterday they were very sore. All right now.

The 28th conducted itself very creditably. The Col. complimented us highly, and said we excelled the others in drill and everything but the manual of arms — in that we knew we were deficient, having had no drill of any account for months. We really did better than I expected.

Yesterday the Cavalry were reviewed. I borrowed a horse of Ammi Hawks and attended as a spectator. It was quite a sight. I wish you could see a review — the bright battle flags floating above the glistening bayonets of the Infantry or drawn sabres of the cavalry — the music of the regimental bands — it is worth seeing & hearing.

I cannot write today — hardly. I have been hard at work at my Pay Rolls and Monthly Return, and am tired and nervous. Shall be all right in an hour or so, for I have got Sergeant Joe Robinson at work making the copies of the rolls, which will save me a heap of work.

The indications now are that the enemy will attack us soon at this Post. The rebels have taken & destroyed a gun boat on White river — & also several transports, as we hear. Quite a force is not far from us. Our fatigue details are to work night and day upon the fortifications until they are completed. How soon they will appear before the walls of Pine Bluff is uncertain — they may be only making a feint, while attacking some other point. But we can hold the place against a much superior force, having our fortifications to fight behind.

I hardly apprehend an attack, though Col. Clayton seems to look for one. If it comes we will try and do our part towards defending the "Stars and Stripes," and will hope to be successful, and come out safely.

. . . .

Camp 28th Wis., Inf., Pine Bluff, Ark., July 5, 1864.

The "Glorious Fourth" is gone, and we have had no battle this time. Everything has been quiet for a few days, except guerrilla bands making raids upon plantations, killing & carrying off negroes, stealing horses, mules &c.

Yesterday we had no celebration in town except the firing of a salute of 34 guns at noon, and reading the Declaration of Independence at parade at the head of each regiment.

A party of officers & citizens went some 3 or 4 miles up the river to a lake and had a time fishing & picnic-ing. I had an "invite" but didn't think it would pay to go, so I stayed in camp. I suppose there was some bad whisky spoiled in the crowd from what I hear.

Some of the soldiers got enough to make themselves happy — some of them getting a little quarrelsome. A few found their way into the guardhouse. Two or three of my men were a little "boozy," but I had no difficulty with them.

I hope we shall hear some more good news from Grant by the next boat. I wonder what he was doing yesterday. Have the scenes at Gettysburgh been repeated during the last 4 or 5 days? If anything has been done, I hope Grant has been successful. I dare not think of the consequences if he should fail. He *must not* fail there.

Ed. Olson was taken sick Saturday night, but is around now feeling much better — will be all right in a day or two. The other sick men are doing pretty well, except Mr. Fritzinger — I don't know what to think about him. He seems to have no energy, or ambition — *hardly life*. He is up a part of the time and walks around a little — *only* a little. I hope he may get better, but I'm afraid he will not.

I still keep well — isn't it a wonder how much better I stand this climate than do a great many better, healthier men? I have no difficulties such as many of them have.

. . . .

Pine Bluff, Ark., July 9, 1864.

. . . .

There is considerable sickness among the troops here — and a *great deal* among the colored people. While I was on duty no less than nine funeral parties passed out through the chain guard. Two of the dead were soldiers (one from the 28th.) seven colored people. Three of our reg't., I think, have died this week, (from Cos. D, F, & G.) The cemetery in town is not used any longer, as it is nearly full, so a new ground has been selected outside of town, and funeral parties have to pass our guard to go there.

My company is getting sick — thirteen were excused by the surgeon this morning. None of them are in hospital, but 4 or 5 of them ought to be in some hospital where they could be well taken care of — the rest will mostly be able to do duty again in a few days, probably. I will send you a list of the sick if I have time to make it before I close this.

Our *night* work on the fortifications has ceased. It is well that it has, for a few weeks more of it would have made all our men sick. There is now, I think no danger of any attack here — our defenses are too good. "Johnny Reb." don't want to "come and see us." I had rather he would come & fight us than have our men worked as they have lately been — we could whip them & lose fewer men than by this heavy work.

We get but few vegetables here, and the heavy food furnished don't all of it agree with the men this hot weather. Their systems become weakened, and when disease comes they are unable to withstand it.

Our pickets & outposts are frequently attacked by straggling parties of rebels, but there is no large force near us now as far as I can learn. Shelby and his "gang" are on White river, Gen. Carr has whipped him at or near Clarendon I hear.[28]

One thing we are all vexed at. Our Chaplain, Rev. E. S. Peake, instead of staying with the regiment where he belongs, stays at Little Rock. He is *detailed* I think in the Sanitary Rooms, but his principal business is, as near as I can get at it, running the secesh Episcopal Church there. *We* have to *borrow* a Chaplain whenever we want one to bury our dead. The Chaplain of the 1st Indiana Cavalry attends all our funerals. He is a good man I think, but is not very brilliant — but he does his duty as far as he knows it & is capable of doing. I wish Mr. Peake would make room for a good man with us. It would suit nine tenths of our line officers, & nearly all the men. Well, I must stop finding fault & close. I'll write again if I can before the mail closes. . . .

Pine Bluff, Arkansas, July 9th., 1864.

. . . .

I have written often, & can't see why three weeks should have passed without a letter reaching you. You must have several when they do get along. Don't feel uneasy about me — I feel just as safe here as if I were in the old Post Office at Oconomowoc — and I think I have gained a little credit in the last 22 months. Not that I wish to *boast* of it, but haven't I a right to feel a little proud of it? — just a little?! I intend to try & do my duty while in the service, & hope past faults may be overlooked or pardoned. I don't feel very ambitious myself, but still if I *could* win a name ——.

I have not been *offered* the Majorship of the reg't. in so many words, but it was intimated to me by influential men *in Wis.* that I could be the next Major. I do not want it. Capt. Williams should be the next one, unless some good reason can be shown for not promoting him. The line officers of the regiment *would choose me before him if they could elect* — at least a good share of them have told me so.

However I take it all as talk, and never expect to rank as more than an *Infantry Captain* — these *hundred day* men will rank just as high and receive just as much honor as we *veterans* who have served *years* where they have served months. It is well! I did not come out for honor — if I had I should be dissatisfied I fear. Look at the ranking Capt. of the 36th. He is already commissioned as Major, having seen *nearly 2 months* service out of the state — I've been out *nearly 2 years* & am still *Captain* Stevens. Bully for him! & *me!*

. . . .

Camp 28th. Wis. Vol. Inf.,
Pine Bluff, Ark., July 17, 1864.

I wrote you last Tuesday when we were on the eve of a *march.* By the date of this you will know that I am back again, and safe. We were called out on Wednesday morning at 1 o'clock by the beating of the drum — fell into line at 2 o'clock and marched down the river some 12 miles, the cavalry passing on some miles further to reconnoiter and ascertain the position of the enemy. They found him in front of us in too heavy force to warrant an attack upon him by our small force. Just before noon of about the hottest day I ever experienced, Wednesday, we received orders to retire to a position some 4 miles in rear of the one we then occupied, on a road passing through the locality known as "the Johnson Plantation", formerly owned by Senator Johnson from this state.[29] After some delays we reached the place, & took a position to protect the right flank of our column in case of any attempt of the rebels to annoy us, remaining here until 2 ½ o'clock next morning, when we fell in & returned to Pine Bluff, our train bringing in some 90 loads of corn, taken almost from under the noses of the enemy. The weather was terribly hot, and the march was a hard one for us "walking companies." Cavalry of course get along easier on a march. Detachments were with us from the 1st Ind., 5th Kansas, 7th Mo. & 13th Ill. Cav. and a few pieces of Light Artillery. Our men some of them gave out, but are *right* again now. We reached here Thursday. On Friday I went on Picket, and got back to camp yesterday forenoon.

Today, (another burning hot one) I have attended the funeral of another of my men — Mr. Fritsinger. He died yesterday. He was sent to Hospital on Tuesday — but hospitals & medicines were of no use to him. He had *made up his mind to die*. I believe that a little of what soldiers call *sand* (others call it grit,) in his composition would have saved his life. But he gave up entirely to his feelings, which, if I have heard aright, were made more melancholy by the sad epistles he received from his wife, in which I am told she assured him that he would die here, & all such nonsense. Surely it was nonsense for her to write even if it were true.

If wives can write nothing but such letters to husbands in the army, they had *better write none*. His death has been occasioned by his own want of energy and her foolishness. I know it is harsh judgment, but I believe it is true.

. . . .

Camp 28th Wis. Inf. Vols.,
Pine Bluff, Ark., July 24, 1864

Another week has gone — a long, long week, and no news from *home* or from "the States." We have had no mail since two weeks ago last Saturday. It seems a terribly long time to wait, but we are "getting used to it!" I heard day before yesterday while on picket that a boat was expected down from Little Rock last evening, but she has not yet made her appearance among us — When she does come we ought to have a *huge* mail with any amount of letters & papers — and the sooner she comes the better we shall be pleased. The boys feel blue at not hearing from home, but joke and make all sorts of fun about it. One said just now that we would be fighting here a month or two after peace is declared, and know nothing about it. Ask then if they want a letter — "no!" will be the answer, "I don't care if I never get one!" — but wouldn't they jump at the chance to get even a word?. . . .

Hoping that "that mail" will soon come, I am, thine.

Pine Bluff, Ark., July 24/64

. . . .

Dearest, I want you to send me some *Quinine*. If the box which Lt. Alvord is to have sent him has not been sent, I want at least 4 bottles of it sent. If it has been sent you can send ¼ or ½ a bottle at a time in a letter, doing it up in a flat thin package so that it will fit an envelope, & seal it up tight all around so that none can come out. Our hospital is destitute of it & I need it for my men. I'm sorry I did not bring more with me. I expect to be sent this week over the river & about 4 miles out, to remain 5 or 6 days with my company. If I go I expect to be in command of 4 companies — 2 from the 28th & 2 from the 62nd Ill. There is not much danger to be apprehended there — the enemy are further down the river. . . .

**Camp Detachment U. S. Forces,
near Pine Bluff, Ark., July 27, 1864.**

Words cannot express my grief upon hearing of the death of our dear father. The tidings came to me so unexpectedly — I can hardly think it true. Can it be that he, so good, so kind and affectionate, so just to all, has left us? Yes, the words are before me — "Pa has passed over the river."

He has gone to his rest. Long and late has he toiled — often has he been wearied under the burden of life which he has been bearing. It shall be so no more. There is no toil in heaven for the ransomed. There is no weariness there for the blessed ones who have gone to their reward. He rests, and forever. We shall miss him from his wonted seat — from all the places in which we have been accustomed to see him — we shall mourn for him — but surely we feel that "our loss is his eternal gain."

I never could — never can — feel grateful enough to "Pa" for his kindness, in word and deed, to me. I loved him, I love him still. How little I thought when I was "at home" last winter that I should never see him again. Oh, that I could have been with you in these sad, sad hours of affliction: But it was not to be. How lonely they must all be at home. God help us all to bear this terrible affliction — this heavy loss.

Yesterday a mail came down from Little Rock for the first time since two weeks ago last Saturday. The only letters I received were your two of June 29 & July 1. It was the first intimation I had of his severe illness. We rec'd our mail just before dark.

I am now stationed across the river 4 miles from Pine Bluff, in command of 4 companies of Infantry ("C" & "G" 28th

Wis., & "G" & "H", 3rd Minn.) a Section and a small detachment of Cavalry for patrols, Messengers &c. I came here yesterday morning. Shall be here a week — that is if the rebels don't drive me away — of which I think there is no danger. We are going at work building some fortifications here. The latest newspaper from the north that I have seen is July 6th, so you see we know but little about "the situation of affairs." Here nothing is going on. . . .

Camp 28th Wis. Inf. Vols., Pine Bluff, Ark., Aug. 3, 1864

I have no idea that I can send a letter for a week yet, but will write so as to have it ready whenever a boat does come down. I wrote you that I went out across the river last week. The next day I was ordered to assume command of *all* the troops on that side of the river, consisting of four companies of infantry, two companies of cavalry & *one section* of artillery — (2 Guns) a very pleasant little force for a captain to have charge of. I had a horse furnished me, as I had to run about considerably, & my force was scattered over some four miles of territory. On Saturday Major Walker of the 5th Kansas Cavalry came over with a part of his regiment & assumed command, leaving me in command of the infantry & 1 Gun. We changed our position that day, moving our front forward half a mile & established a chain guard across the neck of land on which we were. [drawing in original letter] Our line is about a mile & a quarter long there, one flank resting on the river 4 miles above town, while the other is on the river 4 miles below town, the river making a bend in the shape of a horse shoe or ox-bow.

We had quite a pleasant time there, though the musketoes almost killed us. They are big ones. One of the boys told me he saw one *swallowing a frog*! and another lying close by that had swallowed one! but I guess that is a *pretty large story*.

Green corn we had lots of, with a few potatoes & tomatoes, & now and then a chicken, turkey, or something of the kind —

but we were without bread a good share of the time, and short of meat.

Yesterday we were relieved by other companies, and came back to camp. Our duty is heavy here now. Four companies are detailed from the regiment, leaving six to do the duty required. I have 40 men & noncommissioned officers for duty (present) today, of whom *only 32* are on duty already today, & the balance may be called for at any time.

Did I write you about Tommy Carr? He was arrested some 5 or 6 weeks ago for permitting a citizen to come across the river without a pass. Has been in prison ever since. He had his trial last week. The result is not published yet, but I think it will not go very hard with him. I don't think he intended any harm, but he knew he ought not to let the man over. He will not be severely punished I think.

. . . . Our recruits have suffered terribly. Only think! Six out of nineteen are already dead!. . . .

Camp 28th. Reg't. Wis. Inf. Vols.
Pine Bluff, Ark., Aug. 4th, 1864.

. . . .

The letting of the money is all right. Do as you think best. If I had dreamed that no paymaster would be here yet I should have sent for money before now — but *we hope* he will be here next week. We are awfully hard up for money, and have been for a long time. It costs me three times as much to board & live this year as it did last year. We can get nothing scarcely, & have to pay awful prices for everything we do get. Lt. Alvord & I have been messing together hoping to get along cheaper that way, but it costs us $15 to $18 per week, & awful poor living at that. I think I shall go to boarding again today or tomorrow, if I can get a decent place. I think I can get in at Mr. Mills, where Capts Williams, Kenyon, Smith & Billings are boarding. Col. Gray did board there, but left so as to be where he could play poker all night. There is lots of gambling done here — a gang of them play nearly every night at Gray's room — sometimes nearly all day & night. Our Q.M. is another of the same stripe, & quite a number of our officers — captains and lieutenants — mix in very freely. One lieutenant lost $800.00 in one night not long since — so the story goes. He owes the amount — it will take nearly all his 6 months pay to pay it. It is a buming shame — a disgrace to the regiment & the service that officers high in position should conduct themselves as they do — gambling, & leading their inferiors into the same practices — drinking, and many times almost forcing those under them to do the same, holding out every inducement for them to do it at least — running after and around, publicly, with fast women — women whose characters are not in the least questionable, for no one *suspects* them of possessing a spark of virtue or decency — men will do this who possessed good names at home, and who have what ought to be far dearer, respectable families — wives & children — at home. O, shame, where is thy blush? When the command is paid off they will probably receive 6 months pay, and then how gamblers will flourish! Many a man whose family needs his every farthing to live, will hasten to risk and *lose* the reward for their services for months. Why will *men* be so foolish?

A rebel spy was caught here the other day. He had drawings of our works here & particulars as to our strength — valuable information for the enemy. He had obtained a pass, stole a horse belonging to a captain of the 7th Mo. Cav., & had gone outside the chain guard, where he fired upon the officer of the day. He was followed & caught, & will be hung, probably, if he gets his deserts.

. . . .

Mr. Peake, our Chaplain, still remains at Little Rock, running a Secesh Episcopal Church. The line officers of the regiment lately made an application to have him returned to duty with the regiment — & hinted that if he did not choose to come back we would like to select a Chaplain who would remain with us. He has replied that as it is not convenient for him to be with the regiment he will forward his resignation by next mail. That suits us. It is what I wanted & hoped for when I drew up the paper. May his resignation *come soon, & be accepted*.

. . . . There seems to be nothing doing in this department, except our army is staying here, and holding its own. How long this is to continue time will tell — if he lives long enough. I hope it will not be long. We certainly cannot conquer the enemy by lying here — we must fight for it — & the sooner the government raises the men to reinforce our armies & enable us to conquer, the sooner the war will be ended. I wish to find no fault. I think no administration would have done any better — but the great fault has been that we have been too slow to call for men. It takes time to raise & equip so large a body of men, and we ought not to wait until they are *absolutely neded in the field* & before calling for them. Well, I hope it will all come right sometime. *I think it will.* . . .

Camp 28th Wis. Vol. Inf.,
Pine Bluff, Ark., Aug. 7, 1864.

. . . .

I have just come from church. What dull dry discourses some dunces can give us. Nothing interesting — nothing forcible or suggestive of true religion in a sermon of 50 minutes length — nothing but a prosy, montonous string of words — a terrible murdering of the kings English, intermixed with southern slang phrases & monkey faces. Why will such men insist upon being thought & called "men of God," and inflicting themselves upon the people?

Did I tell you what reply our chaplain made to our request that he be returned to duty with the regiment? He says "As *it is not convenient* for me to be with the regiment I will forward my resignation by first mail!" — the puppy! Isn't that impudent? It is not *convenient*! So he came into the service *for his own convenience* did he? pretty talk for a minister of the Gospel. It has been thought by some old-fashioned people that it was the *duty* of such to labor for others & for their Master's cause, without consulting their own convenience. The fact is he came in as *Col. Lewis' Chaplain* — not as a chaplain for the regiment — remained with Col. Lewis until he got out of the service & since then has been running a rebel church at Little Rock, — paying no attention to his duties in the regiment. The sooner he gets out the better we will like it.

. . . .

I am now boarding at Mr. Wm Mills. It is a very pleasant family — Mr. Mills & wife, his wife's mother, Mrs. Griffin, and four children, ranging from 3 to 12 years old. It seems good to have a good place to board. We get good fare, and it is got up in good shape. Five of us captains board there & two or three lieutenants — all of the 28th.

The paymaster is positively expected this week. Then look out for *Greenbacks*. I'm afraid I shall not be able to send *much* money home this time, though I'll do the best I can. My expenses have been heavy lately. An officer has about all he can do now to make both ends meet, though I think I can save something by being economical.

. . . .

Pine Bluff, Arkansas, August 11, 1864.

As the boat is going up today I drop you a line, though I don't feel much like writing. Monday I was "Field Officer of the Day," going on duty at 5 P.M. for 24 hours. Had to ride about half the night visiting the Cavalry outposts, & the next day had to visit them again, riding some 16 miles in the hot sun. Yesterday I went foraging, with a train of about 50 wagons, 10 miles out in the country, and came back yesterday afternoon tired out. I felt pretty near sick last night, but am better this morning.

The 28th was paid off on Monday. I made up a package to send home for the men. Thompson, Chaffee & some others won't send a cent home. Foolish boys. I send you $100. The package is sent to Simmonds to be delivered. You will find yours there. I hope we will be paid again in two or three months — for I haven't money enough to last longer than that. You had better keep this $100. where you can have it to use along, for we will need it if the paymaster stays away 6 months again. I rec'd some papers again by the boat last Sunday, but no letters.

. . . .

Pine Bluff, Arkansas, Sunday, August 14, 1864.

My last letter was short, and perhaps impressed you with the idea that I was sick. I was nearly so. Wednesday & Friday I had a high fever which lasted me nearly all night, and left me very weak next day. Today is my regular day for another fever, but it is now nearly six o'clock P.M., and no signs of it yet — so I think I may safely reckon that my "fever is broken." I succeeded in getting a little quinine, which seems to have done the business. I am weak from the fever, but am able to be around camp, & to walk to my boarding house. When I had the fever Mrs. Mills used to send my meals to me, so I had everything as nice as a soldier could well ask. I am excused from duty for a day or two, but shall soon be at it again as usual. I am also detailed again as President of a Board of Survey — the duties of which position will be the first to attend to. My company was last night detailed to take charge of and run a steam saw mill just at the south side of town. They have moved up there today, ready to go to work tomorrow morning. The details from the regiment for picket & guard are very heavy, as six companies of the 3rd Minn. went home

Friday — also eight companies of the 62nd Ill. & 4 from the 5th Kansas Cav. A portion of the 1st Indiana Cavalry whose time is out are promised that they may go home the last of this week.

. . . .

Pine Bluff, Ark., Aug. 19, 1864.

As I had no letters by the mail which arrived a week ago last Sunday, (Aug 7th) I have been looking forward anxiously to the time when another boat from Little Rock should bring us another instalment of the welcome messengers — waited patiently, and have been cruelly disappointed. The fact is we have lost about a two week's mail. The steamboat "J. H. Miller" left Little Rock on Monday for Pine Bluff with a large mail & a lot of sutler's goods &c. The river is low and she was detained considerably by running upon sand bars. On Wednesday, while lying on a sandbar she was captured by guerrillas, the goods taken off, & the mails &c burned with the boat. I hear that there were 8 large sacks of mail on board, among which I must have had nearly a dozen letters, as I had none last time. Ain't it too bad? We all feel fighting mad over it. Another boat which started a day later, arrived here yesterday afternoon. Chaplain Peake came down on her. It seems he has concluded not to resign. Many different stories are told about the loss of the "Miller." One is that she was captured by three men only — *mere boys*, while another report says there were 30 or 40 of the band. It is also thought by some that the captain of the boat had an understanding with the guerrillas — at any rate it seems that no resistance was made by any one — they were permitted to burn the boat & mails, & carry away the merchandize on board without opposition.

Something is wrong about it we all believe. The Captain, crew & passengers have arrived here. The captain has been arrested I hear. A man of "G" Co. of the 28th. was on board in charge of the mails. They made him help unload the goods & carry them into the "brush" he took advantage of a moment when not guarded very closely & escaped, arriving here last night. The only ones retained by the rebs seem to have been 2 or 3 colored soldiers. They will probably meet with severe usage.

Well! the letters are gone, so if you wrote any particular news in your letters of about July 17th to August 5th or 10th, please repeat it, or I shall not get it. The papers are also "gone up."

. . . .

Pine Bluff, Arkansas, August 28, 1864.

. . . .

This is Sunday again. Mr. Peake officiated at the Presb. Church this morning — he had a very full house — mostly soldiers, however. Yesterday I went out with a forage train of 30 wagons after corn. We went 14 miles down the river on the other side from town. We loaded the wagons on the plantation of a rebel or *guerrilla* captain named Lightfoot. We were told that he was there himself with 75 men the day before. That was just the number we had with us, and we hoped to be able to "scare him up" before coming back, but failed to see any enemy. It was a very hot day, and I came in tired. I left here at 4 a.m., and got back a little after 4 P.M. Of course I had a horse.

. . . . Four or five days ago Maj. Hamilton, Capt. Miller, & Capt. Lambert, all of the 36th. Iowa, who, with most of their regiment were taken prisoners at Mark's Mills during Gen. Steele's campaign last spring, reached here, having escaped from the stockade at Tyler, Texas, where they were confined. They were 32 days coming through, enduring all privations imaginable — almost — living most of the way upon green corn, melons & peaches, killing a hog once in a while. They were hard looking subjects in their "butternut" clothes, when they reached here, weary & worn, with lacerated, blistered, bleeding feet and limbs.

They escaped by forging a pass, & traveled mostly by night, avoiding towns & plantations. They spoke with but one white man & two negroes from the time they escaped until they reached here. The distance is 300 miles, but they probably traveled more than 400 miles on the way, much of the way through forests, wading swamps & bayous, swimming rivers, sleeping by day. What have they not suffered? Not a word from home have they heard during their long imprisonment.

3500 of our men are confined at Tyler, fed on corn meal, fresh beef & salt, — *nothing* more, & not always enough of that. Major Hamilton told me he had tasted neither tea or coffee since he was captured — 4 months ago. The poor fellows feel happy at their escape — and well they may. They state that our troops there (prisoners) are not very sickly — not as much so as here — though much exposed & enduring many privations.

. . . .

We gets lots of rumors here from abroad — but I wait to hear again before mentioning them. The two regiments which arrived here the other day are the 106th & 126th Ill. Inf'ty.

Col. Clayton of the 5th Kansas Cavalry, commanding at this post, has been promoted to Brigadier General.[30] He is a good fighting man when he *fights*.

. . . .

Pine Bluff, Ark., Aug., 30, 1864.

Dear Carrie:

I send you the following photographs of officers &c in the 28th

1 Lt. Col. Edmund B. Gray.

2 Capt. Jas. R. Kenyon, Co. E.

3 " Levi J. Billings, Co. K.
4 " Willis V. Tichenor, Co. G.
5 " Charles B. Slawson, Co. B.
6 1st Lt. Wm E. Bingham, Co. E.
7 1st Lt. Wm E. Coates, Co. A.
8 1st Lt. Alex T. Seymour, Co. I.
9 1st Lt. Geo. F. Cowing, Co. K.
10 2nd Lt. Henry H. Watts, Co. D.
11 2nd Lt. Smith A. Hartwell, Co. I.
12 Sergeant Frederic B. Browne Jr. Co. C. to which number I
   add one of your most affectionate husband,
13

T.N. Stevens.

Pine Bluff, Ark., Aug. 30, 1864

. . . .

I wrote Mr. Fritsinger at the time of his death. He died in Post Hospital. The surgeon would not admit persons very often to see the sick. I called two or three times after he was sent to hospital, but was not permitted to see him. From what I gathered from the attendants I think he died quietly & happily. I sent to Mrs. F. a list of her husband's effects, asking what I should do with them. I shall have to dispose of them soon.

. . . .

If Frank is drafted or leaves Oconomowoc, the office must go into other hands — I shall resign my commission as P.M. Is Guy still at Milwaukee? I failed to get his note. I will write him about it. Have you received the $100. I sent you last pay-day? It was about the 10th of Aug.

. . . .

Pine Bluff, Ark., Sept. 4, 1864.

The boat arrived again today from Little Rock, bringing me 3 letters from you, mailed *July 25* (how did it escape?) Aug.

15 & Aug. 18, the latter containing the first instalment of quinine. *Sent the rest along.* I must have been a little crazy when I told you not to. We shall need the 4 or 6 bottles at least. Let me know the cost so that I may charge it to the Co.

. . . .

I was Field Officer of the day yesterday — rode 16 miles in the middle of the night — narrowly escaped meeting a couple of bushwhackers who were within 20 rods of me. Had to ride 20 miles again yesterday on the same duty — but met with no adventures. — Came back tired out, and almost dead with the heat & dust, as it is very hot now, and I had to ride between 1 ½ & 5 o'clock P.M. — the hottest part of the day. The consequence is that, as it was so hot I could hardly sleep last night, I am very tired, & can't write. The box sent by express was gobbled by guerrillas at the time of the taking & burning of the "Miller." — so I have learned from the Express Agent. What was in it?

. . . .

Pine Bluff, Ark., Sept. 10, 1864.

. . . .

We have news by telegraph from Gen. Steele at Little Rock to the effect that Atlanta is ours — that Forts Gaines & Morgan are ours — & that the traitor Gen. Hardee is killed.[31] God grant it may all prove true. How many thousands of lives have already been sacrificed before Atlanta. O for an end of this terrible war! When will it come?

This is a pleasant moonlight night, just such an one as when we had that pleasant ride from camp-meeting once — do you remember? How I wish I could ride or walk with you tonight, or even sit with you, my own. Wouldn't we talk over old times & old scenes? And wouldn't we be happy, darling. Nothing would make me happier.

All is quiet here. Nothing is transpiring in this department of any public interest. No movements of troops are being made — we are merely holding our position & waiting for events to develop themselves at the east & southeast of us. I presume we will remain here a year longer — & serve our time out here. I hope we will not have to stay here next summer. The sickly season for this year is nearly over. We expect a boat here tomorrow. . . .

Pine Bluff, Ark., Sept. 11, 1864.

It is now evening, and a little cooler, though so warm that I perspire freely sitting in my room in my shirt sleeves. I have been around the line once as "Gen'l Officer of the Day" — have to go again at 12 o'clock tonight & once during the day tomorrow.

Col. Erskine of the 13th I'll. Cavalry who was out with the Cavalry, "raiding" came in with his command tonight. While coming in he met today a force of the enemy about 1000 strong between him & this post, about 20 miles from here. He cut his way through them, with a loss of about 20 men, & came in. One Captain of the 13th was killed, & one is missing; supposed captured. Major Scudder of the 5th Kansas with his men & the 1st Indiana saved the field piece they had along, behaving themselves gallantly. All honor to the brave men.

The boat has not yet arrived, consequently we have no mail yet, & no more news.

. . . .

September 13th.

Capt. Suesbury of the 13th Ill. missing since the affair of Sunday came in today. Quite a force is reported near us, but there is evidently no intention on their part of attacking us here — at least not at present. I am detailed again as "Field Officer of the Day," & go on duty at 5 P.M. — have to visit 3 outposts, on the Sulphur Springs, Warren & upper Monticello roads, at midnight tonight, & again during the day tomorrow — a ride of about 16 miles tonight, & about 25 miles tomorrow.

. . . .

Sept. 14th.

Had another delightful night for a ride last night. Don't I wish you could have gone too, without being exposed to any of the dangers of the trip — wouldn't I have been proud & happy, with my pair of big, jingling spurs on my heels, & rattling sword by my side, sash over my shoulder, *brass buttons* glittering in the bright *moonshine*. Oh, it was *grand*! terribly so! Got back safe at about 3 this morning — went out again at 8 ½ A.M. today & got back at 2 P.M. — had a long, tiresome ride. Met 2 deserters from the rebels coming in. The rebels were some of them last night within 2 ½ miles of where our pickets were today when I visited them. I was fairly out in rebeldom today, with a cavalry escort of *one man*! Strong, wasn't it?. . . .

Have been to hospital to see the sick ones. Robinson is worse, & failing fast I think. Don't think he will live the week out. The doctor reports Hardell "died of congestive fever." The fact is he killed himself eating blackberries & huckleberries. He had had the ague — was excused Tuesday morning by the Surgeon, — went down town & ate, (so the boys say) 2 cans of fruit. In the afternoon he laid down & went to sleep, & never knew anything again, dying the next forenoon. We had a cool, splendid night for sleeping last night. Another man of Co. "H." died last night. One of Co. "A" is thought to be too low to recover. We hope the sickly season is about over. More tomorrow —

Pine Bluff, Ark., Sept. 16, 1864, Noon.

We had a cool, — yes, a *cold* night last night. Today is pleasant, but not as warm as we have been having. The roads

& camp are very dry & dusty — the air is full of dust. How I wish it would rain tonight.

I am officer of the day in camp today, & have a large party of 33 men cleaning, sweeping, "policing" the camp.

Poor James W. Robinson died about half past 10 this forenoon. His brother, Sergeant Robinson, was with him. I left him about 10 minutes before his death. He will probably be buried this evening. What a sad loss to his poor wife and family; and how sad to think that a furlough or discharge a few weeks ago would have saved him for years, probably, to protect his loved ones. I did what I could toward it, & thought I should succeed in getting him home. The Sergeant feels his brother's loss very keenly. Two years ago last Tuesday I left home for camp with my company. How many are missing from the roll now! Death has made sad havoc amongst us — & the end is not yet. More of us must fall ere the survivors are permitted to see their homes. Let those who survive be thankful.

7 P.M.

Just as the sun was setting, we marched to the sound of the fife & muffled drum to the resting place of our brave dead, and, as the day closed, placed in his grave our dead fellow soldier. The burial service was read, the "farewell shot" was fired above his grave, & with sad hearts we returned to camp.

Sept. 17th

. . . .

I don't think Homer will be accepted if he attempts to enlist. I *hope* not, for he can't stand the service. And if he does enlist he had better go to some regiment in a more healthy location than this. Our men die off by dozens & scores here in Arkansas, & with the heavy duty we have to do a sickly or weakly man stands but little chance, as he is expected to do just as much as any one else unless he is sick enough to be excused by the Surgeon. Capt. Billings of "K" Co. & Lt. Chandler of "H" Co. expect to leave for Little Rock tomorrow to enter the Officer's Hospital at that place. They have both been in poor health for some time. I don't know but I shall be detailed as Acting Assistant Adjutant General on Brig. Gen. Clayton's staff. My name has been mentioned in that connection, but it is uncertain so far. If I go there I shall have no picket & officer of the day duty to do, & Lt. Alvord will be in command of the company. My duties there will be in the office almost entirely, unless we go on a march or campaign. Say nothing about it until we know about it. I am tough & hearty now — feel first rate. . . .

Camp 28th Wis. Vol. Inf.
Pine Bluff, Ark., Sept. 18, 1864.

. . . .

Wm Hicks, the spy which the Court Martial of which I am a member tried last month, is to be hung here next Friday. Has the $100. which I sent home about the 10th of Aug. reached you yet? I begin to fear it may be lost, as I hear nothing of it. O, how I wish I had the balance of the Quinine now. I would pay $100. for 5 bottles of it for my company today if I could get it. It could be sold here for $50. pr bottle if one had it & were allowed to sell it to citizens. Our men need it sadly, & the Surgeon is out again, though he had about 40 bottles only a few days ago. I hope that I sent for will arrive soon. I only got some in *one letter*.

. . . .

Camp 28th Wis. Vol. Inf.,
Pine Bluff, Arkansas, Sept. 19, 1864

. . . .

I think there is no danger of *promotion* ever keeping me from you. There is probably "none of that for me."

Carrie, don't *ever again* say you don't care *how* they settle this war with the southern traitors — at least *not to me*. Rather than [have] it settled any way except by making the rebels submit to the laws, & return the seceded states to the Union, I would see the war last twenty years — yes, a lifetime, & while my poor life lasted I would serve my country rather than see her dishonored by yielding to the demands of the wicked crew. I expect to serve no longer than my three years, but the day that sees *such* a peace as northern Copperhead would make, if that day ever comes, then those who have served in the field fighting for a continuation of our liberties, have no country worth claiming. Let me "fight the thing out" ere that comes. I'm not much of a patriot, but I want to see the rebels whipped into submission, & *I want to help whip them.*

I hope the $100. has come to hand before this. You must buy things to make you & the little ones comfortable, if it takes all I earn while I'm gone. Get whatever you need, my own, for you'll have to get lots of things *for me* when I get home, so you must get yours now. I know you will be prudent & careful, dearest, so I think I can trust you with what little I save — & it is not much, is it?

. . . .

September 20. 9 P.M. We have had a pleasant day — pretty warm after the sun got up — cool morning & night. Lt. Alvord is quite unwell — a billious attack I think. Have been writing in my office & reading papers nearly all day. How terribly the 36th has suffered since it went out last May. Five field officers killed & wounded already, with dozens of line officers & nearly all its men! They have had a rough time, sure.

Tell Mrs. Fritsinger, if you think best, that I can't learn as her husband left any word for his family. The attendants in the hospital seem to remember nothing about it, & I couldn't be with him & be miles away with my company at the same time. I regret that it is so.

Sept. 21, 1 ½ P.M.

There, I've just been to dinner — shall I tell you what we had? Well, here's the bill of fare: Beef Soup — Boiled beef, boiled ham, potatoes boiled, tomatoes raw & cooked, corn bread, wheat bread, biscuit, pickled peaches, pickled cucumbers, rice, milk, coffee — how does that suit you — I forgot to mention *Grape Pie* for dessert. I reckon we'll *have a change* if we ever go on a long march.

. . . .

Sept. 22, 6 A.M. Marriages between Union officers or soldiers and southern ladies are quite frequent here. From what I have seen I should suppose many of them are "for three years unless sooner discharged." Quite a number of "wives" have been left behind by soldiers who have gone home, and very likely many of them will never see their "husbands" again, though some of them are in a condition to need a husbands attentions. Last night Lt. Jenkins of the 5th Kansas & a Miss Keeler were married. He is a rough, hard case, and if she don't rue the day in less than a twelve-month, then I lose my guess. She is said to be a very fine girl. Some of the matches made here seem to be happy enough, & both officers & soldiers take their southern brides home with them — but "excuse me" from any such match — even if I were a single young man. "A northern girl for me" every time, for all anything I have seen in "Dixie."

O, how I wish I had that quinine here! Our boys do have the chills so hard — so many of them are down — and nothing but quinine will break it up in this climate — & it takes big doses too. There's no use talking — *quinine is the thing for ague here.* I'd give $100. for 5 bottles today. If you have sent those four bottles get a couple more & send ¼ or ⅓ of a bottle in a letter till it is all sent — we shall need it.

There, it is breakfast time — I'll tell you what we have
when I get back, if I don't eat so much that I can't write.

7 ½ A.M. Sept. 22. Back from breakfast. We had broiled
beef steak, broiled Ham, Wheat bread, corn bread (hot) warm
biscuit, batter cakes, with nice fresh butter, coffee & a glass
of milk, Isn't that good enough for a *"common Infantry Captain?"* ———— It is pleasant this morning — not cold as
yesterday morning — but oh, how dusty — the air is full of
it — we breathe dust, eat dust, drink dust, & live in dust all
the day — if it would only rain & wash the air & lay the
dust, how welcome the falling drops would be!

Well I must quit writing & go to the hospital, & from there
to the company & see how the boys get along. I've got me a
good colored servant now — "Harry" by name — a boy
about 20 years old.

. . . .

Sept. 24th.

Was up at 5 yesterday morning — went up to hospital & to
the company before breakfast. At 8 I mounted my "gallant
steed" & marched the regiment to the scene of the execution
on the opposite side of the river. *As usual* the 28th was the first
regiment on the ground. The troops formed a square about the
gallows. I'll not trouble you with the details — the man didn't
flinch — was brave to the last — & was executed about half
past 9 o'clock, A.M. I don't wish to be compelled to witness
any more executions.

. . . .

Sunday, Oct. 2.

I today rec'd from Little Rock *a furlough for George Osborn* — & he has been dead more than 5 weeks! Aint it a
shame that things go so?

. . . .

Pine Bluff, Ark., Oct. 4, 1864.

. . . .

No, dearest, I am thankful that I do not get *homesick* — if I did I should suffer terribly. If a man *wants to die here*, let him get *homesick*. I suppose some men can't help it. I hope I never shall contract that disease here — it would certainly diminish my chances of getting home. But I do wish many times I could see you and the little ones — oh, how often I wish it?

. . . .

Oct. 4, afternoon.

. . . .

We have a report from Little Rock that Price has been whipped by our army, & Marmaduke killed, the rebels losing heavily in prisoners & artillery.[32] I don't know how true it may be, but hope it is all so. If it is, there is less danger of the enemy attacking us here — so we will hope it is so.

. . . .

Pine Bluff, Ark., Oct. 12, 1864.

. . . .

The *Rebs* that were hovering around Pine Bluff are all gone — there are none of any account this side the Saline river. A large Cavalry force came here last week, & went out on a scout. The *rebs* fell back before them & avoided a fight. As far as a fight goes we are as safe here as in Wisconsin — just about —

I am so sorry that quinine is not here — it does take so long to get anything here from home. If I had had it all sent by mail I might have got part of it. Well, we did the best we could.

. . . .

Pine Bluff, Oct. 20, 1864.

. . . .

On Tuesday I rec'd from Brig. Gen. Clayton an order to take command of the regiment — so I am, *pro tem*, the *big bug*! Shall be able to go to work by Saturday or Monday I think.

Feller & his brother arrived here Saturday night. I rec'd by them my coat, 4 bots. Quinine, 3 H'd'kfs, the locket & the two-cent piece — for all of which, dear one, I think you so much . . . .

Head Quarters 28th, Wis. Vols.
Pine Bluff, Oct. 22, 1864.

. . . . I am very much better — am able to be on duty again, and am still in command of the 28th. Shall probably remain in command for some little time — perhaps all the fall and winter. The weather is very fine yet, & seems likely to continue so. The river is getting lower and lower, so that no boats are arriving — & we may possibly have none for six weeks or two months to come. Our mails will probably come overland if at all . . . .

H'd Qrs. 28th Wis. Vol. Inf.
Pine Bluff, Ark., Oct. 23,/64.

. . . .

I still command the 28th. Am going to have dress parade at 5 o'clock — in about half an hour . . . .

There is the call for dress parade, so I must get on my "good clothes," sash, belt and sword, and place myself in position to command the parade.

7 P.M. Well, we had a nice dress parade. Quite a large number of spectators were present to witness it. I put the boys through the manual of arms & they did well. Among the

spectators were Mr. & Mrs. Mills, (the people I board with) accompanied by three young ladies. Two of them, Miss Mollie Tisdale & Miss *Lamb* Key, (isn't that last a funny name for a girl?) I had met yesterday at the house. Who do you think the other was? No one but "my cousin," Miss Ruth Stevens! I had not met her before since my return to the regiment from Wis. Mr. Mills, after the parade was dismissed, invited myself & two other officers to go home with him, and I had the happiness to escort Miss Ruth. She was very agreeable. This is the first time I have walked with a lady in Dixie. *Now I've got started*, you see! *Driven to it by your desperate flirting with Hurlbut & those fellows! Aren't you mighty sorry?*

Miss Ruth says she thinks I "wasn't mightily pleased with my "relations," or I would have called again before now — which is, perhaps, *more than half true*! However, I think I shall call upon her now, some of these days.

General Clayton, with an escort, has gone to Little Rock today — on business, I suppose. He went overland. Hope we will have a mail when the party returns.

. . . .

Oct. 25th.

One year ago today I was at Helena, having gone there on business for the regiment. One year ago today the rebels 3,600 strong, under Marmaduke, attacked Col. Clayton with his 600 heroes at Pine Bluff, and got most *beautifully whipped.*

Today we have had some rain, which has laid the dust. It has been a very quiet day. I am General Officer of the Day, and have a dark, wet ride before me at 12 o'clock tonight. Wish I could postpone it till some bright, pleasant night!

There is a report in town today from Monticello *via "Grape Vine telegraph,"* that we have been badly whipped at Richmond. I hardly believe it can be true — *hope not.*

Oct. 26

Last night it rained very hard & we had a heavy wind when I went to bed. I directed the guard to call me at midnight, so that I could go on my ride. It rained & blew very hard still when I was called, so I left orders to call me at 2 o'clock & went to bed again. At 2 o'clock it rained still — so I laid quiet for 15 or 20 minutes, and all at once it stopped raining — so up I got, went & got my horse & off I went. It was dark, muddy & slippery, but I didn't have any rain while visiting the outposts, and got back just before daylight, well covered with mud — went to bed & had a good snooze before breakfast — after which it rained again. Wasn't I lucky? It cleared off again before I went out at noon — so I escaped the rain, though I found plenty of mud. The party out repairing the telegraph between here & Little Rock were attacked yesterday, & one man of the 13th Ill. Cavalry was killed. A Cavalry scout has gone out that way today to hunt for the rebels. Hope they will find them.

Pine Bluff, Ark., Oct. 28, 1864.

I've something to tell you once more. Will you believe it? We got a mail — a large one — at eight o'clock last night, by train overland from Little Rock. I rec'd 4 letters from you, dated *Sept. 14!* Oct. 1,3, & *6 - 11.* Also 1 from Homer dated Oct 11. We had had no mail for nearly 3 weeks, and this one was very welcome, I assure you . . . .

Pine Bluff, Ark., Nov. 8th., 1864.

. . . .

Election passed off quietly to-day. Co. "C." polled 44 votes — *all for Lincoln.* The Regt. gives about 350 majority for

"old Abe." There were a few McClellan votes — about 35 I
think.

. . . .

**Headquarters 28th Wis. Vol. Inf.,
Pine Bluff, Ark., Nov. 18, 1864.**

. . . . We have news by Telegraph that Sherman has burnt
Atlanta & gone off in the direction of Charleston — . Also that
Illinois has given Lincoln 30,000 majority. Shall wonder if it
is true or not till I hear again.

I have been commanding the regiment just one month today.
Don't think much of having the *responsibility* without the *rank*
of field officer, though the *honor* may be something. I think
Gen. Clayton is perfectly satisfied with the manner in which I
have discharged the duties of regimental commander thus far
— hope I shall have no more serious trouble than I have had
for the past 30 days. I don't believe there is an infantry regiment at the post, better managed & cared for than the 28th (—
"though I say it as shouldn't!") and I know we have a better
reputation for orderly conduct than any regiment that ever was
here - either Union or rebel. The citizens nearly all dislike to
have us leave — they think ours a "model regiment."

I have been reading "Casey's Tactics" so hard for a few days
that I can't write — my noodle is too full of "By Battalion in
mass on third battalion," "deploy column," "Forward on the
center in four ranks to form square," & such like — I believe
I'm getting my little brain mixed — *if I have any!*

. . . .

**H'd Qrs. 28th. Wis. Vol. Inf.,
Pine Bluff, Ark., Nov. 24, 1864.**

This is Thanksgiving Day, & I have been thinking how
much I would like to be at home with you & the rest of "our

folks." Not much has been going on with us today. Had an inspection this forenoon by Gen. Steele's Inspector General. I have been around the lines once, & have to go again at twelve o'clock to-night. Chaplain Roseborough of the 126th Ill. delivers an address at the Presbyterian church this evening, but as I wish to get a good sleep before my ride I do not attend.

The boat from Little Rock did bring a small mail last night. I rec'd two letters from you, dated Nov. 7 & 10 - & "Sentinels" as late as the 9th. I also rec'd a letter from Homer.

Carrie, I don't see but you will have to draw a part of that money from Chadbourne, for I don't see as we are going to be paid off very soon, and you will need the money. I may have to send for some for all I know — I don't see how we officers are going to live if we are only paid once in six months. It is really too bad — but I suppose the gov't does as well as possible, & it can't be helped.

. . . .

Today has been a delightful day — so much warmer than for several days past. The warm sunshine has invited me out several times. I shall not have so cold a ride tonight as I had last Sunday night.

I send $12. which George Osborn had when he died. You will please send word to Mr. Osborn that you have it, & pay it over to him when he calls for it. Tell him that George had been paid no bounty since he came here, though $40. was due last pay-day. The pay-master had not funds enough to pay the bounties due recruits — so he paid none. George had only the $12. when he died. I don't remember now how much, if any, he sent home after pay-day, but the list I sent to Mr. Simmonds will show whether there was any or not — & if so how much. I wrote to Mr. Osborn about some accounts I found in George's pocket book. I have not yet been able to collect them. — Boys in the company have since told me that the accounts belonged to John Hollenbeck, who was discharged — that he left them with George to be collected. Please tell Mr. Osborn this. Perhaps he can see Hollenbeck & find out about it. Hollenbeck is a son of Mrs. Lyman Annis who lives above Monterey. Pay the money to Mr. Osborn as soon as you can. I sent Georges clothes home by express — all except those he was buried in — & wrote Mr. Osborn.

The things were not sent as soon as they should have been — but boats would carry nothing but government freight when the river was so low. The medicines that Mrs. Osborn sent to George were received by Lieut. Alvord I think — he being in command of the company. *I* did not receive them. You will please read so much of the letter as relates to these things to Mr. or Mrs. Osborn.

Hoping you have had a pleasant Thanksgiving — sending kind regards to all — and with love & kisses for my dear ones at home, I'll to bed & rest a while before my "grand rounds."
. . . .

Headquarters 28th Wis. Vol. Inf., Pine Bluff, Ark., Nov. 27, 1864.

. . . .

No, my dear little wife, I do not draw Colonel's pay while commanding the reg't. — on the contrary I draw $10. per month *less than if I were commanding a company. Lieut. Alvord gets the same pay now that I do —* he commanding a *company —* I a *regiment!*

My company was relieved from duty at the saw mill this afternoon — preparatory to leaving, I presume. Well, if we are going I don't care how soon we go — but hope they will send us by river instead of by land, for 'twould be a terribly hard march at this time.

No sings of a paymaster yet. Why don't he come? We do all need our pay so much. How we are going to live when we get to Little Rock I don't know, I'm sure.

You ask what supplies we have received from the Sanitary

Commission. None of the supplies which have been shipped
direct to the regiment have ever reached us — at least I am so
informed by Surgeon Smith who has had charge of supplies
from the San. Com.

Last May he received a small amount of *crackers* and *dried
fruit,* and this fall *3 or 4 barrels each* of *Potatoes, Onions, &
Pickles.* These, he tells me, are all that the regiment has received this year. The Post Surgeon, has, however, rec'd quite
an amount of sanitary stores, which have been used in the Post
Hospital, and as a small number of our sick have been there,
we have been benefitted thereby to some extent. Supplies sent
direct to a regiment fall into the hands of agents of the commission along the river, and go into the general store of supplies — at least that is my impression.

Nov. 28. All well this morning. No boat & no news. . . .

**H'd Qrs. 28th. Wis. Vol. Inf.,
Little Rock, Ark., Dec 4/64**

Well, we have finally got here! Last Tuesday at 11 A.M. we
rec'd orders to march next morning at 8 for Little Rock. At
that time I was having a fine shake, which was followed by a
decidedly uncomfortable fever, but I managed to get everything ready, and at the appointed time had my regiment in line,
ready to move. We were escorted out of Pine Bluff by the
remnant of the 1st Indiana Cavalry — soldiers whom we are
proud to have served with, as we have for nearly two years
past.

Brig. Gen. Clayton sent to me, the evening previous to our
departure, an address to the officers and men of the regiment,
which is highly complimentary to us. I shall try and preserve it
for myself, and send it home for safe keeping.

Leaving Pine Bluff we marched 18 miles on Wednesday,
bivouacing for the night at a point called Rock Spring. Started
at daylight on Thursday, marching 19 miles that day. We
reached Little Rock a little before noon on Friday. Brig. Gen.

Salomon & Staff came out about two miles to meet us. The reg't. gave him three rousing cheers. As we approached the town the Brigade Band met us & escorted us to the camp of the 9th Wis., where we were treated very kindly — the soldiers being furnished with coffee & lunch by the soldiers of the 9th., & the officers with a very good dinner — after which we gave "three times three" for the 9th Wisconsin, & were then escorted by the band through the city to our present location. Were we not very highly honored? We were indeed, I think. I felt proud of being at the head, even for a time, of an organization which is as highly thought of as the old 28th. It rained for an hour or two Friday morning, & the boys had got wet, but it cleared off before we got in, & we had a very pleasant time. I felt better than I expected, after my chills — I had one the first night out, and got no sleep, but stood the march pretty well, as I had a horse to ride. Wasn't I lucky?

The barracks we now occupy are not half large enough for our reg't — the buildings have no doors or windows — only places for them. We are at work building new building, for which we have to haul logs about four miles. It makes a great deal of work.

. . . .

Little Rock, Arkansas Dec. 8th, 1864.

I haven't had time to write since my last — have been very busy trying to take care of the reg't. & men. Col. Gray is released from arrest, and has assumed command of the regiment once more — taking a load from my shoulders, of which I am heartily glad. I am once more in command of "C" Co. Lieut. Alvord is sick, though not very seriously, and is in officer's hospital. Our regiment is worse situated than for a long time before. The quarters we occupy are not half large enough — there is not a window or door in the whole camp — everything is open, and the weather has suddenly become freezing cold. Add to all this the fact that the men packed their clothing, except what they wore on the march, (and it was warm at the time we left Pine Bluff.) & left it to come on the boat, which has not yet arrived, and you can guess that they suffer from cold. Another feather still is to be added to the load — we haven't the means to supply the reg't. with wood enough, as it has to be hauled some 3 or 4 miles. O, we suffer!

It is now 4 P.M. I am warm now for the first time since last evening. I laid & shivered with the cold all night — well, I was better off than many of the men, so I ought not to complain.

If we could only have remained at the Bluff this winter I'd have been glad. If we were enduring this on a march, or could see that our removal from Pine Bluff to this place was for the good of the service, we would try & not complain — but this all seems to have been done merely to gratify one man's personal feelings — or those of a few men. Well, we are subject to orders, & we'll let it rest at that. The boat with our sick has not arrived. I'm afraid they will suffer before reaching here. . . . I am boarding here at $1. pr day. That is the best I can do here. Have almost starved since coming here. This is one of the meanest places on the footstool, if I am any judge. It will take a month or more, in the dead of winter, to complete our barracks. Till then — I dread to think of it — how many of our men will die from exposure? . . . .

Little Rock, Ark., Dec. 9, 1864.

The note written yesterday I have not been able to mail yet, so I'll inclose another to tell you that we are still situated as before. Last night I managed to sleep warm by keeping on all my clothes. Am Brigade officer of the Day to-day — have not yet visited the pickets — have to go out this P.M. & during the night. The boat with our sick & clothing is aground ten miles below here — teams have been sent with provisions for the men, & ambulances will probably be sent for the sick. It is so dark here I can't see the lines, & I don't know as you can read this. Hope we will get settled after awhile so that I can write more comfortably. It is cold, disagreeable weather. I was told today that we will not be paid off until the 15th or 20th of Jan'y. I must have some money if it can be got — if you can, please send me $100. by Express. When we are paid I can probably send home a considerable amount. I don't like to use the money which is drawing interest, but cant get along without it as we have everything to buy at big prices. Board of self & servant costs $9. pr week beside extras, and I have to borrow all the time. Am sorry I have to be so *extravagant*, but it is the best I can do. I get no later news. . . . .

Little Rock, Arkansas, December 10th, 1864.

. . . .

Reports, said to be reliable, state that Maj. Gen. Steele is relieved from the command of this Department, & that he is to be succeeded by Gen. Reynolds.[33] Hope it will be an improvement. Everything remains about as usual hereabouts. Lt. Col. Gray was released from arrest last Tuesday & resumed command of the regiment — I have returned to "C" Co. I commanded the regiment just seven weeks. . . .

It is a bright but cold day, but the weather is moderating, I think. Hope it may remain warmer until we get our barracks somewhat advanced. It seems it will be next to impossible to procure glass for windows, or brick for chimneys — but we will get along in some way, I think. No news. . . . .

Jany 7, 1865.

I was at the camp of the regiment this P.M., and while looking over some papers in the desk, found the above letter, written the day before I came into hospital. There is nothing important in it, but I'll forward it, and let it take the place of a better one.

Lt. Alvord is getting along with the quarters, and I shall certainly go over there on Monday to remain — *I think*. The chimney is being built of stone, sticks & mud. We will have no floor but the ground — and that will be pretty damp till the fire dries it out. — Very pleasant to-day.

. . . .

Officer's Hospital, Little Rock, Dec. 13, 1864.

Don't be frightened because I write you from hospital. I am here because I had no half way comfortable place in camp to stay & nurse my chills & fever — am not seriously ill, but feel so *decidedly mean* that they wanted to get me out of camp, I suppose, so the Doctor sent me here last Sunday — 11th. I would have written you sooner, but the big doses of quinine &c. which I have taken keep my head in a continual whirl. Dr. Miller says he shall keep me here only a week or ten days. Dr. Smith sent me here to keep me from getting down sick — as I think I should have done if I had remained in camp. Lt. Alvord is still here — will go to the reg't in a couple of days if he has no more chills — in the mean time Co. C. is without an officer.

It costs me $1.30 per day here for myself & servant — which amount will be stopped from my pay whenever we are paid off — *if that ever happens again.*

I rec'd a letter from you the day I came here — a long nice one of 3 sheets, dated Nov. 27.

I had written you for money, but shall have to recall the request if it is placed where you can't get it at present. I heard yesterday that we *may* be paid off soon, but have heard so so many times that I put no faith in the rumor. Never mind, dearest, better times will come by and by — but really it is sometimes very humiliating to be entirely out of money — ain't it

. . . .

Officer's Hospital, Little Rock, Dec 14/64.

I wrote yesterday to let you know how I was. Today is my well day, and I feel a great deal better. I have a hard cold, & am *dosing* for it. Hope not to have any more chills. If there was any chance to get home I should improve it — but there is not. I'm not sick enough to get a "surgeon's certificate," and that's the only way a man can get away now. If I could in any manner get my resignation accepted, I would do it in a minute, but there's no chance for it now. Never mind — a few months more will finish my "three years of war." I am very comfortably situated here for a man who is not well. Have a pretty fair mattress to sleep on, on an iron cot — white sheets & pillow cases, (! what an idea for a soldier!) woolen blankets, a large room (6 of us in it) with a big fireplace & plenty of wood.

Get up at 7 A.M. — have breakfast half an hour later — baked potatoes, beef-steak, bread & butter, coffee, tea, hash, soda crackers &c. Dinner to-day consisted of Potatoes, cabbage, onions, (boiled & raw) bread & butter, crackers & Pudding — Everything is well cooked. If a man is to be sick down here, this is the place to be.

The building used for Officer's hospital is larger than the main part of the LaBelle House in O——. It was the residence of a wealthy secessionist named Woodruff. He was here when Little Rock fell into our hands, remained & took the oath, but secretly corresponded with rebels & sympathized with them. Some of his letters fell into the hands of the Military authorities & he was banished to rebeldom last winter.

In the room with me there are two captains, beside myself, & three lieutenants. Lt. Alvord rooms across the hall. There are six or seven there.

Yes, darling, I'd be glad to see you, but *not here*, even "if you had no children." If you were here now I'd be in a pretty fix, with no money, & no place to borrow enough to pay a week's board. I'd have a good time paying $25. a week *at least* for board for us two! No, dear, wait until I come home, "that's a good girl!"

Am sorry you have to go to Waukesha — but you must get along the best you can. I am sorry to hear that you are so hard up for wood, or have been. I can't collect a cent where I owe it, for the simple reason that no one has been paid, & consequently I have as much money as the rest. I didn't think people would try to impose upon you during my absence; but we'll see *by & by,* dear. How much would our house & lot sell for darling? Had we better stay in Oconomowoc, or go somewhere else? What think you.

. . . .

Officer's Hospital, Little Rock, Ark., Dec 16/64

Am feeling very well this morning — have had no shake since I wrote you. Hope I shall have no more, though the Doctor says he shall keep me here ten days or two weeks longer, so as to be sure I'll have no more shakes. I hate to have my company without an officer, but a *sick* one is of but little account. The weather is a great deal warmer than when I came here, but it will be cold enough in a week or two again, I have no doubt.

My own wife, if I could get money you should have a Christmas present of some kind — but not a dollar is to be had, and no signs of any. It seems too bad, but I don't know as it can be helped. Probably the Army in this Department receives, as much attention as its works entitle it to but that don't help *me* any — nor does it provide for my suffering family at home. Darling, I'm thinking of you all the time, and wondering how you will get along if I'm not paid off this winter? I don't see what we *can* do, for my part, unless we can borrow — and where to apply I really don't know. I have friends enough at home as long as I want nothing of them, but when I would use them, that's another thing. I *hope* I shall come home a *more selfish man* than ever, for I never can make a living unless I am, among such people as we live with. As for clothing, I can get along with what I have, I think, though it is, some of it, rather seedy. I'll make it do in some shape. Ezra Feller is still at Pine Bluff. When he gets here I'll try & find out about the pants & the box, but don't expect to get them. Of course he won't know anything about them. I don't know how the boys at the company are getting along — have not seen one of them since coming here. Gen. Steele had a large party at the "Anthony House" night before last — in honor of *himself* I suppose. I shall not give *mine* at present!

Once more, dear, don't worry about me. You probably hear all sorts of stories of my being in hospital &c., but I'm *not* badly off. I am able to go out doors every day, & have taken a walk this morning. If I was in the regiment instead of here, I should be doing duty with the rest. You shall know if I get really very sick. . . .

Officers Hospital, Little Rock, Ark., Dec. 18, 1864.

Your dear letter of the 7th just came to hand, relieving me from one thing — the fear that you would have *no* money to use this winter. It relieves me to know that Mrs. Gilmore has been able to forward the amound due me.

If you are unable to obtain any money beside this, don't think of sending me a cent — I'll get along some way — perhaps we may be paid off sooner than I think. At any rate I'll borrow and try & get along some way.

. . . .

Gen. Steele left here yesterday. He is to go to Cairo, I believe, & report by letter to the Adjt. Gen. for instructions. Gen. Reynolds has not arrived yet, I think.

. . . .

Officer's Hospital, Little Rock, Ark., Dec. 19, 1864.

Dear Father:

As I am feeling pretty well to-day, and lying around the hospital is dull business, I'll try and write a few words to you. I am not seriously ill, and have not been, but the chills & fever have clung to me so stubbornly for about two months, that the Surgeon thought I had better go to hospital, as I had no comfortable place to stay in our camp. I had my first chill since coming south about the 17th of Oct. The next day I was ordered by Brig. Gen. Clayton to take command of the regiment, Lt. Col. Gray having been placed in arrest. I was in command from that time until Dec. 6th, when Lt. Col. Gray was released from arrest and resumed command of the regiment. I had been having chills & fever off and on for the seven weeks, and as long as I was at the head of the regiment, and could keep around, I was bound to do so. On the 29th of November I received orders to have my regiment ready to leave Pine Bluff for Little Rock at 8 A.M. next day. It was short notice, and I was down with a fever, but went to work, and we were ready on time. We marched to this place in a little over two days. The distance on this side of the river is 45 miles. I had chills both nights we were out, but as I had a horse to ride I managed to get through, though it was hard work. We hated to leave Pine Bluff, for we were very comfortably situated there, having nice winter quarters &c. Here we have some little huts without doors, or windows, and most of them without floors — and hardly room in them for the men to lie down. The cold weather which came on at the time we came here rendered it very uncomfortable for us all.

Brig. Gen. Clayton, in an address to the regiment, complimented us very highly, upon our leaving Pine Bluff. He disliked to let us go. Here we had a flattering reception. Gen. Salomon & Staff came out to meet us, and we were escorted through the city to camp by the brigade band — a Milwaukee band, by the way.

The regiment had a right to feel highly honored, and I felt a little proud of being at its head upon that occasion.

They are now building new barracks. I selected the ground and got the work well started while I was in command. We will have a pleasant camp, I think. I came into the hospital on the 11th. Shall be out again in a few days. Have had no chill for 5 days. The chills we get here are as much worse than Wisconsin ague as you can think. They just *use me up.*

Of course you have seen the result of the election in the 28th. Didn't we do pretty near the *clean thing?* A majority of about 400 for Lincoln we think was pretty good.

The third year of our term of service is pretty well started. Whatever is left of us will probably be home in ten months longer. I wish I could think the war would be over by that time, but I can hardly see it so.

. . . .

Officer's Hospital, Little Rock, Ark., Dec. 24, 1864.

My darling Carrie:

To-day & to-night you are as busy as you can be, I suppose, with your Christmas Tree and other holiday arrangements for the children, but not too busy, I know, to think of me and wish I could be with you to see and to help, as I am wishing I could be, even if only for a day. I hope the work and exposure will not make you entirely down sick, as I fear, for what would or could you do if you were? Be very careful, darling, for I'm sure there is necessity for care, your health is and has for so long been so bad.

Here I have done but little but sit about and read all day, and can do nothing else this evening except sit & think of my own wife and our little ones, and all our friends at home, and wish them a Merry Christmas. To-morrow we are to have a Christmas dinner at our hospital — don't know as it will be anything extra, and don't care, so long as my loved ones cannot share it with me. I have thought I would *hang up my stocking* tonight, for I feel almost certain I should get something in it — say a dose of pills or a quinine powder! I'll think of it and make up my mind before bed-time.

. . . . Some boats left here yesterday or the day before for

Fort Smith. Report says that that post is to be evacuated, & that the boats have gone to bring down the troops and government property there. I can hardly believe that we are to abandon that point, notwithstanding officers say it is so, I can't see the object — but probably the authorities can.

Gen. Gilmore is here with Gen. Reynolds.[34] I understand that he received a dispatch night before last from Duvall's Bluff, stating that Sherman had captured Savannah — good news — *if true* — as I hope it will prove to be.

Lt. Col. Drake of the 36th Iowa has been promoted to Brigadier General for bravery at the Mark's Mills fight, between here & Camden last spring, where he was in command of a brigade escorting a large train of several hundred wagons to Little Rock or Pine Bluff, and, allowing his command to get stretched over 5 or 6 miles of bad road, was attacked by the rebels, and badly whipped, losing the entire train (6 mules with each wagon) and a large portion of his men. If it had been a captain in command with our third the force, & he had lost the train under the same circumstances, he would have been dismissed the service before now. I hope the Senate will refuse to confirm the appointment, for those who have served with Lt. Col. Drake do not consider him fit for the position.

I am getting all right now. I think I shall go back to the regiment the first of next week — then look out for breakers, as Lt. Col. Gray has been misusing me lately.

. . . .

Little Rock, Ark., Dec. 25/64.

Merry Christmas, dearest! and a right Merry one may it be to you all at home. Here it is anything else, almost. It is a dull, dreary, gloomy, solemn, drizzly Sunday, compelling one to have the blues whether he will or no. I'm glad I'm not to spend another one in the army.

We have had enough to eat here at the hospital, and that

which is good enough. Shall I tell you what we had for dinner? The doctor got up a good one in honor of the day. We had roast pig, chicken, mashed potatoes, raw onions, cold slaw, boiled cabbage, kraut, parsnips, Jelly, Apple-pie, mince pie (both kinds horrible) coffee, & bread and butter. Wasn't that good enough?

I am improving, but the doctor thinks I'm not quite ready to go to the regiment, as I would have no comfortable place to stay, so I must stay here a few days longer. I hope you are not having as dreary a day at home. How I want to be with you to-day — but it's no use wishing *that*. Shall be there a year from now, — that's one comfort.

The boys at the company are mostly well, I believe. No news here. . . . .

Officer's Hospital, Little Rock, Dec. 28, 1864.

I haven't a word to write — only to tell you that I am still gaining ground, and have had no more shakes, though the doctor protests that I shall not go to the regiment until next week — the more particularly as my *house* is not yet finished. I want to get back to the Reg't., and shall probably do so the first of next week. I feel better than I have for three months, but expect to get the chills again when I get on picket & other duty which will keep me out nights.

The boys are nearly all well, I hear, but the Lieut. don't carry himself very straight, I am told. I have been down town twice since coming to hospital, but have not been over as far as the regiment.

Lt. Col. Gray called to see me a day or two ago. He has made a requisition for conscripts enough to fill up the regiment, so that he can be mustered as Colonel. He says Capt. Williams can't be a field officer in the regiment with him, and intimated that if the regiment should be filled, he should have me promoted to Major. "I hear ducks!" I have often hear their "quack! quack!" before now. I'll trust a great deal to what he said — *only I won't!*

. . . .

P.S. About selling the house I don't know what to say. $800. is not as much as it cost me — for "greenbacks" are not *gold.* At the rate of gold now, it cost me about the worth of $1,000 in "Greenbacks," besides the improvements. Still if you had any place to go it might be as well to sell it, perhaps — though I can't tell what I shall do, or where I shall go after next fall. I don't feel very much attached to Oconomowoc, though I have lots of *"fair weather friends"* there. Still, I think it would be better to keep the place than sell for $800. & then pay $100. or more for rent, moving, & fitting up another house — if you stay in O—— till I get home. I shall, however, be satisfied if you think otherwise & conclude to sell. If I *knew* that gold would be down to $1.50, even then $900. in "Greenbacks" would no more than pay what it has cost us, counting improvements & interest.

. . . .

Little Rock, Dec. 30, 1864.

. . . .

I yesterday received your letter of the 18th., with my holiday present. It is a *sweet* little neck tie — I think it will be long enough, though I have not tried it on. Thank you, love, for it. I think I'll hang up my stocking tomorrow night, & hire my boy to put the neck-tie in it, *unknown to me!* then I'll have a nice *New Year's present!* At any rate I shall not wear it till New Year's day — shall consider it a present *then.*

Isn't the news from Sherman and Thomas *glorious!* Hood cleaned out — routed — & sixty pieces of his artillery captured — Ft. McAllister and Savannah ours, with lots of guns & cotton — *hurrah! Hit 'em again!*[35]

How I'd like to participate in some of the glory of it all. I consider it no honor to belong to this army, or to be an officer in the 28th. I wish I was out of it. We may have a chance to redeem our character the next spring.

I heard a rumor yesterday that we will be paid off about the middle of January — don't know how true it is — & don't believe it — though I wish it might be true.

. . . .

Little Rock, Arkansas, Sunday, Jan'y 1st 1865.

Wouldn't you like a good long letter for a New Year's present? I'm going to try and fill this *small* sheet, hoping you will have time & patience to read it all, for I would hate to spend all the time necessary for filling up the letter, and then have it go for naught.

First let me tell you how I have spent the day. To commence with I rose at 7 o'clock — after breakfast went down to Brigade Head-quarters in company with Capt. Towne of the 126th. Ill. who is sick here. After chatting with Col. Mackey a short time we all went down to Presbyterian Church where we heard a passable sermon. After dinner I went down town to the scene of a fire which occurred early this morning. From there I went up to our new camp, Co. C having moved into their new quarters there yesterday. Found the boys mostly well, though Dodge, Baxter & Briggs are in hospital. I did not see them as the hospital is some distance off, and I did not feel able to go there. Had a visit with Lieut. Alvord and the men and came back to camp — by which time supper was ready, after which I sat a little while with the officers in my room, then a little while with Doctor Miller, and *then commenced* this letter — when will I get it done, think you?

The Lieut. has done nothing of any account to our quarters since I came to hospital, but promised me today that he will try

& finish it up tomorrow & next day. I hope he will, for I want
to get there, for there I am needed — but I don't want to go
until I can have a comfortable place to lie down.

. . . .

Lieut. Col. Gray is to be tried. The order for the court is
issued, and the court will meet next Thursday, I believe. Brig.
Gen. Bussey is President of the court, and no officer is of
lower grade than Lieut Colonel.[36] When the time comes I shall
be in command of the regiment again, I suppose, if I am there.
Perhaps that will be better than being on picket.

. . . .

How different the holidays seem here from what they do at
home. There peacefully you go about your enjoyments and
your duties. Here one is reminded by everything he sees that
he is away from home — that he is near, if not among enemies.
The iron bed-steads — the sheets & pillow cases are all
marked "Hosp. Dept. U.S.A." Almost every one you see has
on the "blue coat & breeches" denoting that he is one of
"Lincoln's boys." You are surrounded by muskets, revolvers
& sabres, while from every breast work the "grim dogs of
war" poke out their ugly noses, standing ready to vomit death
upon the first approaching enemy. The roll of drums may be
heard almost any hour of the day, and the sound of bugles
marks each passing hour. We work, and write, and work, and
write, and all our work reminds us of our position, & that we
are taking care of military men & military property. When will
this end? Who can tell? The year just passed has been fruitful
of victories — successes of our arms, while some reverses for
us have to be recorded. But taking it all in all have we not
much to cheer us? Atlanta is ours! Sherman and his heroic
army — an army of heroes! — have marched through the heart
of Georgia, and Savannah lies beneath the folds of the good
old flag. Hood has been terribly whipped in Tennessee, & his

rebel crew are scattered — where? Grant & Sherman can now unite their armies at any time — and with *such* armies what glorious deeds may not be done? What we may do during the present year we can only conjecture — but I think we ought to do much. It may be that our little army may do something this year, though it has accomplished very little during the last 12 months. It seems probable now that an expedition will be fitted out and start from here for the south west about the first of March — though that is all guesswork. It will be better for us all to go on a campaign than for us to remain here in camp during the coming summer. I hope that if we start we shall accomplish something worth telling of when we get home — something that will tell towards putting down the rebellion & closing up this terrible war. General Reynolds will not prove such an officer as General Steele, we think here — we hope not. He has commenced by removing from their positions several officers. He saw a couple of officers in the street intoxicated. He immediately dismissed them from the service of the United States. He has also instituted other reforms, and has given "notice to quit" to several rebel citizens whom General Steele had permitted to remain in the city. If he will only keep on in the same way, he may be able to accomplish something in the "Department of Arkansas." Of course we shall have many things to grumble at — everything will not be done just right — but we hope that he will do much better than his predecessor.

. . . .

Officer's Hospital, Little Rock, Ark., Jan. 8, 1865.

. . . .

Capt. Williams arrived here from Pine Bluff yesterday, having been summoned as a witness at the trial of Lt. Col. Gray, which has not yet come off. I saw him last evening. He is looking & feeling well, and appears to be very confident that Lt. Col. Gray will "go up the spout" — as the *poet* says! He certainly is anxious that that shall be the result, and will probably do all he can to bring it about. I think, however, that when he commenced the thing he forgot the old saying about "glass houses" and throwing stones. (This in relation to officers is all *private* remember.) Insinuations have been whispered in my hearing that he never will be promoted — in fact that if Gray is dismissed, Williams will follow him — and if Gray beats him, wo unto thee, Williams! The officers of the regiment have expressed themselves against his promotion in either event. I'm too modest to suppose they want me for a field officer, and wonder who the lucky one will be, if any promotion takes place. Enough of this.

A report reached the hospital last evening that two rebel regiments had come in and given themselves up. I doubt it, but it may prove true. If so, it will probably be only the beginning of such movements on the part of the defeated and discouraged men who four years ago threw off their allegiance to the government represented by our victorious "stars and stripes."

Last evening, by invitation of Dr. Miller, I went with him to the theatre — and wasn't I sorry? A more beggerly attempt at acting I have not seen — this side of Pine Bluff! The singing was horrible, and I was pleased to notice that the greater part of the house was filled with — empty benches! the other, (there are two *theatres* here,) is said to be poorer than the one we attended. What can it be?!

. . . .

Little Rock, Ark., Jan'y 12, 1865.

I left the hospital yesterday morning & returned to the regiment. Found Lt. Alvord having the ague. Briggs is very sick in the hospital again. Dodge is getting pretty nearly well. Baxter is worse again — I fear he will never be any better. I went up to see him this morning. He looks bad. The men in camp are suffering from want of wood. Our teams are in poor condition — our Q.M. is drunk a good share of the time, & as there is a great deal of hauling to do, & the business not properly attended to, wood is scarce. I have had none since yesterday morning, except what the "contraband" could pick up. Hope to get a lot tomorrow. Arrangements have been made so that we officers who are out of money can draw rations & have them charged to us & stopped from our pay. It is great bother to get our provisions so, but better than to go hungry. We get Flour, meat, coffee, sugar, beans, rice, vinegar, salt, candles & soap. If we want anything else we have to buy it — if we can! I drew a months rations for myself, Lt. Alvord & our servants today. They cost us $37.$^{20}/_{100}$ — then everything else is to be bought. Last night was very cold — froze hard. I couldn't get warm, & had no wood for a fire. The ground is wet & cold, & as it is our only floor, it is rather uncomfortable. The chimney to my shanty is built of stones & old bricks about four feet of the way up, then finished off with sticks. The window sash is of soldier's manufacture, as is all the rest of the house & trimmings. Wish you could look in and see us.

. . . .

Camp 28th. Wis. Inf.
Little Rock, Jan. 17, 1865.

Yours of Dec. 26th by express with the money ($100.) was received yesterday. Thank you, darling! — but I'm afraid you need it worse than I do and am half inclined to send it home again — and would if I could see my way through, so as to get along in some way.

. . . .

Camp 28th. Wis. Inf.
Little Rock, Jan. 20, 1865.
Jan'y. 21.

I went so far as to date this last evening, when I was called upon to make some reports, which occupied me till nearly bed-time — so the letter failed to get written. I commence again this morning, but can't promise to write a long letter, for I may be interrupted at any moment.

First: Lt. Col. Gray came in a few minutes ago & said he had rec'd an intimation this morning that our brigade would march to-day for some where — *where* I could not learn. He had rec'd no *orders*. I can't guess in which direction we will move, if we move at all. No one in the regiment knows, I think. I will try & keep this open till we are about to leave & see if I can find out.

I was on duty yesterday. Started out at about day-light — went over the river with 50 men, took charge of a train of sixty 6-mule wagons & went into the country to haul wood for steamboats. Returned at 4 ½ P.M. Had a *very* fine day, & not very hard work.

. . . .

What an amount of suffering there is among the refugees about here. Yesterday I saw in the woods, on my way out, a *shed* — a roof set up on poles, merely, where, with bed quilts hung up on three sides to keep out the wind, & a fire built on the other side, were living five or six women with nearly a dozen children, from the babe to girls of eleven or twelve, & three or four men — their blankets & beds lying on the ground, & no household goods or conveniences at all, scarcely. Only think! little ones like our darlings, — our Lulu & Mary — living in this style — & women, like my own wife! It is terrible! Dirty they can hardly help being, under such circumstances — and many of them were ragged enough, & half barefooted. I thank my God that *we* lived not in the south, to suffer as these people suffer — to be the victims of this terrible rebellion. I had far rather die battling for my country, knowing you are no worse off then you are. People living at the north have no idea of what misery & destitution is existing here.

Not a word of news. We hope to hear soon further glad tidings from Sherman and his gallant army. How I wish the 28th. was there *to share in their labors & their honors*.

. . . .

3 P.M. We march tomorrow at 9 A.M. I have no idea where we are going — can find out nothing — will write at every oportunity. Good bye.

Little Rock, Ark., Jan'y 21, 1865, 9 P.M.

We are nearly packed up for the march — that is, as far as we can tonight. We take but little baggage — only our blankets & a change of underclothes, socks, handkerchiefs, towels &c. Four of us (officers of Cos "G" & "C", pack our clothing in one carpet sack. The officers of three companies mess together, as we cannot take a mess chest for each Co. Co. K. is detached. Co. F. is without an officer, so it is divided up among the other eight companies — so we go with eight companies, as an odd one is much in the way — or out of the way — in battalion movements. I go with about 35 men. Corp. Jacobson, Baxter, Briggs, Cole, Dodge, Stinson, Parish, Hinkley, Kinne, Palmer, Tom Carr, Kimball, Lillie, Lewis & McIalwain remain here. I heard to-night that we would probably go to Pine Bluff, & thence on to the south or south west. I'll write as soon and as often as possible. The object of our expedition I know nothing of, and cannot learn — shall find out, I expect. This is a drizzly, dreary night. I expect it will rain now, as we are going to march.

. . . .

Pine Bluff, Ark., Jany 25, 1865.

We left Little Rock Sunday (22) at 11 A.M. Reached here at 11 ½ AM to-day. I came in in advance of the reg't. They reached here at 2 P.M. I hear we are to leave here at 6 A.M. tomorrow. It commenced snowing at noon the day we left, & we have had a rough time, I assure you, — mud, wet feet, freezing cold nights & all that. I have only time to say I am well. — have stood it first rate thus far — had to get me some boots & Gloves here, & other things. No news.

Pleasant today, but cold.

Pine Bluff, Ark., Jany 25, 1865,

I wrote just a line to-day to announce my arrival here. We had a rough time coming here — and probably shall have more of the same sort before getting back. Mr. Mills people seemed much pleased to see me — I dined with them — had one more good meal. I have had wet, cold, half-frozen feet all along the road, as my boots leaked & all that — my feet were as wet as [ ]. Here I got a pair of boots & pair of gloves — they cost me $23! but I was compelled to buy them or suffer. I bo't a pair of gloves at the Rock when we started, which cost $3 ½. They are worn out! I bought a new sword at Little Rock, paid $7⁵⁰ for it, *Cash*. The gloves & boots I had chg'd.

Mrs. Mills said "Cousin Ruth" wanted to see the 28th officers — so I called for a few minutes. Both Ruth and her mother professed to be pleased to see me. I showed her your & the children's pictures. She called you all *her cousins* — said Lulu's picture was the neatest one she ever saw — said it looked just as if she would scream if the picture was not taken pretty soon. She said you looked like one of her friends here. I ret'd to camp just at dark. We are to be in readiness to march at 6 ½ A.M. tomorrow. Mr. Mills wanted me to stay there, but I couldn't. I wish I could pay him the $60. I owe him for board. I had to buy a bottle of Castor oil, for which I paid $1.50! I have had a couple of boils *on my nose* — they made a beauty of me — are getting better, but with them & my cold my nose is *horrid sore.*

We have with us the 9th Wis. 43 Ill. 33 Iowa, 50 Ind. — all Infantry — the 25th O. Battery & 1st Iowa Cavalry. The 106 & 126 Ill Inf go from here — also part of the 13 Ill Cavalry & part of 1st Ark. Battery.

It seems to be a secret where we are to go, but I think the object is to attract the attention of the enemy so that another force can strike some where else — but that is only conjecture. . . .

Camp 28th. Wis. Inf.,
Mt. Elba, Ark., Jan. 29, 1865.

This Sabbath day, for a wonder, finds us lying in camp, with but little to do. We left Pine Bluff on the 26th (Thursday) at daylight, & reached this place Friday afternoon. After putting down the pontoon Bridge which we brought with us, the cavalry crossed the river, and are now "raiding," I suppose. I was on picket yesterday & last night, below town on the river road — had a cold, freezing night, but got along with it with little difficulty. Our cavalry had a slight skirmish here — lost one man. The rebels lost about 10. We have picked up about 25 prisoners since leaving Pine Bluff. We expect to return in a day or two, as it seems unlikely that we will go any further, and we are getting short of rations. Shall probably have none the last day or two out, except what we can find in the country — & that will be nothing but meat.

I left two of my men at Pine Bluff — Batchelder was sick — Kimmerly was sore footed *and a sneak.* I did not know he was left till too late. We have hard weather to be out nights — but no storms since about a week ago. We have just tent enough for the officers to sleep in, but they are nearly as cold as out of doors, as we can build no fires in them. I am very well, but have had a cold, & have a *terribly sore nose*. Don't you pity me? My hands & lips, too are badly chapped, & the smoke of the camp fires, which a soldier cannot avoid, troubles my eyes considerably. I wish you could for half an hour look down upon our camp fires — see them blazing in every direction around us, & see the men & servants preparing food for supper on the next day's march. There is much about an army that is interesting to see.

If we had rations the men generally would rather move forward toward the Red river than return to Little Rock — & so had I.

The object of this expedition seems to have been to divert attention from some other point at which some part of our army has probably struck ere now. May the blow be a deadly one to the rebellion.

. . . .

Feb. 4, 3 P.M.

Safe at Little Rock again. I greet you with a kiss, my darling. Have just got here. Will write as soon as I can.

Report says we are to leave here in a few days for New Orleans.[37]

NOTES

1. For operations in Arkansas in 1863 and 1864, see the two biographies of Sterling Price listed previously and Robert L. Kerby, *Kirby Smith's Confederacy: The Trans-Mississippi South, 1863–1865* (New York, 1972). For a specific study, see Thomas L. Snead, "The Conquest of Arkansas," *Battles and Leaders*, III, 441–61. For accounts of the Battle of Helena, see Edwin C. Bearss, "The Battle of Helena," *Arkansas Historical Quarterly*, XX (Autumn, 1961), 258–93, as well as the above.

2. Charles E. Hovey, founder of the first Illinois Normal College in 1857, raised the regiment, the Illinois 33rd Infantry, from its students and teachers and became its colonel. Promoted to brigadier general in September, 1862, he commanded a division in the Yazoo Expedition; he also commanded a division at Arkansas Post, where he was badly wounded. His appointment expired in March, 1863, and he went into the practice of law.

3. These reports were not accurate. Joseph Hooker was not extensively engaged with Confederate forces until May, when his army, however, was badly defeated by Robert E. Lee at Chancellorsville. William Rosecrans was inactive in Tennessee from the time of the Battle of Murfreesboro at the end of 1862 until the Chickamauga campaign in the fall of 1863. Nor had there been an attack on Charleston for some weeks before the diary entry. Frederick H. Dyer, *A Compendium of the War of the Rebellion* (3 vols., New York, 1959), II, 833.

4. Benjamin Prentiss, 1819–1901, from Illinois, was promoted from colonel to brigadier general in May, 1861; captured at Shiloh, he was exchanged and later promoted to major general in November, 1862. He was commander of the district of eastern Arkansas from February until August, 1863. Prentiss then returned to civilian life.

Willis Gorman, 1816–76, a Kentuckian, moved to Minnesota, where he was active in politics and commissioned a colonel in April 1861. Promoted to brigadier general in September, 1861, he fought in various battles in the East in 1861 and 1862 and then was transferred to command at Helena, Arkansas; he was mustered out of service and resumed the practice of law in 1864.

5. John S. Marmaduke, 1833–87, was an 1857 West Point graduate. From Missouri, he became colonel, brigadier general, and finally major general. He was a cavalry commander and one of the principal aides of Sterling Price.

6. Kenner Garrard, 1828–79, was an 1851 West Point grad-

uate. Captured early in the war, he did not take command until 1862; he participated in many battles in the East in 1862 and 1863 and then transferred to the West. He ultimately reached the rank of major general.

7. Though Stevens clearly did not like White, nevertheless White seems to have been an unusually ambitious and successful person. Born in upstate New York in 1830, he moved to Wisconsin, practiced law, and became district attorney in Waukesha in 1861. He was very active in raising at least one company of the 28th Wisconsin. During the war he went from captain to lieutenant colonel; at the end of the war he was Provost Marshall for the state of Arkansas. Upon discharge from service, he went to Little Rock and entered a law partnership with Colonel Augustus Garland, who later became Senator from Arkansas. White's health deteriorated, however, and he started north to return to his family in Wisconsin when he died at Evanston, Illinois, in November, 1866. *History of Waukesha*. . . . (Chicago, 1880), 594.

8. Theophilus Holmes, 1804–80, was an 1829 graduate of West Point. A lieutenant-general in the Confederate army, he held various positions before being appointed commander of the Trans-Mississippi Department. Severely criticized and old, he temporarily relinquished his command after the battle at Helena.

Dandridge McCrae was a brigade commander of General Price's division, as was Mosby Parsons, 1819–65, who was instrumental in raising the Missouri State Guard and fought in a series of battles in Arkansas and Missouri.

Despite Stevens' statement, Daniel Frost was not at the Battle of Helena; *Battles and Leaders*, III, 461. James F. Fagan, 1828–93, commanded a brigade in Price's division. Born in Kentucky, he lived in Missouri before the Civil War, fought in the Mexican War, was appointed colonel in an Arkansas regiment, and promoted ultimately to major general in the Confederate service.

The report of the death of McCrea and Fagan was inaccurate; both were actively engaged in Confederate service until the end of the war.

Sterling Price, 1809–67, had served in the Mexican War and had been governor of Missouri in 1852. As commander of the Missouri state troops in 1860, he joined the Confederacy. Fighting in numerous battles in the West, Price commanded a division at Helena. After the war he went to Mexico, returning after the collapse of Maximilian's empire.

9. E. Kirby Smith, 1824–93, an 1845 West Point graduate, served in the U. S. Army on the frontier and in Mexico, resigning in 1861 to enter the Confederate Army. After extensive service in Virginia and the West, he was promoted to lieutenant general and, in early 1863, was transferred to the trans-Mississippi department. In March, 1863, Smith was appointed to command the department, a position he retained until the end of the war. For Smith, see Robert L. Kerby, *Kirby Smith's Confederacy: The Trans-Mississippi South, 1863–1865* (New York, 1972).

10. John Davidson, 1823–81, an 1845 West Point graduate was a Virginian who chose to stay with the Union. After service on the frontier and in Mexico, he fought in various Eastern campaigns in 1861 and 1862; from August, 1862, until the end of the war he held various commands west of the Mississippi. He was promoted to brigadier general in February, 1862.

James Blunt, 1826–81, a native of Ohio, an ardent abolitionist and associate of John Brown in Kansas, held commands in Kansas and Arkansas. He became a brigadier general in April 1862, and a major general in November, 1862.

11. Theophilus Holmes did not die until 1880. Stevens appears to have been mistaken; the Confederates lost no generals up to the time of his diary entry who had fought at Helena.

12. Frederick Steele, 1819–68, a New Yorker and an 1843 West Point graduate, served on the frontier and in the Mexican

War. He held numerous commands in the Mississippi Valley; promoted to brigadier general in January, 1862, he was made major general in November, 1862. He was associated with the 28th Wisconsin Infantry from this point until nearly the end of the war.

13. Spelled variously: "Bayou Metoe" in the *Official Records,* Atlas I, Plate 32. In such secondary sources as Kerby's *Kirby Smith,* p. 229, it is spelled "Bayou Meto."

14. Samuel Rice, 1828–64, a native of New York, was a lawyer and politician in Iowa. In command of the 3rd Division during the expedition against Little Rock (where the 28th Wisconsin was assigned), Rice held several commands in Arkansas operations until he was mortally wounded in April, 1864.

15. Carrie would have had a hard time finding the quotation in her bible. The same words, by an unknown author were published in 1656. Very similar words, however, were written in Greek and Roman times; Burton Stevenson, *The Home Book of Quotations* (New York, 1967), 456–57.

16. Lucius Walker, 1829–63, from Tennessee, was an 1850 West Point graduate. A brigadier general, he led a cavalry brigade under Marmaduke at Helena. Hostility between the two men led to a duel on September 6, in which Walker was killed; Kerby, *Kirby Smith's Confederacy,* 231.

17. James T. Lewis was Secretary of State in the administration of Wisconsin Governor Salomon. A convert from the Democrats in 1860, he was expected to appeal to members of his former party. He did and was elected governor overwhelmingly. Current, *Wisconsin in the Civil War Era,* 327, 408.

18. Arkansas was one of the last southern states to secede. The first state, South Carolina, left the Union on December 20, 1860, followed by the lower southern states in the first two months of 1861. Only after the firing on Fort Sumter and

Abraham Lincoln's call for troops in April did the upper southern states secede, Arkansas on May 6, 1861.

19. Unlike the report of the Walker-Marmaduke duel, this report was not true.

20. There was a modicum of truth in the report. After the Battle of Helena, an ill, elderly Holmes turned over command of the District of Arkansas to Price on July 23. After Price evacuated Little Rock and retreated to Arkadelphia, Holmes resumed command on September 25. Price, however, still retained command of a division of Confederate troops. *Battles and Leaders,* III, 456, 457; Castel, *Price,* 161–62.

21. Clement Vallandigham, an Ohio Democrat, was an outspoken critic of the Lincoln administration. Arrested by military officials, Lincoln placed him behind Confederate lines from where he made his way to Canada. Nominated by Ohio democrats for the governorship, Vallandigham was defeated in 1863.

22. Napoleon Buford, 1807–83, was a half-brother of the better known John Buford of Gettysburg fame. Napoleon was an 1827 West Point graduate. Promoted to major general in November, 1862, Buford exercised several commands in the Mississippi Valley, including District of East Arkansas at the time of the General Order mentioned by Stevens.

23. Stevens is referring to Ulysses S. Grant's major victory at Chattanooga over Braxton Bragg in the battle fought November 23–25, 1863.

24. The Red River Campaign, March–May, 1864, indeed was a failure. General Nathaniel Banks was to advance up the Red River from his base at New Orleans; Frederick Steele was to move south from Little Rock, and a third force of William Sherman's men was to move eastward from Vicksburg. Bitter recriminations followed the northern failure.

25. The reference is to Grant's Wilderness Campaign which began on May 4, 1864.

26. Cadwallader Washburn, 1818–82, a lawyer and land speculator in Wisconsin as well as a Republican Congressman, raised a cavalry unit and became the colonel. Promoted to brigadier general and major general in 1862, he was in command of the District of Western Tennessee in May, 1864. After the war, he became a governor of Wisconsin, 1872–73.

Ralph Buckland, 1819–92, lawyer and state senator, went into service as a colonel of an Ohio regiment; in May 1864, he was a brigadier general in command of the 16th Corps, District of Memphis.

27. The reports that Price was planning a movement were premature. In August, Price did cross the Arkansas River between Little Rock and Fort Smith unmolested, and then carried out his raid into Missouri.

28. For a summary of the 28th Wisconsin's operations from October, 1863 to May, 1864, see Lt. Col. Sray's report, *Official Record*, Series 1, Vol. XXXIV, Part 1, 775–76.

Eugene Carr, 1820–1910, an 1850 West Point graduate, was in the regular army at the outbreak of the war, became colonel of an Illinois cavalry regiment, and was promoted to brigadier general for bravery. Holding various commands in the West, Carr in June, 1864, commanded the District of Little Rock during the fighting at Clarendon with Joseph Shelby's Confederate cavalry.

Joseph Shelby, 1830–97, a wealthy plantation owner, entered the Confederate Army as a captain of the cavalry under Sterling Price. Engaged in many of the battles of the trans-Mississippi West, he rose to brigadier general and command of a cavalry division. Like Price, after the war he went to Mexico for a time.

29. Robert W. Johnson, 1814–79, was a Senator from 1853 to 1861; during the war he was a member of the Confederate Senate.

30. Powell Clayton, 1833–1914, a Pennsylvanian, moved rapidly from captain of the 1st Kansas Regiment in 1861 to

brigadier general. After the war he settled in Arkansas, became governor of the state in 1868, senator in 1871, and was a lifelong Republican boss of Arkansas.

31.Confederate forces evacuated Atlanta September 1, 1864, and Union forces under William T. Sherman occupied the city the next day. Union forces occupied Fort Gaines August 8 and Fort Morgan August 23; these forts commanded the entrance to Mobile, Alabama. In 1865, the 28th Wisconsin was part of an expedition which occupied Mobile itself. William Hardee, 1815–73, a Confederate lieutenant general, participated in the Battle of Atlanta, but was not killed; indeed, he was given the thankless task of commanding the few Confederates who vainly opposed Sherman's March to the Sea.

32. On his Missouri raid, Price attacked Union forces in southern Missouri and suffered a bad defeat; Marmaduke, however, was not killed.

33. Joseph Reynolds, 1822–99, was an 1843 West Point graduate. During the war he was promoted to major general and performed service largely in Kentucky and Tennessee. In December, 1864, he was placed in command of the Department of Arkansas.

34. Quincy Gillmore, 1825–88, a West Point graduate in 1849, attained the rank of major general in 1863. After numerous commands in the East, he was severely injured in a fall from a horse in July, 1864; thereafter, he served on numerous boards and commissions.

35. The reference is to George Thomas' rout of John Hood at Nashville, December 15–16, 1864, and William Sherman's capture of Savannah, December 21, 1864. Fort McAllister, part of the defense structure for Savannah, had fallen December 13; its capture reopened Sherman's communications with the outside world.

36. Cyrus Bussey, 1833–98, entered service as colonel of the 3rd Iowa Cavalry regiment. He commanded a cavalry division during most of the war in Arkansas. Although Stevens

made several references to Gray's court martial, he never spec-
ified the charges against Gray.

37. This time the report was accurate — the 28th Wisconsin
was under orders to proceed to New Orleans. On January 21,
1865, the major general commanding New Orleans directed
General Reynolds, commanding the department of Arkansas,
to send 3,000 infantry from Arkansas to New Orleans. This
order was delivered by personal courier on January 30. On
January 31 Arkansas headquarters issued orders that six regiments were to proceed "without delay" to New Orleans. The
28th Wisconsin left Little Rock on February 11. *Official Records,* Series I, Vol. XLVIII, Part I, 603, 691–92.

Part IV: MOBILE CAMPAIGN

The Union blockade of the Confederacy was immeasurably strengthened by the capture of Southern ports. Most notable of these was the capture of New Orleans in April, 1862, by a fleet under the command of Admiral David Farragut. Soon thereafter, Farragut proposed that Union forces seize Mobile. It was not until February, 1864, however, that Farragut secured permission to seal off Mobile.

On February 6, Farragut's fleet ran past Forts Morgan and Gaines, which protected the harbor, and attacked and defeated the Confederate fleet located there. It was in that engagement that Farragut reportedly said, "Damn the torpedoes." Soon thereafter, Forts Morgan and Gaines were captured by Union forces.

In the spring of 1865, the Union made plans to capture the city of Mobile itself. In overall command of the operation was General Edward R. S. Canby, who was ultimately assigned some 45,000 men. Since the Confederates had long expected an attack, the city was well fortified, though their troops numbered only some 10,000 men. Canby initially concentrated on Spanish Fort, located east of Mobile. Following a seige of approximately two weeks, the Confederates abandoned it. Already Union forces were besieging nearby Fort Blakely, and that, too, fell to Union forces on April 9. The 28th Wisconsin was involved in the siege of Spanish Fort, and Stevens proudly records that he had the honor of leading his company into the fort, the first organization, he claimed, to enter the work. Stevens' regiment marched to Blakely but arrived just after Union forces captured that Confederate fort.

Canby then transferred his army to Fort Gaines, from where he expected to attack Mobile directly. The Confederates, however, abandoned the city, and Union forces occupied it on April 12.[1]

Stm'r Sir WM. Wallac, Just below St. Charles, Ark., Sunday, Feby 12, 1865

Here we are, on our way to New Orleans, or some other point. Whether we are to go there or not I don't know. Some pretend to say we are to stop at the mouth of White river until the balance of the brigade is brought down from Little Rock — and I think it very probable that we will do so.

All this last week we have had all we could do getting ready to leave — have been at work about every night till 11 o'clock — and have had no time to write. On Friday we rec'd orders to leave by the train Saturday morning for Duvall's Bluff. We left camp at 4 A.M., having moved our "traps" Saturday evening, — left Little Rock about sunrise, & reached Duvall's Bluff before noon. Went immediately on board the boat, and at 1:10 P.M. were on our way down the White river. Lt. Bennett got left at Brownville, where he got off the train — and a man of Co. "B" was left behind at Duvall's Bluff. He followed the boat a short distance along the river bank, when, in attempting to cross a bayou on a log, he slipped off & went in all over. Whether he got out or not is uncertain — several men were near and went to his assistance. We run about 80 miles yesterday — got started at daylight this morning and are coming along finely. We passed St. Charles about half past 8 this A.M.

Lt. Alvord & I shipped to Walter S. Dibble (in a trunk) some articles we could not carry.

Mine are 1 Mattress, 2 Blankets, a bundle of papers, orders &c — that is all I think of, though there may be some other little articles. I think I shall send home to you my old sword as soon as I can get a chance. The things were sent by Express. I will send my diary as soon as I can spare it.

I have 53 men with me. Lewis & Palmer are left in Gen. Hospital at Little Rock. Baker was taken sick on the boat yesterday - has fever. Hope it will not be serious. Adj't. Kindrick is detailed at Little Rock as A.A.A. Gen. to Gen. Salomon.

. . . .

Steamer St. Nicholas,
Mississippi River, Tuesday, Feb'y 14, 1865.

We reached the mouth of White river about half past two o'clock on Sunday. Went ashore, men & baggage & camped near the landing — put up what few tents we had, & prepared to wait for a boat bound down river. We found here some old friends — the 126th Ill. having arrived from Pine Bluff early in the morning of the same day. Capt. Towne of that reg't. was in hospital with me at Little Rock — and a pleasant gentleman he is. Had quite a visit with him & Major Morris of the 126th — We also met Capt. Payne, Lt. Ellsworth & others of the 1st Ind. Cavalry, who were at Pine Bluff all the time we were there. Brig. Gen. McGinniss (of Ind. I think,) is in command at the mouth of White river.[2]

Early Monday morning another boat from Duvall's Bluff arrived, bringing Lt. Bennett & Sorenson of Co. B. who were left behind — also J. M. Alvord of "C" Co. has been relieved from "detached service" at Little Rock. It commenced raining in the forenoon & rained nearly all day. During Sunday & Sunday night large boats were continually passing down the river, heavily loaded with troops & stores. Some 50 boats are said to have left Memphis with troops. Some big expedition is ahead when we get down the river, I reckon.

About noon yesterday the St. Nicholas came along loaded with freight, but with no troops. Four companies left here in the forenoon on the "J. C. Swon," & the balance of us were put aboard the St. Nicholas, & left about half past 2 P.M. This is a new boat, on her first trip. It rained very hard nearly all night last night, & is raining some to-day — making it very gloomy & unpleasant.

I understand we are to stop at a place a few miles above New Orleans, where the troops are to rendezvous. Gen. Steele is to command, I learn. Hope he will do better than he did as a Dept. commander in Arkansas.

We are now (the troops at Little Rock having been re-organized) in what is called the "Detached Brigade of the 7th Army Corps" — "head-quarters in the field." Brig. Gen. Carr was placed in command of this brigade, but Maj. Gen. Reynolds relieved him before we left Little Rock — *for drunkenness* it is said. Gen. Veatch is now assigned to the command.[3]

Our brigade consists of the 28th & 27th. Wis. 29th & 33rd Iowa, 50th Ind. & 77th Ohio. It was said at Little Rock that we would return to that place in 6 or 8 weeks, but we have no desire to go there again. We all say heartily, "Good bye, Arkansas!"

. . . .

14th 2 ½ P.M. Just arrived at Vicksburg — all well.

Natchez, Miss., Feby. 15, 1865

We reached Vicksburg yesterday at about 2 ½ P.M. I went ashore while the boat was landing freight, & went up town to send my sword home by Express. I will send the receipt herewith — if I don't forget it! While running about town with Capt. Kenyon, we went into an eating saloon, when who should I see seated at one of the tables but — guess who? Give it up? Well, it was none other than Charley Randall — poor, dissipated, much-to-be-pitied Charley. "I looked at him — he looked at me" — finally I approached him & he asked me if I was not a Wisconsin man. I told him who I was & that I believed he was Charles Randall — He said he was Clerk at the "Washington House," a large hotel in Vicksburg. He showed certain signs of drunkenness — his red, watery eyes, his trembling hand — everything about him told me he was the passive slave of Alcohol. Isn't it too bad! Poor Mary is to be pitied. Charley invited me up to the hotel, but I had no time to go, as I feared the boat would leave. She finally did not leave till about dark. The "Swon" with our 4 other companies was there when we left. About 8 ½ o'clock last evening, while the passengers were sitting in the cabin, we felt a severe shock to the boat. We supposed she had run upon a snag, & some were mightily scared. We soon found that in the fog we had run ashore in a bend of the river. It took till after midnight to get off again.

Yesterday was a gloomy, rainy day. To-day is bright & pleasant — and is quite warm, compared with what we have had lately. We are getting south is one reason I suppose. We reached this place at 10 A.M. to-day. I bought some oranges here — 4 for a quarter. How I wanted to send you some, for they are nice ones. I think of you & the children while eating them. They are larger than the apples that are sold for 10¢ to 1/- each in Arkansas. I believe I have not bought an apple this winter — they taste too strong for money.

When we left Vicksburg yesterday it was amusing to see the apple & orange peddlers (women) throw fruit to the soldiers after the boat had pushed off. They kept it up as long as they could throw them aboard the boat — they as well as the soldiers enjoying the fun.

I have mailed to you from here, to-day, some old Arkansas papers; — you will find in them advertisements of runaway slaves — keep them as a relic of barbarism which has been tolerated in the United States — thank God, it is disappearing!

Rumor says that Maximilian, Emperor of Mexico, has formed an alliance, offensive & defensive with Jeff. Davis, &

it is suspected by some that if this is so, our destination is
Mexico — or at least the frontier along the Rio Grande. We
shall see!

When we passed Vicksburg yesterday the flags on the fortifications were at half mast — for what reason I could not
learn.

We arrived here ahead of the Swon. When she landed alongside of our boat, the officers came over to see us.

I have been looking about town a little. Natchez is a much
larger town that I thought — but little of it is visible from the
river, it being situated, for the most part, at the top & back of
the bluff. Some store houses &c are built on the levee next the
river. It is quite a nice place - nicer in my opinion than any
town along the river — excepting, possibly, Memphis & New
Orleans.

. . . .

H'd Qrs. 28th. Wis. Vol. Inf.,
Algiers, (opposite N.O.,) La.,
Friday evening Feb. 17, 1865

We landed here yesterday afternoon — got into camp just
before dark — that is, got to the ground we are to occupy
while here. We had no teams to haul our traps up from the
boat, and it was late in the evening before we got it done. Then
we were without wood to cook with. This last was the occasion
for the disgrace of the regiment. It happened in this manner.
The Lt. Col. ordered the men to abstain from destroying
fences or other property. Early this morning the men went at
work and tore down about 100 rods of fence near the camp, &
commenced bringing in the rails & posts. Being pretty well
tired out last night I had gone to bed, & slept pretty late this
morning, though I was officer of the day. When I got up I
discovered what they were at, and immediately ordered the
men to stop, & made them carry the rails back. I got many a

curse for it, and I'm afraid some of the men got "left handed blessings" in return, for I got my dander up to see them disobey positive orders in the way they did. All that could be done was done to supply them with wood, by the Q.M. dep't., and they could well wait a few hours longer. Some of my men thought I was very hard on them and misused them. Let them think so — *thieves* are apt to get misused now and then. Let them obey orders, and I'll use them well every time — but men who won't do it need ask no favors from me. I hope they will be punished for their disobedience.

To-day I went over to New Orleans. After running about town awhile with Capt. Tichenor, we went to the office of E. M. Randall, brother of Governor Randall, — found him in and had quite a visit with him.[4] I used to be acquainted with him — he lived at Waukesha. Upon enquiry I found that he knew Harry Lester, and he went down to the Canal Basin with me to find him. Harry was there on board his boat — I took him by surprise. Had a chat with him, and then went home with him & took tea with him & his wife. Didn't I enjoy the visit, though? They were both well. Tell Aunty Lester that I have seen Harry. He had lots to say about you. He had just this day received a letter from Lavantia. He only got in from a trip this forenoon at 11 o'clock, and goes out again at 6 in the morning, to be gone 10 days to 2 weeks. Had a good supper — Ham & eggs, fresh fish, biscuit & butter, tea, cake & peach sauce — to all of which I did ample justice. I got photographs of Harry & his wife, & told him you would send him yours. Please do so when you get some. I'll send them to you.

We are probably going to Mobile — or *towards* there — perhaps we may not get there. It is thought here that we will start in about a week. I hear that Gen. Steele has had some trouble with Gen. Canby, & has been deprived of the command which he expected to have.[5]

We are to go from here with as little load of baggage as possible — the men carrying a blanket, shirt, drawers & socks in their knapsacks — *nothing else* except what they have on them. Officers may take a small valise only, — even our desks with our company records will be left behind. Whether we will go by land from here, or on board transports is uncertain.

    . . . .

Steamship Belvidere,
Near Mouth of Mississippi River,
(South East Pass,) Feby 23, 1865.

My last letter I mailed to you from Algiers, night before last, after coming on board this vessel. We broke camp and marched to the levee — embarked in a drenching storm of rain, just before dark on that day. Five companies went upon the hurricane deck, where they were exposed all night to the rain and a hard wind.

All our wagons (nine) and about 60 mules & horses of ours are on board — and as many belonging to the 33rd Iowa, so yesterday four more companies were ordered on the upper deck, leaving but one below. It rained by spells all day yesterday & all night last night, & for a while this morning, but has now (1 P.M.) partially cleared off. It has been a rough trip so far, but fortunately we are so far south that the weather is not cold. We did not leave Algiers till about 3 P.M. yesterday. About dark we anchored in the river some 30 miles below the town, & laid there till morning.

Reached here about 1 P.M. today, & anchored just below a man-of-war lying here. I left two men (Ole Nelson & Henry Weaver,) sick at New Orleans. Both were down with pneumonia, I believe.

I don't think we will leave the mouth of the Pass before tomorrow, as the weather is rough, & the Captain of the boat says he will not take us out in a storm — so we may count on having good weather on the gulf. We have only about 75 miles to steam across salt water, & can cross it by daylight.

. . . .

A large number of troops were arriving & landing just below New Orleans when we left — suppose they will be part of our army. I understand we are now in the 13th Army Corps but have not seen the order — will send the address as soon as I get it. In the mean time you can address "detached brigade 7 A.C. Via New Orleans." I think they will come all right. I had to buy me a new rubber coat at New Orleans. It cost a dreadful sight of money, ($18.) but I had to have it, & I got $5. worth of wear out of it night before last in the rain. I think it will pay for itself in a month — but I did need the money to live on. I *do* wish the paymaster would come! It costs me a great deal to live — & buying on credit is worse than paying down for goods.

. . . .

Camp 28th. Wis. Vol. Inf.,
Fort Morgan, mouth of Mobile Bay,
Saturday, Feb'y 25, 1865.

Two weeks, filled up with pleasure & privation, happiness & hardship, have brought us thus far from Little Rock. I wrote you from the mouth of the Mississippi river, but was unable to mail my letter there, and have bro't it thus far with me — so you will receive it with this.

We left the mouth of the river yesterday, passing over the bar at 8 A.M. in a dense fog. The pilot left us there. The sea was rough when we got out upon the gulf, and as our direction took us right along the trough of the sea, the ship tossed about right merrily, making lots of us seasick. Nearly all the officers, & lots of the men had a turn at it. I stood it till about half past ten, when I had to make for the ship's side and toss my breakfast to the fishes. To add to our discomforts we had a heavy rain storm in the after-noon, accompanied by a very heavy thunder. The steamer was a neat thing to run about on at that time!

I was sick till night. We came 69 miles yesterday, but, on account of the fog, were unable to run into the harbor last night, so we anchored & tossed about till morning. I didn't get up till just as we were landing here, as the sea was rougher still after daylight, and my stomach threatened to rebel, though I had eaten nothing for 24 hours. We come to anchor off Fort Morgan about 9 A.M., but did not land till about noon. I don't want any more *sea* in mine at present! The land reels with me yet, — but I'll soon get over *that*. Have had some bread & butter & a good cup of coffee since we landed, & feel better. Expect to have a big appetite for the next few days.

. . . .

My men are mostly feeling pretty well, though the thorough vomiting yesterday makes us victims feel weak! McIalwain is pretty sick with diarrhea — brought on by his own imprudence in drink — & eating all the trash he could hold. I *think* he will not live a week. He has made up his mind to be sick if he can, and now he has got sick he gives up entirely to it. He is good for nothing as a soldier — & was no better at home — Harsh language you may think, but it is *true*. If we leave here, while he lives, we shall have to leave him behind unless he is better.

This is a barren portion of earth — sure. Nothing here but sand & weeds — to which I may add the various shells which abound on the sea shore, & the *water*! We are some 30 or 35 miles from Mobile.

I have not been inside the Fort yet — but the exterior shows marks without number of the bombardment at the time it fell into the hands of "Lincoln's Boys." It is a stronghold, sure. Quite a large number of vessels are lying here — men-of-war — transports &c. — both steam and sail. I have heard nothing yet of the number of troops in the vicinity, but reckon that a large army is coming if not already here — for I am told that quite a number of Generals are here & at Fort Gaines, waiting to be assigned commands. Where we will go I can only *guess* — & *my guess* has already gone home to you in a previous letter — (Selma & Montgomery.) Those points captured, Mobile would be worth little to the rebs.

. . . .

Mobile Point, Alabama March 5, 1865.

. . . .

We heard day before yesterday that Charleston was ours — that our flag floats over Sumter. Hurrah! One more step towards crushing out treason. Now for the next.

A blockade runner loaded with liquors was caught a few nights while trying to run into Mobile. How are you "Frenchy?"

. . . . We are now in the 3rd Brigade, 3rd Division, 13th Army Corps. Direct to "Mobile Point, Alabama" . . . .

Mobile Point, Ala., M'ch 8th, 1865.

. . . .

We moved four miles up the point yesterday to a point called "Navy Cave," where the 20th Wisconsin have been lying. They left here, to go a few miles further up, this morning. The gunboats, ships &c. lie opposite our camp - quite a number of them. We are on the south side of Bonsecour Bay.[6] It is only about half a mile across this neck of land from the bay to the Gulf. It is a sandy, airy plain.

We had a drenching rain nearly all night last night. We all got more or less wet in our "dog tents," but I'm used to that — it don't hurt me a bit. I have seen no late papers. I got one from Homer of Jan. 29!

. . . .

Mobile Point, Alabama, Sunday, M'ch 21, 1865.

Sunday has come again, and finds us lying here still. No movement has been commenced yet *by us*, but we are ordered to be ready to march at short notice. We were inspected, on Thursday, I think, by Maj. Gen. Osterhaus.[7] We have fatigue parties at work each day on the railroad which is being built along the south shore of Bonsecour Bay. How far it is to be built I don't know.

Thursday night was a terribly rainy, windy night. In the morning it cleared off, but continued to blow, and it was very cold all day — *not freezing cold* — but cold enough to pinch us up & chill us through after the warm days we had previously. Yesterday was more pleasant, & very comfortable in the afternoon. To-day is bright & beautiful. We had regimental inspection this morning.

The news of the capture of Wilmington, & the other successes of our arms, is cheering to us who have toiled so long, even if we have done but little towards the accomplishment of these objects. Some of our officers even express their belief that the war will be ended before our time expires. I hope it may, but hardly think it will. Be that as it may, much is being done towards ending the war, and it does seem that the rebels must soon be overcome — *conquered*. When that is done the war is ended — *and not till then*.

Several iron-clads from here went off yesterday in the direction of Mobile, and all day long we heard the thunder of their guns as they hurled their missiles against the enemy's batteries or vessels. How far they went or what they acomplished we have been unable to learn, though the iron-clads have returned. We have no other news . . . .

Mobile Point, Ala. March 16, 1865.

Still we wait here — waiting for news — waiting to know when we are to move & to what place. Orders, without number almost, are being issued, not half of which are ever enforced, except in exceptional cases, but no movement yet. I do wish the officers who command would get ready, and let us do what we have to do. Here we are lying in the sand, exposed on this narrow point to every gale from the gulf or the bay — and the "gentle zephyrs" are blowing nearly all the time, from one direction or the other, almost hard enough to sweep our tents from the face of this desert.

I got tired of lying in my kennel as it was, and yesterday set my darkey at work & dug into the sand & set my tent *over the cellar*, thereby making my *house* much more spacious. I can *almost* stand up in it to dress! I'm *proud* now! We had another drenching rain night before last, and another yesterday after-noon, with wind enough to blow the water through a board — if there was a big hole through it!

There! just now, *since I commenced writing*, we have re-ceived orders to move at an early hour in the morning, with three days rations in our haversacks. That is all I know about it yet. I am officer of the day in camp, & have had a detail clearing off a parade ground. Now we are off to leave it. As I have to get my company ready to move. I am compelled to cut this letter short. . . . .

In the Pine Woods
About 30 miles N.E. of Mobile Point, Ala.,
Friday, March 24, 1865.

We left Mobile Point last Friday Morning, as I wrote you we were ordered. Our division (3rd) consisting of 3 Brigades, is commanded by Brig. Gen. W. P. Benton. Our brigade, (3rd) consisting of 27th & 28th Wis. 33rd Iowa & 77th Ohio, is commanded by Col. Krez [?] of the 27th Wis. We moved from camp about 6. A.M. but it took some time to get our trains & all under motion. Had a pleasant day for the march, and marched about 10 miles . . . .

On Saturday we marched about 10 miles again. The road from Mobile Point lies over a sandy ridge, with no vegetation of consequence — a barren, miserable desert is this.

Sunday we marched about 5 miles, lying in a swamp nearly all day, while details of men repaired & "corduroyed" the roads, which now run through low lands, & are cut up long before our train can pass over it. Monday we marched none — lying ready all day, & getting up trains & fixing roads.

On Tuesday the 21st we started early, in a hard rain — Rained all day — Wagons stuck — Marched 3 or 4 miles, stacked arms, & our brigade went back & hauled through cannon, wagons &c. by hand. Mud & water from ankle to waist deep. Every one wet — dreary time. Wednesday we continued work at the roads & trains till 4 ½ P.M. when we started through the mud & marched till 9 P.M. making only about 3 miles.

Yesterday about 3 P.M. we reached here. This point is called Danly's Mills. I "don't see" the Mill. We crossed a stream called Fish river here.

Our Division is now in camp here. A. J. Smiths corps. (the 16th) is here[8] . . . .

H'd Qrs. 28th. Wis. Vol. Inf., In the field, near Spanish Fort, opposite Mobile, M'ch 31, 1865.

I cannot tell when I wrote you last, but, whenever it was, I have had no opportunity to write since. We left Fish River on the 25th about 2 or 3 P.M. & marched till 9 — slept without blankets — cold & damp. Marched next day to a point about 1 ½ mile back of here, & on the 27th moved up to our present position. Here our army (13th & 16th Corps.) is investing a strong fortification of the enemy, called "Spanish Fort." It is on the east side of Mobile bay, & nearly opposite Mobile. From one of our batteries I have seen Mobile with a glass. We have quite an army here & operating in the vicinity. Steele is, I hear, investing Blakely, & has, we hear, cut the railroad above there & captured a train. So far our artillery has affected the enemy but little, if any. Some of our gun-boats have got up near here, & one has been sunk by a rebel torpedo. Artillery firing is going on nearly all the time during the day, & our skirmishers & those of the enemy keep up an almost continual rattle of musketry. The day we came here Corporal Zimmermann of my Co. was wounded by the fall of a limb cut from a tree by one of the enemy's shell. It is not a bad wound, & he will be doing duty again soon. The next day, (28th) Iver Iverson rec'd a severe flesh wound in the shoulder, which will probably lay him up a month or two — *It is not dangerous.* Quite a number of the men of the regiment have been wounded. Hogg of "B" Co. has since died of his wound & Joseph Shabins of "I" Co. was instantly killed while skirmishing with the enemy yesterday. We were out skirmishing when Iverson was wounded. I am well, but pretty well tired out with continual duty — night & day. I have slept but little for the last four nights. Was brigade Officer of the day yesterday & last night, & was out on the skirmish line. The boys who are here are all pretty well except Harris & the wounded ones. Our teams are back, with our valises, & I have been without paper, or any conveniences for writing. We are now "in the field," sure. The fall of this fort & Blakely will be a good start toward the reduction of Mobile. How large an army we have here I don't know, & probably should have to consider the information *contraband* & withhold it if I did know. I *don't think* our part of it is handled with the greatest ability. Smith's Corps. is all right, I guess. Canby is here. No mail & no news, & I am so tired & sleepy that I can hardly write, or hold my eyes open. . . .

Camp 28th Wis. Inf.,
In the Field, Alabama, Saturday, April 1, 1865.

The mail goes in a few minutes. All well this morning. The rebels tried to drive in our skirmishes again at dark last night.

The 7th Vermont, ("the White Reg't." our men call it,) fell back again, like a pack of cowards as they are. This is the second or third time that they have done the same thing. They left me unsupported last Tuesday night when I was out, so that it was only by doing the best I knew that I kept the rebs from flanking me & "gobbling up" my two companies. Capt. Murray of Co. "H." was out yesterday & last night. He had a sharp time holding their ground, & had 1 man killed & 3 wounded. Capt. Williams is now out with his Co. Things are more quiet today. Part of our men in camp live in holes dug in the ground, covered with timbers & earth, to protect them from shot & shell from the enemy's batteries.

I got a fair nights rest last night — the first of any amount since Sunday night. I fell better for it, "you bet."

I send a list of the killed & wounded in the Reg't since we invested this Fort last Monday (27th) —

Mch 27th	Corp.	J. D. Zimmerman,	Co. "C"	—head - slight
" "	"	Vaughn	"	E — shoulder - severe
" 28th	Private	Iver Iverson	"	C — shoulder - severe
" "	"	Robt Spencer	"	K — hip - severe
" "	"	Ezra Diedrich	"	B — Toe - slight
" "	"	Sam'l Hogg	"	B — Bowels - mortally - since died.
" 30th	"	Joseph Shabins	"	"I" — Killed - shot through head
" "	Sergt.	Peter Noblet	"	I — face - severe
" 31st	Private	Matthias Oberbillig	"	H — face - slight
" "	"	Timothy O'Brien	"	H — bowels - dangerous
" "	"	August Iunge	"	H — arm - severe
" "	Corp.	Philip Flood	"	H — Killed - shot through head.

This may be interesting to those who do not hear from their friends — showing that they are safe so far, if their names are not found above.

No more news. Paper & envelopes all back with the wagons, so I borrow to send this.

. . . .

Camp 28th. Wis. Vol. Inf., In the Field, Near Spanish Fort, Ala., April 6, 1865.

Once more I have an opportunity of writing, though I don't know as I shall have time to finish my letter. The investment of this point still progresses — *slowly*, I was going to say — but a vast amount of labor has been done since a week ago last Monday (Mch 27). Our rifle pits are some of them within 150 yards or so of the rebel forts & batteries — the men dig, dig, dig, day & night, with accoutrements on, & their trusty rifles by their sides in the trenches. The rebels dig too, and we have to be cautious not to expose ourselves too far, or *whiz* goes a bullet, much too close to one's head to be pleasant for a timid man. Sometimes they rain around us like hail, and I wonder that the casualties are so few.

Since I wrote last our reg't has lost three men, killed & wounded, namely: Apr 2, Corp Lewis Bloodgood, Co. E, severly wounded in leg — Apr 4 Private Martin Everson, Co "C" shot through shoulder, & Corp. Spencer Weeks, Co. "I", killed by the premature explosion of one of our own shells. Martin Everson is a brother of Iver Iverson [*sic*] who was shot last week — he was out with me Monday night (with a large detail,) at work on a battery which we are building for six 30 pound guns. He & James Hall had laid down together to rest, when a stray rebel bullet wounded him, passing through the flesh of the left shoulder, touching no bones I think, & struck Hall on the left breast, almost directly over the heart, hurting him somewhat, but not breaking the skin. Hall was sore for a day or two, but is now all right. The fact that Everson was before Hall probably saved Hall's life. Everson stood it like a man. His wound is painful, but not at all dangerous. He is in hospital. On the 4th our batteries opened on the rebel works & bombarded them constantly for 2 hours. Some 4000 shots were thrown by our artillery. There is more or less firing all the time. Last night a mortar near our camp threw a shell into the rebel works, once in 15 minutes, all night.

On the night of M'ch 31 the reb's charged our skirmishers — the 7th Vermont run again for the 2d or 3rd time, & left the left of our line exposed, but Capt. Murray with Co. "H" behaved nobly, driving back the enemy & holding the line. The 35th Wis. is also said to have behaved badly. That & the 7th Vt. have been taken from the line & put at fatigue duty — *disgraced* in fact, as we consider it.

Our brigade was moved to our place at the left of the division after dark. We have a much better & safer camp now — not as much exposed to the enemy's fire as the old one.

The enemy has a strong position here, and seems sullen & defiant — how long he can hold out is to be seen.

We heard today that Selma has fallen into our hands. Good! What next?

Capt. Redington & several men of the Reg't. arrived here on the 4th. I. L. Bogart of my Co. came with the rest. Several of my men are ill with diarrhea. And, oh, how they all have to work! Some have been on duty three nights in succession — picket, fatigue, all sorts of work, all the time.

I had an Election on Tuesday — gave Sam. Randles 30 votes — none against him. Several of my men were absent & couldn't vote — for which I was sorry. . . .

Camp 28th. Wis., In the field, Spanish Fort, Ala., Apr 9, 1865.

As far as this work is concerned, the agony is over. Spanish Fort was evacuated by the enemy between 11 & 12 o'clock last night, and soon after midnight I had the honor of leading "C" Co. up the declivity & over the parapet into it. My Co. was the first organization to enter the work, though some straggling officers & men were in ahead of me. I would have given $50. to have had our colors with me so as to have been the first to plant them on the work; but as I was out on the skirmish line away from the reg't. with the Co. we did not have them with us. About 100 guns of ours had shelled the fort for 2 hours last evening continuously, and at intervals during the night till they evacuated. It made the place too hot to hold them. It was a sight to go over the spot & see the effect of our shot & shell.

They left a large amount of ammunition, & several guns — some large ones. The guns were nearly all spiked, but can, probably, be rendered serviceable again. Some are already fit for use.

(9 A.M.) We are now under orders to be ready to march in half an hour. I presume we will now go to Blakely, a few miles above here, where Steele is. I suppose the rebs have gone to Mobile — we could not entirely cut off their communication by water, as the torpedoes were in the way. I was up till about 4 o'clock this morning, when I was relieved & ret'd to camp tired & sleepy, & am so still. It is now raining. We are ready to move, but I don't think we will get away this forenoon — perhaps not today. I don't want to march in the rain, but shall probably be obliged to. I hope Blakely & Mobile will fall soon. You ought to have heard the cheers from the throats of our Yankee soldiers when the stars & stripes were flung to the breeze. The rebs left a large amount of ammunition in their magazines. I don't see why they did not blow them up. The rebels had torpedoes planted in front of the Fort to blow up a charging party, but we didn't run on to any of them, fortunately.

I am well — some boys are not very well. . . . .

Camp 28th Wis. Vol. Inf.
Near Blakely, Ala., Apr. 10,/65

We marched yesterday morning from our camp near Spanish Fort — but did not move far till afternoon — then we were put through till 7 P.M. when we reached this point, just above Blakely. Steele's troops charged the rebel works here just before we arrived, & took them. The black troops behaved well, I am told. The result is that the 28th is fortunate enough to be out of the fight here. In the last two days we have captured about 5000 prisoners & 70 pieces of artillery. Our entire loss since we invested Spanish Fort & the one here, with the adjacent works will probably not exceed 1500. killed, wounded & prisoners. Prisoners with whom I have conversed this morning say Mobile will be evacuated before we get there — that their men will go to Georgia — would go to Texas if they could get there. They say they don't see how "our fellers" can dig & advance our rifle pits so fast under their fire. It puzzles them.

They are generally much finer looking men than those we met in Arkansas — intelligent, well fed, & pretty well clothed. Many of them did not seem to feel very bad at falling into our hands. Those I saw were mostly Alabama & Mississippi men. Steele has gobbled two Brigadier Generals, I am told.

. . . .

Camp 28th. Wis. Vol. Inf., Whistler, Ala., Apr. 15, 1865.

We left Blakely Tuesday night at dark, returning by Spanish Fort to the bay, reaching the landing at about 3 A.M., after a hard march, which nearly played out a good many of us. Here we laid down on the ground till after daylight, when we went aboard of a "tin-clad" gun-boat, & after some delay, started across the bay. We had quite a fleet along with us — gun—boats, men-of-war & transports — having on board our Corps (13th) We approached a landing some 6 miles below Mobile about 10 A.M. One gun was fired from a gun-boat, when a white flag was displayed on shore. A small boat was sent ashore, & returned with the information that no opposition would be made to our landing, no troops being there, & *that*

Mobile had been evacuated by the rebels. We commenced landing our Army. The 28th got on land about noon, but it took till nearly night to get all the troops ashore, as the pier was rotted down in places & some of the vessels could not get very near in shore. After getting a lunch from our haversacks we started for Mobile. The 1st Division occupied the city — ours was camped outside the city, but inside the rebel fortifications. The rebel works here are quite extensive, & very strong — our line, complete in itself, is enclosed within another equally strong. Forts, bastions &c. at every angle, & scores of guns, with large quantities of ammunition are there. Many of the guns are large Caliber — several 7 inch "Blakely" among them. They were all spiked, but most of the spikes can be withdrawn without much trouble.

I believe about 150 cannon, in all, were captured there. The rebs had dismounted many of them, & injured or destroyed the carriages of nearly all. Why they did not destroy the ammunition I do not see. They evidently had not men enough to man their works, or they would never have abandoned such strong ones without giving us a fight — & a hard one. Next morning (Thursday, 13th) our Division marched through the city & up the railroad north of Mobile to *Whistler* (about 7 miles out) where we arrived just in time to drive off some 500 secesh who had been sent down to destroy some locomotives & cars which had been left behind, & burn the workshops & break up the machinery — but after a short skirmish they run, and we saved the property. We had 3 men wounded — none in our Regt.

Before 9 P.M. one of the locomotives (all had been disabled) was put in running order, and was run down to the city the same night. Capt. Redington has been detailed as Military Supt. of the R.R. (Mobile & Ohio) & his Co. ("D") as guard at the depot. Friday we moved a mile or so from the depot, "and here we are." Friday P.M. I went out foraging with 200 men, & brought in about 40 head of cattle. The citizens here many of them claim to be "good Union men," *of course*. They seem to be aware that the "Confederacy" is *played out* — especially since Richmond is in our hands.

Yesterday we rec'd a small mail — By it I rec'd yours of March 29 from Waukesha, 1 from Lavantia of *March* 5! & a notice from Hospital at Little Rock that Stock Lewis is dead. He died March 31, of Consumption. One more gone from our little company. Poor boy, he was a good boy, but a careless one as regards his health.

The fall of Richmond — the surrender of Lee & his army (if he has surrendered, as reported.) all our late victories must be about enough to convince the rebels & everyone else that the rebellion is nearly quelled. How will foreign sympathizers feel now. How will the "com-fed-e-rate" loan be now, I wonder?

Dr. Miller reached here day before yesterday — He is looking well — said he had sent to Mrs. Miller a large picture of the Little Rock, U.S.A. General Hospital, to be handed to you. I engaged it while at the Rock.

I still keep well. Have had no tent or blankets, except my Rubber poncho, since we left Blakely — Don't know when I shall have. Am also out of rations, & don't know when I shall get any, but shall try to-day again — guess I'll make a raise of some hard tack & pork.

. . . .

Camp 28th. Wis. Vol. Inf.,
Whistler, Ala., Apr. 16, 1865.

We are here yet, and don't know but we may remain here for weeks or months, though we are subject to orders to move at any moment. To-day our wagons came up & to-day I have succeeded in getting some *eatables* once more — something beside "hard-tack" & hog meat. No other kind of bread or meat, but something with it — namely, fresh potatoes (only $3.50 pr bbl.) curried cabbage (60¢ pr gallon) sugar & coffee. Coffee is 50¢ (roasted & Ground) Sugar & Pork each 20¢

Beans 4 ¾ cents per pound — dried beef (got none today) is 17¢ Dried Apples 12 ½, Hard bread 8¢, Pickles 55 cents. No apples or pickles to be had now, but those are the prices when we do get them.

Dr. Miller very kindly lent me $20. without my asking (oh, he has a big heart!) I bought 3 bbls potatoes for my company — they needed something of the kind. . . .

A Dispatch was rec'd this P.M. confirming the report of the Surrender of Lee & his army. Didn't we cheer? We all feel better for the news. I hope the war will close by the time we get home — and is not there a good hope of it now. It seems so to me, but I may be deceived. At any rate I will *hope* for it
. . . .

Camp 28th. Wis.,
on Tombigbee River. In the field, Ala.,
Saturday, Apr 22, 1865.

We left Whistler Wednesday morning early — marched till 2 P.M., when we camped, & I went on picket with 100 men & 2 Lieutenants from our brigade. It was a very warm day, & a great many of our men gave out. All came up at night, though. Had a pleasant night on picket, & we marched at 5 A.M. on Thursday — marched all day except a while in the afternoon when we were waiting to build a bridge — crossed Cedar Creek after dark & went into camp. It rained before morning, & we got breakfast in a wet spot next morning — marched at 5 A.M. — rained nearly all day — We had to wade streams where the water was over our knees, & the mud was bad enough. I fell down once full length in the yellow clay — daubed myself from head to foot — you'd have laughed yourself sore to have seen me then, I'll bet. Had to pull off & wash my clothes in the creek & then go "marching on" to catch up with the regiment. We camped in the rain about 2 P.M., on wet

ground. As the train came up I was able to change my clothes
so I got along comfortably after all.

. . . .

**Camp 28th Wis. Vol. Inf.,
Nannahubba Bluff, (on Tombigbee river,) Ala.,
Sunday, April 23rd, 1865.**

Sunday has come again, but is anything but a day of peace
and quiet for us — in our *minds* at least. Early this morning we
received the terrible news of the assassination of our faithful and
upright Chief Magistrate, Abraham Lincoln, and his able Secretary of State, W. H. Seward.[9] Words fail to express the in-
dignation felt by the soldiery at these cowardly murders. He
who had so nobly stood at the helm of the Ship of State during
the dark night of trial & storm of rebellion through which she is
passing is treacherously murdered by those who have sought to
destroy the noble vessel. Doubtless the rebel authorities will
disclaim all connection with those who struck the blow — we expect they will, but we *know* too well that they & their press have
advocated the commission of this very act ever since the Election of Lincoln in 1860. Lies are useless now — or *should be*.
     What will be the result. We in the army hope that all will be
well — that the government is left in the hands of men who
will do there whole duty; but this is what we wish — that the
dogs of war may be let loose upon these treacherous, dastardly
curses — let the army destroy everything from the face of the
land they claim — burn every city they capture, every building
along their line of march — destroy every animal & every
pound of food we cannot use — leave them houseless & home-
less, and *kill* every rebel we can find. Harsh punishment it may
seem — they have well deserved it. True the innocent must
suffer — women & children — if this is done. Are their wives
& sisters & mothers & sons & daughters better loved or more
innocent & worthy than are ours — than are those of the tens

of thousands of patriots who have fallen in defending our glorious Union — those who now suffer all but — even more than death now, since their supporters & protectors are gone? No! If we have to deal with friends, or we fail to punish them as we ought. —

If our leaders will but give us the word, we'll sweep over their states like a besom [!] of destruction — fire & sword will desolate all they have. The wind of rebellion they have sown — let them reap the whirlwind of destruction & shame, desolation & sorrow. If we *knew* the war would *now* be conducted in this manner, two thirds of the army would reenlist *to-day for ten years or during the war.* I would for one, as much as I long to go back to the dear ones & the home I love so well. Curses on the fiends who have committed so cowardly an act. May perdition seize their souls forever.

. . . .

Camp 28th. Wis. Vol. Inf., McIntosh Bluff, Ala., Apr. 27th., 1865

We finally left Nannahubba Bluff on Tuesday and came to this place by river, on the steamer "James Battle", reaching here about 5 P.M. It is only a small place, but the rebels have had something of a Navy Yard here — they burnt some vessels a few days ago, which they found they had not time to complete.

Yesterday we moved our camp — now we are located in quite a comfortable place, and it looks as if we were to remain here for the present — though we may leave in two hours.

Flat boats loaded with negroes are passing down the river every day. They report that Wilson's Cavalry is raiding the country up the river. Bully for them. No more mail & no news. We are still in doubt as to whether Johnston has surrendered or not.

We are all ready for another inspection, and are expecting

every minute to hear the drums beat the assembly for us to fall
in. Lt. Alvord has just gone on picket. Have just been having a
little rain. It is quite warm. There goes the drums. Good bye.
. . . .

Camp 28th Wis. Vol. Inf.
McIntosh Bluff, Alabama. Saturday, May 6, 1865.

This is a lovely morning — as it should be — for is it not my
birth-day. I have just reached another mile-stone on the journey of life, and surrounding nature smiles, as if in salutation
for my arrival at this point, midway between the cradle and the
grave. My country, too, is smiling, laughing, shouting in glee
upon this day, for are not her troubles almost at an end? It
seems so, even now when so dark a cloud has just passed over
our heads. There go the guns! Hark! Their sullen growling
speaks of victories won. A Boat has just arrived from Mobile,
bringing news of the surrender of Johnston (hope it is true this
time) and *official* news of the surrender of Dick Taylor & his
command, and the rebel navy on the Tombigbee. A flag of
truce boat has just gone up to bring down the vessels. Work on
the fort here is discontinued, and the men are set at work
cutting wood for fuel to run the vessels down the river. Three
times three cheers! Let the glad "hurrah!" ring loud along the
shores of our rivers, through the streets of all our towns &
cities & in the peaceful country! Once again, hurrah! and
hurrah!! — and then I'm not done talking of it. The surrender
of Kirby Smith, which we daily look for, will be about the
last.[10] Won't we all be glad to know that the glad days of peace
are dawning? That the soldiery are not to be led to bloody
fields any more — in our own land? We are having a glad day
of rejoicing. Each one is congratulating his fellow upon the
glorious news — we are all too happy to work, or write — all
who can — and like it — are drinking poor whiskey to our
success. I, for myself, prefer to do something that everyone
else does not, — so I'll keep sober. But I'll quit — no chance
to send a letter, so I'll keep this open for a day or two, merely

adding that we are going down the river to Mobile on the rebel boats when they get here.

. . . .

Camp 28th, Wis. Vol. Inf., Near Mobile, Ala., May 11, 1865.

As you see by the date of this we have moved again. On Monday the rebel fleet of Gunboats & transports begun to arrive at McIntosh Bluff, and the soldiers there were set at work putting wood aboard of them, & loading them with our own stores of different kinds, preparatory to a move to this place. I was out until 12 o'clock Monday night loading wagons, mules & all sorts of property. I had charge of seven companies who were at work. Got to bed a little before 1 A.M. — up again at 3, got my breakfast, packed up, & at 5 A.M. Tuesday we were in line at the landing waiting to go on board. Here we waited, & "wearied with waiting," but finally go aboard about noon, but the fleet was not ready to move till about 2 P.M. We reached Mobile late in the evening, after which we marched about three miles into the country, & went into camp about 11 P.M., tired & cross.

Yesterday we moved into a new position & put up our tents — & here we are, wondering what we are to do next. Some think we will go to Galveston next time we move, while others predict that we will go up the Mississippi — perhaps *home*. No one here knows anything about it, as far as I can learn. Time will tell after a little. I wish we might be paid here — we all need money — I got the $25. from Lt. Bingham, but that will go but a little way. . . .

Camp 28th. Wis. Inf., Near Mobile, May 19, 1865. Saturday, 20th.

. . . .

We rec'd the news of the capture of Jeff. Davis several days ago. Hope they will hang him, sure. If they do not, justice will not be done.

We are anxiously waiting to hear whether the rebels in Texas are going to still try and hold out. If they surrender now, we hope not to be obliged to go there. "Come down, Johnnies!"

There does finally seem to be a prospect of our getting a little money. We are promised eight month's pay next Monday. That will pay us up to the last of February. They ought to pay to April 30th — but won't now. However 8 months pay will be a "heap" "*better nor none.*" When we get it, I will try & send home a few shillings — if I have any left after paying my debts — so you'll have a little something more to live on till I get home again. Can you use any of it?(!)

. . . .

**Camp 28th Wis. Inf.,
Near Mobile, May 26, 1865.**

I have something startling to tell you — we have been *paid off*! On the 23rd we were paid-up to Feby 28th only — so we have yet nearly three months pay due us. I enclose a check on Summit Bank for $678.75 which you can take care of. Perhaps you had better lend it to Chadbourn, or deposit it there, so that you can get it any time. Do just as you think best. If you want some where you can get it any day, Mr. Metcalf would probably keep it for you — & it would be safe.

. . . .

A terrible accident occurred in Mobile yesterday. I was in the city at the time, & came near being nearly on the ground. The Ordnance Depot in the city blew up killing hundreds of soldiers & citizens, & wounding hundreds more. Whole squares of brick buildings were blown down & destroyed, while windows & doors were forced out nearly all over the city. A number of buildings were burned, as well as several steamboats, & trains of cars standing on the rail-road track. It seemed to lift the whole city from its foundations. I never heard such a terrible roaring, & never expect to see such a sight again. I send you a paper with an account of the catastrophe. We have no other news of importance.

. . . .

**Camp 28th Wis. Inf'ty,
Near Mobile, Ala., May 27/65.**

We had pretty nearly made up our minds that we would remain here awhile, but last evening we rec'd marching orders again. We are ordered to hold ourselves in readiness to march at two hours notice, and as the 1st Division of our Corps is embarking on transports to-day, it looks as if we would move soon — for I understand we are to follow them. They go to New-Orleans first, I hear, and Lt. Frank Lull, who is on Gen. Veatch's Staff, told me they expected to up Red river. That may not, however, be our destination. Some think we will go to Galveston, while others think we are only going up the river to *get ready* and go home. We will know soon, I presume. I yesterday send you a check for $678.75. Hope it will go safe. Sent it in a letter. I also sent to Mrs. Strem & Mrs. Decker checks for the amounts due them from sale of their late husbands' effects.

We have another report today that Kirby Smith has surrendered. I doubt it yet, for we have had such news so many times that I can't believe all the reports I hear — even though they are said to be "official."

. . . .

NOTES

1. For the naval history of the Civil War, of which the capture of Mobile was a part, see Bern Anderson, *By Sea and By River; the Naval History of the Civil War* (New York, 1962). For specifics regarding the capture of Mobile, see *Battles and Leaders*, IV, 379–412; most of the account deals with

Farragut's capture of Mobile Bay in 1864; 410–2 deal specifically with land operations in 1865 which resulted in the capture of Mobile itself.

2. George McGinnis, 1826–?, was born in Massachusetts but enlisted as a private in an Indiana regiment in April, 1861; he was a lieutenant colonel by April 25, a colonel in September, and a brigadier general in November, 1862. He remained in command at the mouth of the White River until the end of the war.

3. Carr commanded a division in the Mobile campaign, the next major activity of the 28th Wisconsin. Carr remained in the regular army after the war and became a noted Indian fighter.

James Veatch, 1819–95, an Indiana lawyer, was colonel of an Indiana regiment in August, 1861, and was promoted to brigadier general in April, 1862. He also was a division commander at Mobile.

4. Alexander Randall, 1819–72, served as governor of Wisconsin from 1858 to 1862. He was noted for his vigorous organization of the state for participation in the Civil War.

5. Edward Canby, 1817–83, an 1839 West Point graduate, served on the frontier and in Mexico, and held New Mexico for the Union early in the war. After service in the East, Canby was promoted to major general in 1864 and placed in command at New Orleans. He led the assault on Mobile.

Frederick Steele, commanded the Department of Arkansas in 1864; he led a division in the assault on Mobile.

6. In the map accompanying the Union report of Mobile's capture in the *Official Records*, this place is listed as Bon Secours Bay.

7. Peter Osterhaus, 1823–1917, entered service as a major in a Missouri regiment and was eventually promoted to major general. He served in the Missouri-Arkansas theatre in 1861–62, at Vicksburg and Mssionary Ridge among other

campaigns. At this time he was the chief of staff to General Canby.

8. Andrew Jackson Smith, 1815–97, an 1838 West Point graduate, saw extensive service in Tennessee and Mississippi. Most recently, he had been involved at the Battle of Nashville.

9. John Wilkes Booth and his fellow conspirators planned on assassinating not only President Lincoln but also several other high officials. The only other official attacked, however, was William Seward, Secretary of State, who was severely — but not fatally — stabbed.

10. Kirby Smith's surrender, on June 2, was the last Confederate surrender.

Part V: TEXAS EXPEDITION

When the 28th Wisconsin was ordered to the Texas-Mexican border, Stevens grumbled that his men had to stay in service even though the war was over. He guessed that stationing additional soldiers in Mexico was related to the Maximilian government in Mexico. Stevens was right.

Shortly after the Civil War began, Britain, France, and Spain agreed to use force to collect debts from a defaulting Mexico. While the parties specifically agreed not to secure any "peculiar advantage," already Napoleon III, Emperor of France, had made overtures to Maximilian, a young scion of the House of Hapsburg, to become the emperor of Mexico. After learning about the French goals, the British and Spanish withdrew from the tri-partite mission, thus leaving the French a free hand. The result was that a minority of Mexicans under the protection of French bayonets, offered the throne to Maximilian, which he unwisely accepted in April, 1864.

The reaction of the United States to these events is understandable. On the one hand, Americans were furious at French intervention in Mexico, thus violating the Monroe Doctrine. On the other hand, the federal govenment was in no position to take forceful action and contented itself with registering a protest and reserving freedom of action for the future.

With the end of the Civil War, however, the federal government could take strong action. Washington ordered 50,000 troops under the command of General Philip Sheridan to the Texas-Mexican border. Another general, John Scofield, was sent to Paris; as he summarized his instructions, he was to get his legs "under Napoleon's mahogany and tell him he must get out of Mexico." Involved in an increasingly unpopular and costly expedition, with Mexicans resisting valiantly, Napoleon had no choice but to withdraw troops from a situation resembling American intervention in Vietnam. Napoleon reached this decision before the end of 1865, though it was some time before face-saving devices could be planned. Maximilian's puppet regime collapsed soon after the withdrawal of French troops, and the unfortunate emperor was executed in June, 1867.[1]

Long before that time, of course, Stevens and the 28th Wisconsin had been mustered out of service. For that unit the Civil War, belatedly, was over.

On board steamship "Continental", Mobile Bay, June 1, 1865.

We went on board the "Peerless" at about 5 P.M. yesterday and were brought to this vessel, she being too large to run up to the city, on account of the shallowness of the water. We reached her about dark, & came on board, & the "Peerless" has returned for the 33d Iowa which is also to come on board the "Continental" with us. We are lying about 15 miles from Mobile. We are told that our destination is Texas, though whether we shall land at Galveston, or go to the Rio Grande I am not able to learn for a certainty — probably the latter. . . .

On Board Steamship Continental, Off Brazos, Santiago, June 6, 1865. 10 A.M.

We left Mobile Bay finally on Saturday about 9 A.M., and here we are after a fair passage. It was a little rough yesterday

& last night, & we had some seasickness on board, but I escaped it — that is *partially.* This point is about 7 miles from the Mouth of the Rio Grande river, at the south end of Padre Island. The "Continental" arrived here early this morning. The "Clinton" which started one day in advance is now unloading. We can not get in near the shore, & will have to go on smaller boats in order to land.

My men are mostly well, I believe, except a little sea sickness. The weather is very warm, and we are crowded here, having about 1150 men on board this ship. It is a low, sandy coast, with hardly a tree or shrub in sight — hope we will not have to remain on this spot a great while — I want to get where there is *some* shade, at least.

I think we will see some hard soldiering here. Gen. Steele is in command of this expedition, I learn. What its object is, I have yet to learn. It seems rough that we have to come here *after "the war is over,"* when the Government has so many Veterans, new troops & negroes to do the work. We 1862 soldiers, with no bounties ($100. only) have to do the hard, rough work. These $800 and $1000 men are the *gentlemen* I suppose. Well, it will soon be over I hope, & *next October* will take us home again, though many a poor fellow will fall by the way before then, if we have to stay here all summer. A little over four months & you may look for me home — *perhaps sooner* — we will hope so. I would give a good deal if I could send my men home *now* instead of keeping them till October — I can probably get along, but It will go hard with some of them, I fear.

If you think best you may invest what money you have to spare, in "7-30 bonds." What do you think?

. . . .

H'd Qrs. 28th. Wis. Inf.,
Brazos, Santiago, June 9, 1865

I am finally on land once more, if the low, sandy beach, destitute of trees, shrubs, or grass, can be called land. It is only just above the water, & the island we are on is small. Owing to the storm the sea was so rough that we were unable to get ashore until late yesterday afternoon. There is no water here except the "briny deep." The army is supplied by distilling fresh water from the sea water. It is issued to us at the rate of about one gallon per day. I hope we will soon go where we can get plenty of water, so that we can cook & wash all we want to — it will be a luxury. There is some talk of our regiment leaving here & going 12 miles up country tomorrow to Clark's Ranch, Clarksburgh, or some such place. . . .

The object of our expedition I don't know, but suppose we will go to Brownsville, & probably beyond there. So mote it be. I will write all I learn about it, & as often as possible. It is very hot here on the sand, in our little shelter tents. Were it not for the sea breeze it would be unendurable. I send kisses to wife & children. If I can, I will send some shells from here, but doubt being able to send them — I could get *a lot.* . . .

Camp 28th. Wis. Inf.,
Brazos, Santiago, June 11, 1865.

. . . .

Lt. Col. Gray & some of the Captains have gone to Bagdad, Mexico, to-day. It is just across the mouth of the Rio Grande, about seven miles from here. If we stay here a few days longer I shall try and go there myself. Goods are said to be very cheap there, & I want a shirt & pair of pants, blouse & some socks — if I can get them very cheap.

I have got a tin can filled with shells, but don't know as I can send them home, there being no Express office here. Perhaps I can send them to New Orleans. If I do send them you can keep them, or distribute them, as you see fit. How I wish Lulu & Mary could go down to the beach and pick up shells for an hour, and see the waves of the sea come tumbling in — Wouldn't they be happy? I guess you would enjoy it, too, wouldn't you — that is, if I went with you? When I get rich we will go to the sea-shore — all of us.

. . . .

**Camp 28th Wis. Vol. Inf.,
Brazos, Santiago, June 12, 1865.
6 ½ o'clock, P.M.**

I have this day been out of the United States. I left here at 6 A.M. with Dr. Miller, Capt. Williams, Smith & Tichenor for Bagdad, Mexico. It was a pleasant morning, & a cool breeze was blowing off the gulf. We rode in a wagon, & reached there before 8 A.M., crossing the Rio Grande in a row boat.

Bagdad is a small, dirty little place, built up almost entirely during the rebellion, by the illicit trade with the rebels. There is quite a large lot of goods there, & as they can only be taken out of Mexico for sale by paying a heavy duty on them to the Mexican Government, they are some of them being sold quite low. I bought me 2 shirts for $4. four pairs cotton socks for $1. 1 silk Hdk'f for $1.25 2 pr Drawers for $2. &c. Capts Williams, Tichenor & myself bought 3 collars for our wives. Yours & Mrs. Tichenor's are just alike. Mrs. Williams' is of the same quality, but a little different pattern. I enclose yours. I want you to write me what it is worth — enquire of the merchants & judge yourself too, — then I'll tell what it cost. We just got back.

We are to move at 4 o'clock in the morning. Will write when we get somewhere. Must stop now & get ready to march. . . .

**Camp 28th Wis. Inf.,
Clarksville, Texas, June 15, 1865**

We have moved once more, you see. We marched early Tuesday morning from Brazos, reaching here before 10 o'clock A.M., the same day. Clarksville is a place — no, *a spot* — immediately opposite Bagdad, Mexico. It contains, at present, some half a dozen buildings, such as they are. It has been something more of a settlement, but the buildings have either been removed or destroyed. Our brigade is camped along a series of hillocks of sand, about 100 rods from the beach, (shore of the Gulf,) & our regiment, which is on the left of the line, lies about that distance from the Rio Grande. We have no shade, for there is no timber here — no vegetation except a few weeds which have sprung up in the almost barren sand. Wood we have none of except what little drift wood we can pick up. For water we have the Rio Grande — but it is terribly muddy. A pail-ful standing over night will contain about three inches of thick mud in the morning — but it is a deal better than *no water*. The fresh sea breeze tempers the heat in some degree, but, exposed as we are to the direct rays of the burning summer's sun, it is very hot at noon-day — & *all* day, for that matter. The nights are very comfortable. A great many of the men have been over the river to Bagdad — some with passes, but more without — and a good share of them have had a spree there — got drunk, in fact, abusing the Mexican Guards & police. — The consequence is that the Mexican commandant there has ordered his guards not to al-low American soldiers to land on that side the river. Officers are permitted to land, if in uniform, though some of them do not deserve the privilege — even some of the gallant 28th! I intend to go there again to-day or to-morrow — I have got to buy me a blouse & a cheap pair of pants. They will cost $10. or $12. The inhabitants of Bagdad are the very scum of the earth — criminals, renegades from all nations — and the worst of them all are run-away "Yankees." They are a mean set of cut-throats.

. . . .

This *staying about* in a place like this is *hard work* for us citizen soldiers. If there was fighting to be done we would be more contented, but to be kept here doing nothing except guard & fatigue duty, when we want to be going home, it grinds us. Well, four months more will end our term. "Fly swifter round, ye wheels of Time!"

. . . .

P.S. June 17, 5 A.M. All well. I send a view of Bagdad for Mary & Lulu. Mamma must put it in the album or a book & not let the girls spoil it. I could find nothing to send them. Brig. Gen. Slack has assumed command of the troops at this place.[2]

Camp 28th Wis. Inf., Clarksville, Texas, June 21, 1865.

My mind seems to-day as desolate, and my thoughts as barren of sense, as are the sand banks on which we at present *exist* — not live — of vegetation. Since we came here we have had a sun, burning hot, shining brightly down on us day after day — and oh, how hot it would be all the time were it not for the sea-breeze which just renders the heat endurable. We have nothing going on to relieve the monotony. Two hours drill each morning, with a dress parade at night, together with our guard & fatigue duties fill up the time — except when we have writing to do, which we can hardly do in such weather. No mails & no newspapers have yet reached us — when will we get some, I wonder. We are tired of waiting for letters from home. I was over at Bagdad again yesterday, but there is nothing scarcely there to interest one, unless he is a billiard player or a gambler, — and I don't indulge in either, even if I have been nearly three years in the army. I do sometimes sit down to a quiet game of euchre or whist with some of my friends, but with the understanding *always* that we play *only for fun*. I have played only once in a long time.

A regiment or two of negro troops arrived here yesterday. I don't know what we are to do any better than when we came here. The citizens, of Mexico, — & officers of the Imperial army too, I hear — think we are going to invade Mexico soon, but I think otherwise. We have now no hope of being mustered out before Oct. 13th. — *I never have had.*

. . . .

Clarksville, Texas, June 24, 1865, 5 A.M.

. . . .

The object of our coming here developes so very slowly that I am not yet able to state what it is. Some still insist that we are to have trouble with the Franco-Austro-Mexican power across the Rio Grande, but I can hardly believe it yet, but shall try and not be surprised at whatever may turn up.

. . . . Weitzel's negro Corps has been arriving & landing at Brazos for some ten days. It is reported here that the 4th Corps is also coming here.

Capt. Lacey, A.A.G. on Gen. Steele's staff told me he thought we would remain along the Rio Grande during the remainder of our term. It is rather a dreary prospect to look forward to, but the time will not be long.

. . . .

H'd Qrs. 28th Wis. Inf.,
Clarksville, Texas, June 25, 1865.

Seventeen years ago to-day came upon my heart a great sorrow. 'Twas then my sweet mother passed away to her heavenly rest, after a life in which she had endured much suffering. How well I remember the sad, sad scene — how desolate I felt in my soul, for there were none but her who sympathized with me in my little sorrows, or rejoiced as she did in my hours of happiness. To no one else could I go and open my boyish heart in confidence, knowing I found a willing listener, & one who felt with me & sincerely cared for me. And, oh, how times & often I promised myself that my life should be worthy of her who gave me being, & who so tenderly watched over my

infancy & childhood. Alas! how terribly I have failed to redeem those promises! If, as I have often dreamed, the spirit of
the mother gone before, watches over the children left behind,
how pained must she be to see what I have done, what I have
been & what I am. How her counsels and admonitions have
been unheeded — forgotten. How little have I been influenced
by her example of holiness in life and heart. And yet I sometimes think that but for her memory, I should have been much
worse, if that could be. Thoughts of her have many times kept
me from evil. What may her influence not have been, notwithstanding my neglect of her precepts and her beautiful example.
And perhaps it may yet be good to me. Let us hope that it will.

How changed seems life to me since thirteen years ago.
Then I was a boy, with none to care *much* for me, as I thought
— though in his way Pa had always cared for me — thinking
but little of aught but passing my time pleasantly away. Circumstances called me away from my relatives among strangers. There I met you, my darling, became acquainted with
you, loved you, dear one, but dared not hope for a return of
that love. How happy was I when I found that you did love me!
How many happy hours we have spent together since then.
True we have had hours of sorrow, but have they been hours of
real unhappiness? Some of our trials have been hard ones, but,
leaning upon each other, we have borne them all, and yet look
forward to years of continued joy.

Now a dear wife & two sweet little girls, in our own home,
care for me, and look forward to the time when I shall be with
them. And how I love that dear family of mine — love them
none the less that I have obeyed the call of my country, &
among her loyal sons gone forth to perform my duty to her.
Three years of absence has not conquered that love, dear one
— but it has increased with each day I have been absent from
your side — and when I can be with you once more, feeling
that I may remain with you, I shall be very happy. That happy
hour may not arrive as soon as you have hoped, but three & a

half months will soon pass away, & then you may look for my
return. It is not impossible that our reg't may be mustered out
sooner — but I have no hope of it now. However, don't let that
discourage you. I know but little about what may happen to us.

You have had a hard time of it the past three years — &
more — I shall try to make it easier & more pleasant for you
when I can get home again. *Poverty* will still be ours, but
riches do not always bring happiness. If we are spared our
lives & health, & our dear children, may we not be happy? We
will be, won't we, my darling wife?

One thing is now in our favor — *my* health is far better than
for years before I entered the army — how I wish that yours
were equally improved. There *was* a time when I feared I was
breaking down in health, but now I am well, & hope to remain
so during the remainder of my term of service. Then I hope to
find you all well at home — but, dearest, I fear you are not at
all well. Are you? You must let me know how you are —
always.

. . . .

Gen's Sheridan, Granger & Steele were here yesterday.[3]
They started from here for Brownsville yesterday afternoon,
but had to return as the steamer could not get up the river so
far. They have probably left for Brazos before this time.

No more mail — not much more news. The 33rd Iowas
which was mustered in Oct. 1st 1862, twelve days before we
were, is instructed to get their Muster-out rolls ready. Am glad
they can go home, if *we* cannot. If we could only have been
mustered a little sooner, perhaps we could go too.

If pa wants money, pay him part or the whole that I owe him
— if you pay part, see that it is endorsed upon the note he
holds. Does he talk of going east this season?

It is very warm to-day — but little air stirring — It will be a
long, dreary day. The nights are very comfortable for sleeping,
with the sea breeze — if they were not we could hardly live here.

Well, good bye, dear love. Cheer up! wait a little longer, and you may welcome home

. . . .

Clarksville, Texas, July 1st, 1865.

. . . .

You ask how it happens that I am in command of the Reg't. when the Col.'s gone. — Capt. Williams is detached nearly all the time, & consequently is not with the reg't. Capt. Townsend of Co. "B" was killed, and I am the next in rank — so of course I command. Do you "see it?" Tell Lulu to keep the *Eagle* for papa.

I hardly think the 28th will get out of the service any sooner "for bravery at Mobile", or any where else. We did our part there, & did it well, but the newspaper correspondents & big Generals in the 16th corps claimed & secured all the glory of the Capture of Spanish Fort &c. What's the odds? A few more months & we'll be home for good. So far I have seen no reason to think that the 28th will go home before October — if they do I shall be disappointed — most happily, too! That is the kind of disappointment I like! We may get home sooner, but I can't see as it looks much like it, now they have pushed us away off to this "far corner" of the land of *"Uncul psalm"*. It is a terrible place to stay this hot weather. I have been busy making out my muster rolls, Returns, &c., the past few days, & am not done yet.

Yesterday we had a terrible storm — a regular "norther". Nearly all the tents leaked like sieves under such a deluge of rain — mine I had put up *double* — (one over another) & kept nearly dry — not quite. It has rained a little to-day, & threatens more.

. . . .

H'd Qrs. 28th. Wis. Vols.,
Clarksville Texas., July 7/65.

. . . .

Lt. Col. Gray is very ill. He is to go on board the "Savannah" to-day for New Orleans. He has leave of absence. He has
been quite unwell for some time, and his "Fourth of July"
used him up for the present. It would not surprise me if he did
not live long, though the sea voyage may assist in restoring
him. I shall be in command of the regiment again. . . .

We had a "Fourth of July" celebration here. We went down
on the point where the Rio Grande empties into the Gulf of
Mexico — there on the "jumping-off-place," we had an ora-
tion, the Declaration of Independence was read, & we listened
to short addresses from Generals Slack & Cole. Then the big-
bugs & many others had a *"big drunk."* I was in command of
the regiment, but, strange to say, *kept sober!*

There are now several regiments of negro troops here —
mostly cavalry. Three of them have brass bands with them, so
we have lots of music. . . .

H'd Qrs. 28th Wis. Inf.,
Clarksville, Texas. July 8th, 1865.

As I have an opportunity of sending a letter by Lt. Col. Gray
to New Orleans, I will write just a line, as it will probably
reach you sooner than by the usual channel. Col. Gray went on
board the Savannah yesterday afternoon — I went out with
him — we had a pleasant sail on the lighter out to the steamship. Was on board with him, & left him about 4 P.M. He
seemed to feel much better, & will probably be much stronger
by the time he reaches New Orleans. I presume the trip home
will restore him to his usual health. I regret to have him leave.
The position of commanding officer of the Reg't. is not pleasant for me *as a Captain.* I cannot do as I would were I a field

officer — but I hope I shall succeed in *running the regiment* in passable shape.

. . . .

I feel quite positive that there is no probability of our going home for weeks yet — perhaps months. No orders or instructions in relation to our leaving have been rec'd at Gen. Steele's Headquarters. If we get home before October we will be fortunate. I am glad if our sick have gone from New Orleans, Mobile, &c.

No news from anywhere.

. . . .

**Head Quarters 28th Wis. Vols.,
Clarksville, Texas, July 16, 1865.**

Everything continues so dull here that one can hardly endure it. We get no news except once in a great while, & the papers now a days seem barren of anything worth reading. We soldiers had become so used to reading accounts of battles fought & victories won — of actions still to come off, & speculations as to the next *move* upon the military chessboard, that we almost need a continuation of the like news as our daily food. Reading a late paper, — if one nearly a month old can be called *late* — and finding nothing of the kind, we feel almost like tearing it & throwing it from us. It is now some nine days, I believe, since we had a mail, so we are, of course, anxiously looking for another. I *have* seen one New Orleans paper of the 8th, which came by private hand. By it I learn that four of the conspirators have been hung. It may seem horrible to people at the north, as the dispatches say, but if the punishment of the murderers of our President and of traitors against the government evokes such a feeling among the people, (to a great extent) then, let me ask, why should we punish any criminal — expecially a great one? For my part I think it is but the beginning of justice to ourselves as a nation & to the civilized world, — I am glad they are hung, and hope Jeff. Davis & his fellow leaders in treason will suffer a like fate. I have no place in my heart for this kindly feeling for those who have trampled upon our flag, endeavored to destroy the fair fabric of republican liberty, murdered the noblest & best of our Presidents since the Father of his Country, systematically *starved to death* our soldiers who fell into their hands, robbing them of clothing, food, money — of everything which was entrusted to their care for the poor fellows — I *want no* such *softness* in my bosom.

. . . .

Wood is very scarce here. We have now to send small sail boats up the river some 20 miles for it — they can bring about 8 cords — & it is poor at that. We have lately been unable to get a supply of clothing, consequently our men are mighty ragged just now. Hope to clothe them after a while.

The rations we get here are not very good — they are unfit for food in this climate. Our mess buy beef & bread every day from the market — these with coffee are about all we eat, except dried apples, stewed. Some of the men are getting the scurvy — I wonder more of them do not.

We ought all of us to be *gritty* when we get home. Everything we eat, drink, or wear is full of sand — so are our beds — *if blankets are beds*. Eyes, ears, mouths, hair — all full of *grit*. I've eaten nearly *my peck* of it here.

We get fresh reports every week that we are to be mustered out immediately and sent home — but they all prove unfounded. They create some excitement in camp while they are flying about.

I went over the river with Dr. Miller the other day, into Mexico. We went down the beach & gathered some shells. I shall try & send or bring them home.

You have read of the *mirage* in the desert — we see it here almost every day; looking across the sandy plains we can see what appears to be water. The shadows of men, horses &c., are perfectly plain to be seen in it — but as you approach you find that instead of standing in the water they are upon dry land. The illusion vanishes. What a terrible feeling of despair must fall upon the heart of the thirsty traveller across the deserts, choking for water, fancying he sees it in the distance, but approaching only to learn that the appearance was a mockery.

Monday, 17th, 5 A.M.

While I was writing yesterday morning, Dr. Miller came in and asked me to go with him to gather shells, so I put up my writing, put on my big boots, & off we went.

We crossed the Rio Grande at the ferry, & landed upon Mexican *sand — not soil —* then down to the beach, which we followed for five miles, picking up such shells as we thought would pay for carrying.

I got no very rare specimens, but they will some of them be nice for Lulu & Marrie to play with. I found several "stars," as they are called by the soldiers, a flat, roundish shaped thing, slightly convex upon the upper side, from ¾ inch to 1 ½ inch across, upon the top of which is a representation of a five-pointed star. What they are I can't learn — they appear to be nearer stone than bone, but some claim that they are part of some animal structure. They wash ashore from the sea. They are very fragile, & must be handled carefully. I shall pack them in cotton & try & get them home safely. I brought in my coat pockets full of shells, such as they are. I shall select the nicest ones to carry or send home. The sun shone brightly all day, and burnt my neck almost to a blister, making it quite sore this morning. I also found some nice samples of what the boys call a "sea bean." They are quite pretty, & so are one or two samples of coral which I have obtained. I wish I had room for

more such things — Id like to send or carry home a quantity of
them. . . .

Would you believe it! we got a barrel of pickles from the
Sanitary Commission the other day — the first thing we have
had from them since we came here. Now I'll bet that the negro
regiments here have had ten times that amount at least. They
seem to be always well supplied, whether we "white trash"
have any or not. These "commissions" look out first for the
rebels & their families, then for niggers, & if anything is left,
we can get it by begging for it — *sometimes*. How do you &
ours get along? Well, I hope. Only a few weeks longer, dearest
one, & I'll be with you.

. . . .

P.S. Speaking of the Sanitary Commission "reminds me of
a little joke." Capt. Cowing of "K" Co., who, by the way, is a
bachelor, says that "after the war is over a great many of these
patriotic young ladies at the north will be wishing they had
made those shirts, which they have sent the soldiers, a few
sizes smaller, and kept them at home — for the light infantry!" Ha! *ha!! haw!!!*

Clarksville, Texas. July 26, 1865.

. . . .

Maj. Gen. Sheridan passed up the river a few days ago. He
has gone to Brownsville — Is expected back today, I believe.
The men of the regiment have *petitioned him* to have us mustered out & sent home! — a foolish affair. When he gets
orders to do so, he will let us go — not till then unless our
term expires sooner — and *our term* extends to October 13th.

. . . .

**H'd Qr's 28th Wis. Vol. Inf.,
Clarksville, Texas, July 30, 1865.**

What shall I write about this morning? I hardly know, for we
have nothing going on here to write or think about — it is *so*

monotonous — no change of any kind — no excitement. How long these burning hot days seem! too hot to write, think or hardly live.

One thing is settled — our *term of service* expires Oct. 13th, — and unless the War Dep't. issues an order mustering us out sooner, we will be held till that time. That is the decision of Generals Sheridan & Canby. Well, even at that we have only two and a half months to serve, but it will be a bad time of year for us to go home, I fear. It is injustice to us to hold us till that time — other troops who were enlisted at the same time, & mustered in more than a month later, have already gone home — and *we are not needed here,* & we know it. The only reason we are kept here seems to be to make us serve our full term from date of muster in. I don't think the Generals commanding here are to blame. The War Dept. could easily make it all right.

. . . .

Camp 28th Wis. Vols., Near Brownsville, Texas, Monday, Aug. 21, 1865.

It is over a week since I have written you — & why? I'll tell you. A week ago to-day we rec'd an order for the 27th & 28th Wis. Regts to be mustered out, and since then we have been hard at work night & day on our Muster Out Rolls & other papers. It is a great deal of work to get them done, & *correctly* done, but we will soon be ready to start for home. It will, I presume, be nearly a month before we get there, as we will probably be delayed at New Orleans, & at other places along the route.

Aint we all glad to know that we are soon to be with our loved ones? Won't they all be glad at home, too?

. . . .

No other news here. Don't expect me till you see me, dearest! I'll get there by and by!

. . . .

Cairo, Ill., Sept. 13, 1865.

We arrived here last night. We go direct to Madison, via Freeport. All well. Left Brownsville Aug. 25 & New Orleans Sept. 6. No news. I can't find Mary here. What do you think about coming out to Madison. Do as you think best. If you *do come,* engage a room at the Capitol House, & take along some money, for it will cost us $5. pr day, & I shall have no money till we are paid.

. . . .

Madison, Wis., Sept. 19, 1865.

I reached here at 8 ½ this A.M. all right. Had a cold ride in the stage. Dr. Miller did not come. Have got some work to do — don't know how much.

I hope dear Lulu continues to improve — but I shall worry about her till I get back, which will be as soon as I possibly can. Kiss her for papa & tell her how well he loves her. Kisses to Baby Marrie. Love & kisses to yourself, darling one. Take as good care of yourself as you can. Good bye. In haste

Capital House,
(Wm. E. Mason, Proprietor.)
Madison, Wis., Sept 21, 1865.
7 ½ P.M.

Darling:

We are to be paid to-morrow, & I expect to get home to-morrow night — I shall do so if possible. We have no news here.

I hope dear Lulu is getting better, the darling little girl. Kiss her & Marrie for me, & tell them papa will come as soon as he can.

With a good night kiss, & much love, I am

Thine,
T. N. S.

Footnotes: Texas Expedition

1. For American relations with France during the Maximilian affair, see Henry Blumenthal, *A Reappraisal of Franco-American Relations, 1830–1871* (Chapel Hill, 1959).

2. James Slack, 1818–81, served as a colonel through most of the war, largely in Tennessee and Mississippi. He was promoted to brigadier general in November, 1864.

3. Philip Sheridan, 1831–88, West Point (1853), rose from lieutenant at the beginning of the war to a two-star general with extensive service in several theaters. He was sent to Texas in charge of 50,000 troops after the war to threaten Maximilian.

Gordon Granger, 1822–76, West Point (1845), rose from captain to two-star general. Granger served most notably at Chickamaugua and Chattanooga; he had also participated in the Mobile campaign.